NEW MEDIA AND SOCIETY

New Media and Society

Deana A. Rohlinger

NEW YORK UNIVERSITY PRESS

New York

NEW YORK UNIVERSITY PRESS
New York
www.nyupress.org

References to Internet websites (URLs) were accurate at the time of writing. Neither the author nor New York University Press is responsible for URLs that may have expired or changed since the manuscript was prepared.

Library of Congress Cataloging-in-Publication Data
Names: Rohlinger, Deana A., author.
Title: New media and society / Deana A. Rohlinger.
Description: New York : New York University Press, [2018] |
   Includes bibliographical references and index.
Identifiers: LCCN 2018012219| ISBN 9781479897872 (cl : alk. paper) |
   ISBN 9781479845699 (pb : alk. paper)
Subjects: LCSH: Information technology—Social aspects—United States. | Mass media—
   Social aspects—United States. | Mass media and culture—United States. | Digital media—
   Social aspects—United States.
Classification: LCC HN90.I56 R64 2018 | DDC 302.23—dc23
LC record available at https://lccn.loc.gov/2018012219

Manufactured in the United States of America

10 9 8 7 6 5 4 3 2 1

Also available as an ebook

For my students:

You inspire me.

CONTENTS

FIGURES AND TABLES

TABLES

Introduction

Understanding Social Institutions and Ourselves
in a New Media Society

KEY CONCEPTS

New media are the mass communications that rely on digital technologies such as social media, online games and applications, multimedia, productivity applications, cloud computing, interoperable systems, and mobile devices. New media are part of mass media.

Social institutions are the systems of established social rules that create stable expectations for behavior. Social institutions include family and religion, which provide support and a sense of purpose, and education, government, and law, which help create social order. Mass media are also a social institution.

Structure refers to the rules and practices provided by society and social institutions.

Agency refers to individuals' decisions to conform to or challenge the rules or practices of a social institution.

The *social exchange model* highlights the importance of relational dynamics, or how the behavior of one actor is shaped by the behaviors of other actors and by changes in the institutional context.

The fish will be the last to discover water.

—Anonymous

Can you imagine trying to explain water to fish? Fish know a lot about their watery world. They know where to find food, where they are likely to become food, and where the water is too warm or too cold for them to survive. Fish, however, are unlikely to discover water itself because it is impossible to see. Water is their reality. Water provides the backdrop to everything fish know about living and dying. The only way for fish to understand the importance of water to their lives is to remove them from it.

The same can be said about us and *new media*, or the mass communications that rely on the digital technologies that we use daily. We use devices—cell phones, computers, tablets—to access the internet, read the news, watch television, chat with our friends, make our appointments, and register for school. If you look at figure I.1, which is based on data provided by the Nielsen Research Center, you begin to get a sense of just how important new media are in our lives. As you can see in the figure, 122 million Americans stream video on their smartphones, and 146 million Americans stream video on their computers. We engage one another a lot via new media as well. According to the Nielsen Research Center, 142 million users access social media through apps on their smartphones, and 133 million users access social media through their computers.

Table I.1, which was created using data from Statista, shows our average daily media use in minutes. You can see that Americans increasingly spend time using mobile devices. Over a five-year period, Americans' average daily use of mobile media grew from 88 minutes per day in 2012 to 195 minutes per day in 2017—a difference of 107 minutes. At the same

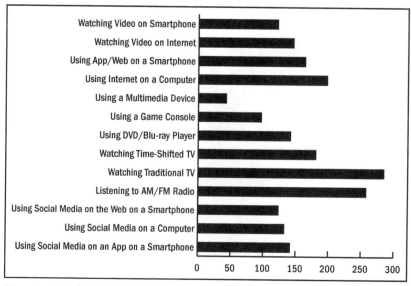

Figure I.1. Number of Users by Device in Millions. Source: Nielsen Research Center.

TABLE I.1. Average Daily Media Use in Minutes, 2012–2018. Source: Statista.

	TV	Desktop/ Laptop	Mobile	Radio	Newspapers	Magazines
2012	278	144	88	92	24	17
2013	271	136	135	90	20	15
2014	262	134	157	88	18	13
2015	251	132	177	87	17	13
2016	245	131	186	87	16	12
2017	240	130	195	86	15	11
2018	235	128	203	85	15	11

time, this doesn't necessarily mean that we are watching less TV. Notice that TV use is only down 38 minutes per day, and desktop/laptop use is only down 14 minutes per day during the same six-year time period.

New media, in short, are our water; they provide the backdrop for most of our encounters. We swim in a technological world, yet like fish, we rarely think about how new media potentially change the ways in which we interact with one another or shape how we live our lives. The social changes resulting from the emergence of new media are consequential. For example, new media alter how we understand our intimate relationships. We may find it easier to text our family good and bad news or find email a convenient way to end a relationship—intimate interactions that had to be done over the phone or face-to-face only twenty years ago. Similarly, we may find it more enjoyable to take a required class online because we can do it from the comfort of our homes, in our pajamas and at our convenience—an option that has only been available in the last decade. New media have fundamentally changed how we interact with one another and how we navigate daily life. This book provides a sociological approach to understanding how new media shape our interactions and our experiences. Specifically, this book explores two related questions:

1. How do new media shape our interactions and experiences with one another?
2. How do new media change the social institutions, or the systems of established social rules that create stable expectations for behavior, governing our lives?

If you are new to sociology, you should know that sociologists study the development and structure of human society. While sociologists are interested in individuals, they analyze how people live together as well as how their lives are organized by social institutions such as family, work, and education. Sociologists, in other words, make clear distinctions between individual experience and the institutional context in which those experiences occur. If this seems confusing, don't worry. In this chapter, I will discuss social institutions in more detail and outline how a sociologist might analyze the effects of new media on social institutions.

SOCIAL INSTITUTIONS EXPLAINED

A *social institution* is an organization that is critical to teaching us the norms and behaviors of a culture. Social institutions provide us with a common identity and give us a sense of order because they establish a sense of purpose and direction as well as dictate clear rules for behavior. For example, we learn a lot more than just our *ABCs* in school. The American education system brings diverse groups of people together and gives them common membership in a group, such as kindergartners or high schoolers, as well as provides them a common sense of direction (to do well in school, graduate, and get a job). Social institutions, in short, give us a sense of purpose and offer us support so that we know what to expect from different social settings and know how to interact with one another.

Generally speaking, there are six social institutions that sociologists study in order to better understand the structure of a society:

1. Family, which teaches us about the world and our place in it
2. Education, which teaches us how to get along with one another and trains us to be good workers
3. Religion, which provides us a unified system of beliefs and a moral code by which we are supposed to live
4. Work, which provides for the production and distribution of goods/services
5. Law, which maintains social order through law enforcement
6. Politics, which maintains social order through policy

These institutions are critical because they encompass every area of social life and because they fulfill essential functions—such as preserving order and perpetuating society—that other groups cannot do. As a result, we know how to behave in a classroom, in the grocery store, and at our workplace—and we expect others to behave in a similar manner or to experience consequences for their failure to do so.

Society, of course, is not static. Social forces such as industrialization, urbanization, globalization, and technological development have made it more difficult for these social institutions to do their jobs. For example, if fewer people attend church or temple services, it becomes more difficult for religious leaders to give individuals a sense of purpose and offer them support. This does not mean that society will fall apart. It's quite the opposite. As our society becomes more complicated, new institutions emerge and help maintain social stability. In fact, mass media are one of the social institutions that have helped maintain social stability in our complex society.

You might be thinking, "Wait a minute. Aren't mass media part of the economy?" After all, like other industries, mass media companies are oriented toward making a profit. This is true. Traditional media outlets, such as newspapers, books, magazines, radio, and television, as well as new media platforms, such as blogs and services like Amazon Prime, Hulu, and Netflix, are all oriented toward profit-making. However, mass media also are a social institution because they teach us the norms and behaviors of our society. Mass media help give meaning to the world around us and provide guidance on how we should behave in it. We don't simply have to rely on our families or our pastors to tell us how to behave; we can watch a movie or go online to learn more about the kinds of rewards and punishments that go along with different kinds of behavior. Similarly, we don't completely rely on educational and religious institutions to integrate us into groups and give us a sense of membership. If we have a particular interest, we can simply go online and find a website, discussion board, or chat room where individuals gather and talk about the interests they have in common.

To be sure, the economic and social functions of mass media do not perfectly complement one another. Since media companies primarily are interested in growing their bottom line, they use content to sell us products and lifestyles. Let's use MTV's hit series *Teen Mom* as an example of how the economic and social functions of mass media can come into conflict. *Teen Mom*, which follows the lives of several teenagers who have had children, is used in more than three thousand middle and high school classrooms across the United States to warn teenagers about the pitfalls of teen parenting. In the reality show, the teen moms are shown struggling to find housing, obtain child care, and stay in school. This, however, is not the only reality the show's audience sees. Since the show also needs to make money, MTV features products in its shows. *Teen Mom* becomes a showcase for products, and the teen moms get extensive makeovers, posh baby accessories, and expensive clothing—none of which most teen moms could afford. The teen moms also are shown engaged in dramatic, and sometimes destructive or violent, behavior. From an economic point of view, emphasizing conflict on the show makes a lot of sense. After all, if the teen moms were only shown changing diapers, MTV probably would not have advertisers or an audience for the program. However, the focus on products and drama arguably undercuts the social message of the program. A viewer of *Teen Mom*, for instance, may not get the message that being a parent during your teenage years is very challenging. Instead, she might think that being a teen mom is glamorous and wonder whether she might be able to get on the show herself. In fact, in 2011, a staff writer for the *New York Post* pointed out that three of *Teen Mom 2*'s Janelle Evans's friends got pregnant within a year of her appearance on the show and that another teen mom roommate, Megan Nelson, became pregnant in an effort to become a regular on the show.

Of course, media companies do not simply drive the desires of Americans. Not all teens want to be moms or get the latest baby swag. New products and platforms emerge in response to what we like and want. Let's use social media as an example. Facebook burst onto the Harvard University scene in 2004. By 2006, Facebook had spread beyond college campuses and had twelve million users worldwide. Given the popularity of Facebook, it is not surprising that other companies tried to create additional social media platforms and that many of these efforts failed. The founder of Monster.com, for instance, created a social media site called Eons for the more-than-fifty crowd in 2007. Given the relative newness of social media and the site's focus on a demographic that was not very familiar with digital technology, Eons did not attract enough users, and it failed. Twitter, in contrast, is an example of a successful social media platform. Founded in 2006, Twitter capitalized on a popular feature of Facebook—the status updates. Twitter allows users to "microblog," or communicate their thoughts, opinions, and activities in 280 characters or less, well beyond their standard friendship networks. Using hashtags, individuals can follow topics and connect with people around the world who share their interests.

The preferences of users have shaped the development of social media in other ways. Both Facebook and Twitter are commercial ventures designed to generate a profit. Both platforms prominently include advertising on their sites and sell user information to corporations. In fact, we've recently seen in the Cambridge Analytica scandal, in which the company accessed the private information of more than fifty million Facebook users and then used this information to influence voter behavior in the 2016 presidential election, just how much of our personal information can be accessed by third parties. While some individuals do not mind the commercial aspects of Facebook and Twitter, others do. New platforms have emerged to address users' concerns regarding the collection and sale of user information. Paul Budnitz, for example, created Ello, an advertiser-free social networking site. As you can see from the Ello Manifesto below, Budnitz rejects the idea that a social networking site needs to be commercially driven to succeed. In an interview with BetaBeat, which is the innovation section of the *New York Observer*, Budnitz argued that "Facebook, Google+, Tumblr, etc. aren't really social networks—they're advertising platforms. They exist to sell ads. That's it." Ello allows users to post content, send messages, and share links; it just prohibits advertising, since it distracts from the users' experiences. Yik Yak, another social media platform, was also created in response to users' concerns over what Facebook, Twitter, Tumblr, and other commercial platforms were doing with their personal information. Yik Yak, which was designed for college students, allowed individuals who were within ten miles of a college or university campus to post content anonymously on a wall. In both of these cases, we can see that social media platforms developed in response to the people who used them.

Ello Manifesto

Your social network is owned by advertisers.

Every post you share, every friend you make, and every link you follow is tracked, recorded, and converted into data. Advertisers buy your data so they can show you more ads. You are the product that's bought and sold.

We believe there is a better way. We believe in audacity. We believe in beauty, simplicity, and transparency. We believe that the people who make things and the people who use them should be in partnership.

We believe a social network can be a tool for empowerment. Not a tool to deceive, coerce, and manipulate—but a place to connect, create, and celebrate life.

You are not a product.

In sum, social institutions such as family, education, government, religion, and work are critical for reproducing American society. Social institutions fulfill our need for learning, provide social order, give us a sense of purpose, and offer us support. As our society has gotten more complicated, however, new social institutions have arisen to help maintain social order. Mass media, including new media, are an example of a social institution that emerged in response to increased social complexity. However, mass media are not just a social institution. Media often are oriented to profit-making, which affects how companies craft the stories they tell us, the products they offer, and, consequently, the messages we receive about the world and how it works.

A SOCIOLOGICAL APPROACH TO STUDYING NEW MEDIA

It can be difficult to assess the effects of new media on our behaviors and lives. Some of our behavioral changes in response to technological innovation are fairly straightforward. The rise in internet-based video streaming services such as Amazon Prime, Hulu, and Netflix, for example, drove video stores out of business and caused some households to drop their cable and satellite services and stream video over televisions and mobile devices instead. Likewise, technological advances in mobile phones have altered who has a phone as well as how mobile phones are used. Motorola brought the first generation of mobile phones (also known as 1G) to the public in 1984. These early mobile phones, which cost more than two thousand dollars each, were largely installed in cars because they were too bulky to carry around. The inconvenience and cost of this mobile technology meant that not many people owned them. Mobile phone usage increased dramatically in the 1990s as second-generation (or 2G) technology made phones smaller, more reliable, and more affordable than in the past. As phones and phone plans became more affordable, more people bought them and integrated this technology into their daily routines.

However, third-generation (3G) and fourth-generation (4G) technology, which is what most of us have today, fundamentally changed how we use our mobile phones. Each new generation transfers data faster and allows us to do more on our mobile phones. As a result, more and more Americans buy mobile "smartphones" and use them for various purposes. You can see in figure I.2 that 45.9 percent of the American population owns a smartphone and that 75 percent own a web-enabled device that is also a mobile phone. The widespread availability of 3G and 4G technology has changed how we use our phones. 3G and 4G technology, for example, allows us to transfer emails, information, and instant messages to one another, which, as you can see in figure I.3, makes it easy for us to use our phones for banking (42.7 percent of mobile phone owners), to check the weather (80.5 percent of mobile phone owners), to keep up with the news (65 percent of mobile phone owners), to listen to internet

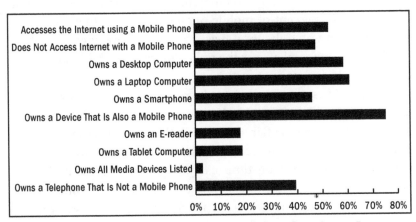

Figure I.2. Percentage of Americans with Different Media Devices. Source: Pew Research Center.

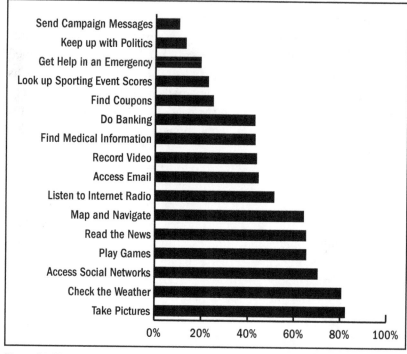

Figure I.3. How Americans Use Their Phones. Source: Pew Research Center.

radio (51.2 percent of mobile phone users), to play games (65.2 percent of mobile phone users), and to communicate with our friends via social networks (70.2 percent of mobile phone users). In other words, we do not need to watch the local news to check the weather or wait for our favorite song to play over the radio. We can do all this, and more, on our mobile devices.

Think of it! Less than one hundred years ago, the television was introduced to the public at the New York World's Fair. President Franklin Roosevelt dedicated the fair and became the first American president to be televised. Now American presidents can speak with us directly through social media at any time of day. Given these dramatic changes, how do we understand the role of new media in our lives? Different disciplines in the social sciences have different approaches for studying the world. Since sociologists study the development and structure of human society, they do not assume that new media are "good" or "bad" for American society. Instead, they examine how new media shape human interaction and institutional life from the perspective of different actors and assess how new media are intentionally (or unintentionally) used to challenge existing institutional arrangements.

Let's extend our discussion of social institutions to better understand how sociologists study the effects of new media on American society. As we discussed above, in America's early history, social institutions such as education, family, religion, and government provided individuals information, tradition, and a moral compass. Technological developments, however, have diminished the roles of traditional social institutions in this regard and, increasingly, mass media have stepped in and picked up the slack. Mass media are a social institution. The relationship between traditional social institutions and new media is complicated by another factor as well. New media are so pervasive that traditional social institutions such as family, education, religion, government, and work are both shaped by and dependent on communication technology to fulfill their functions.

Politics are a good example. Politicians use media to influence the public. Politicians spend millions of dollars on advertising designed to make their opponents look bad and make themselves look good to voters. That said, politicians' actions are also affected by what happens in mass media. For instance, when Barack Obama ran for the Democratic presidential nomination, he focused on new media, such as social media, rather than traditional media outlets, such as broadcast television, to beat his opponent, Hillary Clinton. Obama had a two-pronged approach when it came to using new media. First, he used social media to connect with his supporters directly. In 2007, Obama's staff took to Twitter to connect with and organize voters. In fact, his account was one of the most followed in the world at the time. Second, Obama rewarded bloggers for writing posts that were supportive of his presidential bid by giving them exclusive interviews and campaign information. Lots of bloggers wrote supportive posts because they knew that having insider information and exclusive interviews would draw people to their sites. Hillary Clinton, who made limited use of new media, quickly found herself out of presidential contention as the buzz around Obama and his call for "change" and "hope" grew louder online and offline. Clinton's presidential bid, in short, was shaped by mass media—and new media in particular—even though she made little use of it in her own campaign.

Hillary Clinton upped her social media game during the 2016 presidential campaign cycle and was quite effective. According to the conservative news outlet *National Review*, Clinton's tweets were liked, shared, and commented on more often than her opponent Donald Trump's tweets. Clinton's "Delete your account" tweet, which was a response to Trump criticizing President Obama for endorsing her, was retweeted more than five hundred thousand times. A sarcastic "'I never said that.'—Donald Trump, who said that" with a link to Trump's 2012 tweet claiming global warming was a Chinese hoax posted by a Clinton staffer during a presidential debate also was retweeted more than one hundred thousand times. Additionally, Clinton's Facebook account was more active than Trump's account, although he had more followers. *National Review* reported that Clinton's accounts had almost 190 million likes, comments, and shares. However, this did not translate into presidential victory for Clinton. This, in part, was because Donald Trump's in-your-face, often-offensive tweets were not just retweeted and discussed in online forums such as Reddit but also made it into mainstream and cable news. Anchors and pundits spent countless hours analyzing and, in some instances, deriding Trump's use of Twitter. While Trump's use of Twitter alone doesn't account for his presidential victory, it is clear that new media play a critical role in Americans' understandings of politics.

There are also plenty of instances in which it is unclear how the interactions between humans and technology will shape institutional practices. Let's take the example of Yik Yak. Mostly, Yik Yak provided a virtual public forum for college students, who posted everything from complaints about the food in the student union to jokes about bodily functions. Yik Yak, however, was not always used as the creators intended, and this affected institutional operations. For example, several students used Yik Yak to post anonymous threats against high schools, colleges, and universities—threats that closed schools and triggered police investigations on campuses. Similarly, some students used Yik Yak to post racially charged, sexual, or otherwise disparaging comments about their classmates and professors. These Yik Yak controversies spurred calls for bans on anonymous platforms and faculty action, including "Yak Back" protests in which professors hijacked Yik Yak with their own commentary. Schools across the country banned Yik Yak, and its use plummeted. In 2017, Yik Yak shut down.

So how would a sociologist study Yik Yak and its effects on education? A sociologist would focus on the push and pull between structure and agency. *Structure* refers to the rules and practices provided by society and social institutions. *Agency* refers to individuals' decisions to conform to or challenge the rules or practices of a social institution. Sociologists believe that individuals can make choices and that these choices can have important consequences. Individuals, however, make choices in institutional settings over which they have little control. For example, a student can decide to post on Yik Yak or check her email instead of listening to a course lecture. This is agency. While this choice does not change the fact that she needs to take the required course as part of her major, it may alter whether a professor allows the use of

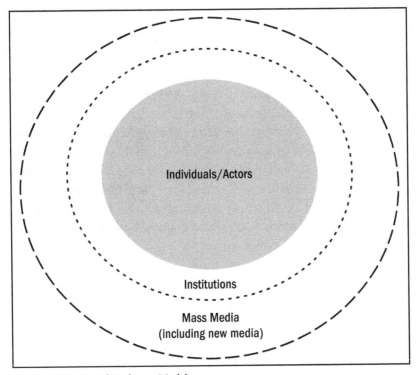

Figure I.4. The Social Exchange Model

devices in his classroom. This is structure. So to better understand how new media affect education a sociologist might study whether professors' policies regarding electronic devices and computers have changed with the introduction of social media platforms such as Yik Yak.

UNDERSTANDING NEW MEDIA IN AMERICAN SOCIETY

Now that we have a better sense of why social institutions matter and understand how sociologists study them, we can begin to make sense of the complex interactions between individuals, institutions, and new media. Figure I.4 provides a simple graphic summary of these relationships. Mass media, which consist of diverse communications technology, including new media, provide a backdrop for our interactions with institutions. In this way, it is the water in which we swim. New media make it easier for us to connect with one another and provide us new ways to engage one another relative to social institutions. For example, we can email or text our colleagues a work-related question after work hours and get a response. This innovation in how we do our work changes the social institution of work. Specifically, it changes bosses' expectations of when our workday ends, and it changes our expectations about whether we should be paid for work done via email and text after regular hours. This model is called the *social exchange model* because it highlights the importance of relational dynamics, or how the behavior of one actor is shaped by the behaviors of other actors and by changes in the institutional context. The consequences associated with these changes may be positive, negative, or both. Again, sociologists are not interested in arguing whether new media are good or bad for a social institution. Instead, sociologists look at the relational dynamics between mass media, social institutions, and individuals/actors and examine how these interactions change our behavior and alter society.

You might still be curious about how individuals fit into the social exchange model. Agency indicates choice, and choice means that we could decide to ignore the guidelines we are given and try to change the social institutions governing us. This is true. Generally speaking, social institutions tell us how to behave and interact in a setting, and we reproduce these rules and expectations every time we engage in them. Sociologists assume that we typically uphold—rather than challenge—the norms and behaviors set out by social institutions because we are rational actors who want to maximize our opportunities (and minimize our personal costs) in a given setting. What distinguishes this logic from a pure cost-benefit calculation that we associate with economics is that sociologists believe that self-interest signals more than competition and the accumulation of wealth. Instead, sociologists argue that we rely on one another in order to accomplish our goals. This is a critical difference. Since we need one another to achieve our goals, we try to create mutually beneficial and stable relationships within an institution. This requires us to form commitments to one another that have more to them than the exchange of money, goods, and services. These relationships involve trust. Understood this way, you can see how the choices we make, which are based on a combination of self-interest and interdependence, end up reinforcing social institutions. To get what we want, we need to have a sense of how others will act in a given situation—and others expect the same from us. Consequently, we generally act in predictable ways, and these behaviors reinforce social institutions. Again, this isn't always the case. If we ignore, replace, or directly challenge social institutions, the rules by which they operate can change over time. We just don't do this daily. We typically behave in ways that reproduce what we already know and do.

In the remainder of the book, I explore a different social institution— family, education, religion, work, law, and politics—in each chapter and outline how new media have changed our expectations as they relate to social institutions and the rules by which they operate. As you will see in the chapters, there generally is not a consensus on the effects new media have on these social institutions. For example, there is a lot of debate over the role of new media in the creation and enforcement of our laws. The purpose of this book then is to give you a sociological framework for understanding these debates and to provide you opportunities to apply sociological concepts to recent cases. Sometimes the material will be uncomfortable and controversial. The goal is to move beyond your personal reaction and think sociologically.

CONCLUSION

In this chapter, we defined social institutions and discussed how sociologists study them. We learned that traditional social institutions, such as family, education, religion, work, politics, and law, have diminished in strength as American society has changed in response to social forces (such as industrialization, urbanization, and technological innovation) and become more complicated. New social institutions emerge in response to these social forces and help fill the gap by teaching us the norms and behaviors associated with American society and by giving us new ways to connect with one another. Mass media, which includes new media, are one of these social institutions.

We also learned that mass media are not just a social institution. Most media companies are oriented toward profit-making, which means that media platforms and content often are shaped by economic concerns. Consequently, we sometimes get distorted messages about social institutions, such as the family. *Teen Mom*, for example, doesn't give a completely accurate view of parenting during your teen years. Showing sleep-deprived teen moms changing diapers would not attract many viewers or make MTV much money. Instead, MTV attracts viewers by focusing on the dramatic aspects of the moms' lives and makes additional money by featuring products in the show. In short, mass media are affected by economics, which shapes what lessons about the world are broadcast throughout society.

We concluded the chapter with a discussion of the social exchange model, which focuses our attention on relational dynamics and helps us better understand how new media change our behavior and society. Specifically, the social exchange model draws attention to the following:

- the different actors engaged in a social institution and their priorities
- how different actors reproduce and challenge the practices and/or structural arrangements of an institution
- how social institutions respond to technological innovation and the shifts in interactions that come with it

As fish swimming in technological waters, it is difficult to determine the effect of new media on our lives. The value of the social exchange model is that it highlights the interaction between structure and agency and allows us to critically examine how new media change our behavior and the social institutions that govern our lives.

In each chapter, we will think about how new media have challenged and changed our expectations as they relate to social institutions and the rules by which they operate. The social exchange model presented here is the underlying framework for the remainder of the book. The social exchange model helps us identify the relevant questions we should ask when analyzing the effects of new media on American social institutions. In this case, the social exchange model focuses on how the introduction of new media into a social institution affects individuals' expectations of an institution as well as how actors within the institutions respond to these new and changing demands. Understanding these relationships is key to a sociological understanding of the role of new media in American society.

There are a couple of notes worth making about the book. As you go through the chapters, you will notice that I included case studies on important issues related to new media, such as countering religious extremism online and dataveillance (which refers to the collection and surveillance of data regarding where we go and what we do). In the case studies, I pose questions for you to think about and specifically ask you to consider these cases relative to course ideas and concepts. I hope that you will use the case studies to explore the relationship between new media and American social institutions in more detail. I've also included a section titled "Reproducing Inequality" in each of the chapters. In this section, I offer you additional information about a topic, such as the costs of online, for-profit education, and note how this reproduces inequality in American society. I hope that these sections will stimulate additional conversation about important sociological topics. At the end of each chapter, you will see a number of links that direct you to articles, talks, and films that will help you learn more about information covered in the chapter. There are also links that will help you learn more about the topics more generally. If you rented or purchased a print version of this book, go to www.deanarohlinger.com to access a document with the "live" links. Finally, I have included a concept index at the end of the book. If you don't remember a term discussed in a previous chapter, navigate to the back of the book to read a definition and see on what page the concept was discussed.

CHAPTER LINKS

"Connecting With the Cosmos: The Total Audience Media Universe." 2015. Nielsen Company. Retrieved March 19, 2015. http://www.nielsen.com/newscenter.

"Average Daily Media Use in the United States from 2012 to 2018, by Device (in Minutes)." 2017. Statista. http://www.statista.com.

Granville, Kevin. 2018. "Facebook and Cambridge Analytica: What You Need to Know as Fallout Widens." *New York Times*. Last modified March 19, 2018. https://www.nytimes.com.

Budnitz, Paul. n.d. "Ello Manifesto." Ello. Retrieved June 2016. http://www.ello.com.

Yack, Austin. 2016. "Clinton Campaign's Social Media Strategy Was More Effective than Trump's." *National Review*. Last modified November 8, 2016. http://www.nationalreview.com.

Dockterman, Eliana. 2014. "Does *16 and Pregnant* Prevent or Promote Teen Pregnancy?" *Time*. Last modified January 13, 2014. http://www.time.com.

Henson, Melissa. 2011. "MTV's 'Teen Mom' Glamorizes Getting Pregnant." *CNN*. Last modified May 4, 2011. http://www.cnn.com.

"Copycat 'Moms.'" 2011. *New York Post*. Last modified February 10, 2011. https://nypost.com.

CHAPTER REVIEW QUESTIONS

1. What are social institutions, and why are they important?
2. Why are mass media, including new media, considered a social institution?
3. How do economics affect the kinds of products and content media companies make?
4. How does the social exchange model explain the effects of new media on American institutions?
5. Does the social exchange model argue that new media has negative consequences for society? Why, or why not?

LEARN MORE

Alter, Alexandra. 2014. "E-book Mingles Love and Product Placement." *New York Times*. Last modified November 2, 2011. http://www.nytimes.com.

"The End of Mass Media: Coming Full Circle." 2011. *Economist*. Last modified July 7, 2011. http://www.economist.com.

Flatow, Ira. 2011. "What Does '4G' Really Mean, Anyway?" *Science Friday*. Last modified January 14, 2011. http://www.npr.org.

———. 2014. "As the Web Turns 25, Where Is It Going Next?" *Science Friday*. Last modified March 14, 2014. http://www.sciencefriday.com.

Geer, John G. 2008. "Attack Ad Hall of Fame." Chicago University Press. http://www.press.uchicago.edu.

Hendricks, Drew. 2013. "Complete History of Social Media: Then and Now." *Small Business Trends*. Last modified May 8, 2013. http://www.smallbiztrends.com.

Ives, Nat. 2011. "Product Placement Hits High Gear on 'American Idol,' Broadcast's Top Series for Brand Mentions: Coca-Cola Top's Nielsen's Chart of Top Brands by Prime-Time Integrations." *Ad Age*. Last modified April 18, 2011. http://www.adage.com.

Kelly, Heather. 2012. "OMG, the Text Message Turns 20. But Has SMS Peaked?" *CNN*. Last modified December 3, 2012. http://www.cnn.com.

Meyers, Justin. 2011. "Watch the Incredible 70-Year Evolution of the Cell Phone." *Business Insider*. Last modified May 6, 2011. http:// www.businessinsider.com.

Sauer, Abe. 2014. "The Envelope, Please: The 2014 Brandcameo Product Placement Awards." BrandChannel. Last modified February 27, 2014. http://www .brandchannel.com.

Toothman, Jessika. n.d. "What's The Difference between the Internet and the World Wide Web?" How Stuff Works. http://www.howstuffworks.com.

VIDEOS AND MOVIES

"Sociological Imagination." 2015. *Sociology Live!* Last modified October 22, 2015. http:// www.youtube.com.

von Baldegg, Kasia Cieplak-Mayr. 2012. "60 Years of Presidential Attack Ads, in One Video." *Atlantic*. Last modified September 10, 2012. http://www.theatlantic.com.

"What Is Sociology?" 2015. *Sociology Live!* Last modified September 18, 2015. http:// www.youtube.com.

CHAPTER REFERENCES

Berger, Peter, and Thomas Luckmann. 1967. *The Social Construction of Reality: A Treatise in the Sociology of Knowledge*. Norwell, MA: Anchor Press.

Best, Joel. 1995. *Images of Issues*. Hawthorne, NY: Aldine de Gruyter.

Crouteau, David, and William Hoynes. 2005. *The Business of Media: Corporate Media and the Public Interest*. Thousand Oaks, CA: Sage.

DiMaggio, Paul, Eszter Hargittai, W. Russell Neuman, and John Robinson. 2001. "Social Implications of the Internet." *Annual Review of Sociology* 27:307–36.

Fuchs, Christian. 2008. *Internet and Society: Social Theory in the Information Age*. New York: Routledge.

Hepp, Andreas. 2012. *Cultures of Mediatization*. Cambridge, UK: Polity Press.

Howard, Philip N., and Steve Jones. 2003. *Society Online: The Internet in Context*. Thousand Oaks, CA: Sage.

Kreiss, Daniel. 2012. *Taking Our Country Back: The Crafting of Networked Politics from Howard Dean to Barrack Obama*. New York: Oxford University Press.

———. 2016. *Prototype Politics: Technology-Intensive Campaigning and the Data of Democracy*. New York: Oxford University Press.

Livingstone, Sonia. 2009. "On the Mediation of Everything: ICA Presidential Address 2008." *Journal of Communication* 59 (1): 1–18.

Mead, George. 1934. *In Mind, Self and Society*. Edited by Charles Morris. Chicago: University of Chicago Press.

Ogburn, W. F. 1937. "The Influence of Inventions on American Social Institutions in the Future." *American Journal of Sociology* 63 (3): 365–76.

———. 1957. "How Technology Causes Social Change." In *Technology and Social Change*, edited by F. R. Allen, 12–26. New York: Appleton-Century-Crofts.

Parsons, Talcott. 1951. *The Social System*. New York: Free Press.

Ruane, Janet, and Karen Cerulo. 2004. *Second Thoughts: Seeing Conventional Wisdom through the Sociological Eye*. Thousand Oaks, CA: Pine Forge.

Scott, Richard. 2003. *Organizations: Rational, Natural, and Open Systems*. 5th ed. Upper Saddle River, NJ: Prentice Hall.

Silverblatt, Art. 2004. "Media as Social Institution." *American Behavioral Scientist* 40 (1): 35–41.

Su, Hua. 2016. "Constant Connection as the Media Condition of Love: Where Bonds Become Bondage." *Media, Culture & Society* 38 (2): 232–47.

Villegas, Alessondra. 2012. "The Influence of Technology of Family Dynamics." *Proceedings of the New York State Communication Association* 1 (10). http://www.rwu.edu.

1

Virtual Selves and Textual Encounters

KEY CONCEPTS

Self refers to the relatively stable set of perceptions we have about who we are relative to others. The self is shaped through interaction with others in a variety of settings.

Identity is the behaviors we perform in a setting that are related to the self. We perform many identities including student, sibling, child, friend, worker, partner, and so on—all of which make up the self.

Family consists of people who consider themselves related by blood, marriage, or adoption. Family is a universal social institution. This means that while its form may vary, no matter where you go in the world or how remote the culture, you will find family.

Socialization is a major job of family. Socialization refers to teaching children the language, social skills, and values of a society so that they can fit into a larger community.

Ontological security refers to our existential sense of self. According to Anthony Giddens, ontological security comes from our relationships with family members and friends and is achieved when we experience the positive and stable emotions that help us deal with events beyond our control.

If you have taken a sociology class, you probably have spent some amount of time contemplating the effects of mass media on the *self*, or the relatively stable set of perceptions we have about who we are relative to others. We compare ourselves to what we see in glossy magazine pages or on the screen and often find ourselves lacking. If you are a woman, then you may find yourself wondering how you measure up to the models and actresses you see. The points of comparison will vary.

Some women will focus on how their bodies compare with those of celebrities. Others will pay attention to actresses' clothing, hair, facial features, and skin tone. Most women, however, find themselves not quite measuring up and looking for exercise programs, diets, and products that will help them inch closer to the ideal we see in virtually every place we look. This is no less true for men, who compare their looks, bodies, abilities, and successes to the images of muscle-bound, handsome actors, musicians, and athletes that dominate the media landscape. Now imagine that you don't fit one of these gender ideals and neither set of images reflects your lived experiences. This is true for more than a million transgender individuals in the United States who, until recently, were almost completely absent from the media landscape. The absence of narratives is just as affecting as skewed ones. When there is no one that looks, feels, or has experiences like you in the vast offerings of mass media, it is easy to think that something about you is wrong—even when it's not true. Mass media, in other words, influence how we think about ourselves—our looks, our intelligence, our abilities, and our worth.

Mass media also can affect how we behave in the world. The gorgeous actors, actresses, musicians, and athletes that we see are successful. They have wealth and fame. They have made it, and we pay attention to their behavior. We look for cues on how to make it too. As we discussed in the introduction, the behaviors that lead to celebrity are not always socially desirable. For example, if *Teen Mom* actually causes young women to get pregnant because they see the show as a way to fame and fortune, then the show has the opposite of the desired effect, which is to reduce teen pregnancy. This, of course, is a dramatic example. Mass media can affect how we behave in more subtle ways—how we walk or dance and what products we think express our identities.

To get a better sense of how this works, watch the *PBS Frontline* video "The Merchants of Cool" (the link is at the end of this chapter). While it is a bit dated (Britney Spears was at the top of her game in 2001 rather than trying to make a comeback), the video illustrates two important points. First, the video shows how the economic function of mass media affect what and how products are sold to us. Recall from the introduction that we discussed how mass media are a social institution but that they have a profit-making function as well. As a result, television programs sometimes give mixed messages to the audience. *Teen Mom* is designed to prevent teen pregnancy but also uses the episodes to show-case clothing and products that are too expensive for the average young mother. In "The Merchants of Cool," the narrator of the video Douglas Rushkoff explains how media giant Viacom packages and markets "cool" to teens on MTV. Second, and more important for this discussion, the video shows how the teens, who gobble up MTV's programing, mimic what they see. In a particularly poignant scene, a group of teens realize the cameras are taping them at a dance and they begin cheering and dancing just like the musicians, dancers, and spring breakers featured on MTV. The teens are presenting what they believe is desirable behavior. In short, the video shows how mass media shape our behavior, or, more specifically, how we present ourselves to others—even if we cannot see them.

You can start to see why sociologists are interested in studying the self. As we talked about in the previous chapter, sociologists are interested in how individuals reproduce and challenge social institutions. Remember that the behavior of one actor is shaped by the behaviors of other actors and by changes in the institutional context. We generally behave in predictable ways because it allows us to achieve our goals. At a more basic level, the interactions we have with one another also shape the self. Sociologist Erving Goffman used the theatre as a metaphor to explain how our interactions affect the ways in which we think about ourselves. Goffman argues that we can understand how we craft our sense of self by studying how we "perform" in front of others in differ-ent "settings" or different social situations where interactions take place. Think of it this way. In a setting, we are on stage, and we perform an *identity*—or a particular version of our self—for an "audience" through our language, gestures, and actions. This performance is calculated. We behave in ways that are consistent with the situation and the expecta-tions of the audience.

As you can probably guess, there is more than one stage, and we give more than one performance over the course of the day. Since there are multiple settings where we interact with others, we have multiple identi-ties, many of which are associated with a social institution. For example, student, sibling or son, congregant, and friend are all identities that we may have that correspond with different behaviors and settings. As a result, how you interact with a religious leader in a place of worship is probably very different than how you interact with your friends at a party. This does not mean we lack an authentic identity or that we simply perform for whomever we are interacting with. We are able to navigate the social world because our different identities fit together in the "back stage." Like the theatre, the back stage is the place where the audience cannot see us and, consequently, we can be ourselves and drop the identities that we enact when we are in front of others. In the back stage, we can make sense of our various identities and their importance in our lives. While the relationship between self and identity can be complicated, Goffman's point is that we shouldn't understand the self as a biological characteristic that we are born with. The self develops through interaction as we anticipate, interpret, and respond to others.

Now imagine all the stages available to us in the digital age. It is not uncommon for individuals to have several different profiles so that they can perform different identities to several different audiences simultaneously. For example, my personal website, WordPress site, LinkedIn, Academia.edu, Research Gate, Facebook, and Twitter profiles are all slightly different. I present my professional self on my website and WordPress site. These sites are full of information regarding research I've done and interviews and talks I've given. I view this website as my first point of contact with the larger professional world, and I spend time updating the content and minimizing the information that is available about my personal life. This is far less true of my LinkedIn, Academic.edu, and Research Gate profiles, which I spend very little time working on. Here, I present myself as a colleague. Since I know that my colleagues—other academics—often are pressed for time and have a lot of professional demands, they won't care that my profiles are updated sporadically and, in fact, will understand exactly why this is the case. I communicate with my friends and close colleagues primarily through Facebook, so what I post is far more personal. I present myself as a friend and person with an active life so I share my political views, headlines from the *Onion*, and lots of family photos. I use Twitter as a semiprofessional place, since I also use it to post relevant material to my course websites. The identity that I perform is "professor who is interested in engaging with the world and who also is a person with a life and some opinions." My Twitter profile includes a picture of me with family, but I am careful not to tweet too many of my personal opinions, since I don't want my students to view my classes as biased. Once I am done teaching, I am a bit freer with my political and social commentary as well as the pictures of my kids—although I try to remember that students can search the last couple months of tweets.

None of these identities are inauthentic. My profiles simply reflect different identities and meet the expectations of the intended audience. Journalists who visit my website want to quickly figure out if I am the appropriate person to weigh in on their story and, in the case of live radio or television, see if I have any media experience. My colleagues who visit my professional pages want to see if I have uploaded copies of recent publications, and my friends who follow me on Facebook want to know what I think of different issues and what my family is up to. Of course, this scenario was not envisioned by Goffman. For one thing, our interactions transcend time and space, meaning we do not have to be in the same place at the same time to interact with one another. Email and texting do not require us to be anywhere near the person or people we are interacting with, nor do they require an instant response. For another thing, the back stage envisioned by Goffman isn't completely outside of the view of the audience. We reveal so much about ourselves online that audiences can easily find the different ways that we narrate our lives.

In this chapter, we will explore how new media have changed our relationships. We will begin by looking at the family, since, as we discuss below, familial relationships play a critical role in our overall well-being and affect how we interact with one another. As we will see, it is not clear how new media affects socialization, or how parents teach their children about the world and their place in it. This is not completely surprising. Social scientists have always struggled to determine when and how mass media affect socialization and this research is not easier to do in the digital age. However, we can see that new media have altered how parents and teens communicate dramatically. Then we will turn our attention to how new media have changed the ways in which teens interact with their friends. We will see that new media can make teen friendships more guarded and superficial. In the digital age, sometimes the number of connections becomes more important than the quality of the connection, which makes friendships less secure. At the same time, it is impossible to deny that new media allow teens to connect with others in ways that were impossible just twenty years ago. Social media, for instance, allow teens to make and maintain virtual friendships with people on the other side of the world. In short, we will see that new media shape relationships and our sense of self in complex and contradictory ways.

CASE STUDY

TallHotBlonde

Have you ever pretended to be someone else online?

In 2006, a forty-six-year-old father of two named Thomas Montgomery killed his coworker over an eighteen-year-old woman named Jessi, whose handle was TallHotBlonde. They met online in a teen chat room. In this deadly love triangle, however, almost no one was who they said they were. Jessi claimed to be a high school senior who loved to play softball. When Jessi sent Montgomery provocative pictures of herself, Montgomery, who went by the handle MarineSniper, sent Jessi thirty-year-old pictures of himself from boot camp. That's right. Montgomery pretended he was eighteen instead of forty-six years old. Before long, Montgomery and TallHotBlonde were engaged in an online sexual relationship.

Montgomery's wife learned about the affair and sent Jessi pictures of her, her husband, and their family. Horrified, Jessi ended the relationship. She told Montgomery that she hated him. Then Jessi began an online relationship with Montgomery's coworker, Brian Barrett, a twenty-two-year-old part-time machinist and college student. Montgomery watched their romance blossom in the same chat rooms he used to frequent with Jessi. Montgomery became jealous, made threats online, and then shot and killed Barrett after work one day. Police quickly learned about the love triangle and went to question Jessi. They learned that Jessi's mother, Mary, had been impersonating her daughter online. Mary had sent all the messages. Montgomery pleaded guilty to murder and received a twenty-year sentence. Mary's husband filed for a divorce and the real Jessi moved away from her mother.

You can watch the video about the case at ABCNews.com. Discuss the following questions:

• How might Goffman explain these presentations of self?
• Can we be authentic and pretend to be someone else? Why or why not?
• Is it ethical to pretend to be someone else online? Why or why not?

CYBER FAMILY

Family, which consists of people who consider themselves related by blood, marriage, or adoption, is universal. While its form may vary, no matter where you go in the world or how remote the culture, you will find family. As mentioned in the previous chapter, family is an important social institution that helps maintain social stability and keeps society working. Family fulfills several important functions, three of which we will discuss here. First, the family plays a central role in *socialization*, or teaching children the language, social skills, and values of a society, so that they can fit into a larger community. Second, the family is a source of practical and emotional support for its members. Parents provide children with the essentials—food, shelter, and clothing—as well as love and, when needed, comfort. Finally, family gives us a basic sense of self. Our first interactions are with family members, and they provide us with our first set of beliefs and values that tell us how to navigate a confusing world.

Family, of course, is not the only influence on us during our formative years. During your youth, you probably watched a bit of TV now and then and used the characters and plots you saw on programs in your own play. You may even recall a parent or relative instructing you to watch programs such as *Sesame Street, Dora the Explorer*, or *Go, Diego! Go!* because they were educational. You may not have considered how media content has shaped your sense of self. Social scientists and pediatricians have been concerned over the effects of mass media on the family for a long time. A central concern is over the role mass media play in socializing America's youth. Movies and television programs sometimes show individuals rewarded for behavior that families or society may not find desirable, and musicians occasionally talk about issues (and use language) that many parents may find unsavory. Interestingly, we most often debate the role of mass media in the socialization of children, and implicitly if it is more influential than family, in the wake of tragedy. One of the most discussed tragedies is the 1999 shootings at Columbine High School. On April 20, 1999, Eric Harris, eighteen years old, and Dylan Klebold, seventeen years old, set two propane bombs in Columbine High School. When the bombs failed to detonate, the boys went on a shooting spree, killing thirteen people and wounding more than twenty others before committing suicide.

The incident, which was the worst high school shooting in US history at the time, prompted a national debate on the role of mass media in the crime. This was different from more recent school shootings, such as the tragedies at Sandy Hook Elementary and Virginia Tech, because there wasn't evidence that Harris or Klebold were mentally ill. Parents, politicians, citizens, and journalists pointed to their media consumption. In particular, the video game *Doom* and the music of Marilyn Manson came under fire. It turns out that Harris and Klebold were avid players of *Doom*, which was an early first-person-shooter game. You can check out a clip that gives you a sense of what the game looked like on YouTube (there is a link at the end of this chapter). You will see that the game features an unnamed space marine who battles invading demons from Hell. The game was already controversial because of its graphic violence and satanic imagery. The debate about the negative effects of *Doom* on kids, their values, and their behavior reached new heights when law enforcement found Harris's journal. In it, Harris compared killing real people to playing the game and bragged that the gun he bought was just like the one in *Doom*.

Pundits and military personnel criticized *Doom* for teaching the boys to be killers. The game, they argued, socialized the boys to be soldiers. One former army colonel, who appeared on both *60 Minutes* and the *Today Show*, described the game as a "mass murder simulator" that provides military-type training. *Doom*, the colonel argued, taught Harris and Klebold how to make "kill shots" so that they could save ammunition as they moved through the game. The colonel also suggested that the violent game ultimately desensitized them against the gory results of taking a life. According to the *60 Minutes* report, *Doom* was used by the military to teach soldiers how to move slowly through a building as well as to shoot and kill targets. The report clearly suggested that the game socialized the boys to devalue and take lives.

Rocker Marilyn Manson was also blamed for the tragedy. News media outlets falsely reported that Harris and Klebold were big fans of Manson's music and styled their gothic look, which included a trench coat, on his. Manson, who had long been the enemy of religious organizations, became a national scapegoat and was accused of targeting his messages of violence, hate, and celebration of suicide squarely at teens. Manson's critics argued that his music basically taught kids that violence and even suicide were acceptable solutions to life's problems. Manson dismissed these claims. He argued that his music was misunderstood. His main goal was to challenge social norms and values so that those who felt out of place in the world knew that they were not alone. In an article Manson wrote for *Rolling Stone* (June 24, 1999), he notes that entertainment has always been an easy scapegoat for American society's tragedies. He writes, "America loves to find an icon to hang its guilt on. But, admittedly, I have assumed the role of Antichrist; I am the Nineties voice of individuality, and people tend to associate anyone who looks and behaves differently with illegal or immoral activity. Deep down, most adults hate people who go against the grain. It's comical that people are naive enough to have forgotten Elvis, Jim Morrison and Ozzy so quickly. All of them were subjected to the same age-old arguments, scrutiny and prejudice."

Later in the article, Manson points out that scapegoating entertainers and video games is far easier than going after the National Rifle Association, which he suggests should carry some of the blame for Harris and Klebold's ability to easily get guns and ammunition. Manson notes,

So is entertainment to blame? I'd like media commentators to ask themselves, because their coverage of the event was some of the most gruesome entertainment any of us have seen. I think that the National Rifle Association is far too powerful to take on, so most people choose *Doom*, *The Basketball Diaries* or yours truly. This kind of controversy does not help me sell records or tickets, and I wouldn't want it to. I'm a controversial artist, one who dares to have an opinion and bothers to create music and videos that challenge people's ideas in a world that is watered-down and hollow. In my work I examine the America we live in, and I've always tried to show people that the devil we blame our atrocities on is really just each one of us. So don't expect the end of the world to come one day out of the blue—it's been happening every day for a long time.

This discussion should make it clear that it is very difficult to figure out how mass media matter to socialization because there are other factors that play a role in socialization as well. In addition to family and mass media, our friends, our communities, our schools, and our group affiliations (such as those with religious groups or gangs) all affect how we think about the world and our role in it. More important, the Columbine case highlights our tendency to talk about mass media as either a positive or negative influence on socialization. On the one hand, this makes a lot of sense. We want to know what is good or bad for us and our kids. On the other hand, socialization is far too complicated for scientists to say little more than mass media play a role in it.

The concern over mass media's effect on socialization hasn't changed in the digital age. We see this concern most clearly in efforts to track how much time American youth spend with new media and what they are doing with their digital devices. For example, Common Sense Media does a yearly census tracking how much time tweens and teens spend using mass media. In its 2015 census on media use by tweens and teens, Common Sense found that kids spend on average nine hours per day engaged with new media, not including their use for school and homework. If you look at the charts below (figures 1.1 and 1.2), you will see that the Common Sense Media Census considers tweens and teens separately and that they break users down into different categories based on the activities in which they most engage: light users, readers, mobile gamers, heavy viewers, video gamers, and social networkers. You probably immediately noticed that overall teens (thirteen- to seventeen-year-olds) spend more time using media than tweens and that a lot of media use involves mobile or computer gaming. Teens spend nine hours and seventeen minutes per day on average gaming. Tweens only spend about six hours engaged in the same activity. In its census, Common Sense Media also notes that most of the new media use happens while kids are supposed to be doing their homework. Remember, the census focuses on new media use unrelated to school work and homework. The census suggests that new media are a potential distraction for kids.

Surveys that track teens' new media use also show that kids share and are exposed to inappropriate content in the digital age. A survey published by the *Journal of Pediatricians* found that 58 percent of teens (fourteen- to seventeen-year-olds) have viewed pornography on a computer or mobile phone and 37 percent of teens have received a link to sexually explicit content. Additionally, an anonymous survey of undergraduates found that more than half of the participants admitted to sending sexually explicit material via a text, or sexting, in high school.

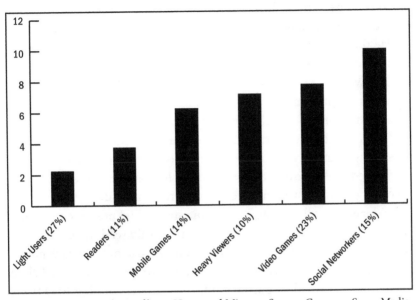

Figure 1.1. Tween Media Profiles in Hours and Minutes. Source: Common Sense Media.

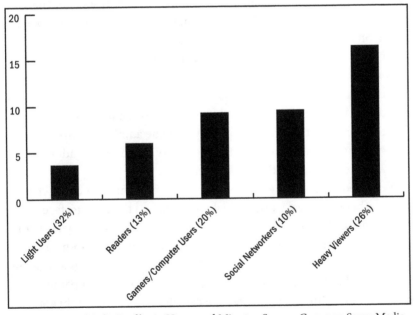

Figure 1.2. Teen Media Profiles in Hours and Minutes. Source: Common Sense Media.

Up to 61 percent of those surveyed also admitted that they did not realize that underage sexting is illegal in some states, nor did they realize the steep punishments, including jail time and being labeled a sex offender, that accompanied a conviction. If you go to Mobile Media Guard's website, you can look up pending and existing legislation. In Texas, for instance, minors who are caught sexting can be charged with a misdemeanor and forced to attend a state-sponsored sexting education class with a parent. If the minor is caught creating, distributing, or possessing a sexually explicit image of another minor, he or she could be charged under Texas's child pornography statutes. Some states, like Wyoming, don't distinguish between minors and adults, and charge individuals, regardless of age, under the state's child pornography laws. What is implicit in the results, which are mostly read by parents and educators, is that grownups need to be concerned about how new media shape the core beliefs, values, and behavior of America's children. While these surveys provide a partial context for understanding how teens connect with one another in the digital age, we cannot use these surveys to make arguments regarding the role of new media in socialization.

So what can social scientists study when it comes to the effects of new media on the relationships between parents and children? They can analyze how new media change the way parents and children communicate with one another. New media provide families with some basic conveniences that almost go without saying. It is much easier for families to coordinate busy schedules and to keep track of one another in the digital world. Parents and children frequently text one another regarding after-school plans and late practices, making it easy for parents to adjust when and where they pick up their kids after work.

New media also change how well parents and children connect with one another in the real world. Social scientists find that face-to-face interactions are critical to parent-child relationships because they give conversations context. When parents and kids can see one another's facial cues and body language, they can gauge each other's reactions and assess what the other person needs from the conversation—a sympathetic ear, praise, admonishment, or advice. We can all probably remember at least one time where we had a terrible day at school but told a parent that everything was fine. If our loved ones were paying attention and noticed our slumped shoulders and the tone of our voices, they pressed the issue to make sure we were OK or at least gave us a sympathetic hug. New media can be distractions that take attention away from these important face-to-face encounters. It is easy to imagine family members, each with their noses buried in a phone or tablet, gathered around a shared table, eating dinner and engaging with someone or something else.

Social scientists do have insight into how new media potentially undermine the quality of the face-to-face interactions between parents and children. For instance, Sherry Turkle, a professor at the Massachusetts Institute of Technology who interviewed dozens of adults and teens, found that we are generally obsessed with being connected. We check our email, texts, and social media accounts constantly in order to make sure that we are not "missing out" on news or events of interest. Our smartphones, laptops, and tablets, as a result, are a distraction during our face-to-face encounters. This is something that teens complain about. Teens told Turkle that they felt distant from their parents even when they were in the same room engaged in a shared activity. For example, one teen noted that his father and he watch sports together but complained that his dad was constantly on his mobile phone. His dad's behavior bothered him because it made him seem disinterested and disconnected. Another teen expressed frustration that her mom was always on the phone when she picked her up after school. She wished that her mom would get off the phone and talk to her instead. Moreover, teens did not consider connecting online through social media or via text message an acceptable substitute for face-to-face interaction. "Friending" them on social media platforms such as Facebook and Instagram as well as texting them when they were out with their friends were regarded as attempts to keep tabs on them rather than an effort to connect. In short, Turkle consistently found that teens want to spend more quality time with their parents in the "real" world.

You might be thinking that the solution to this problem is obvious. Parents simply need to put their phones down and connect with their children. You wouldn't be alone in that thought. If you go online, you will quickly see that there is no shortage of suggestions on how parents can make sure that they are connecting with their kids in the digital age. Social scientists, however, find that the problem may not be so not easily solved. As we will discuss in more detail in another chapter, new media make employees available for work after hours and on vacations. Many employees are expected to answer their phones, emails, and even do work outside the regular workday. These work demands intrude on family time in ways that parents cannot always control. Additionally, social scientists find that new media can help teens transition into adulthood. The distance that new media create between parents and children can be good for teens as they develop identities outside of the family. As we discuss in more detail in the following section, new media provide forums where teens can experiment with their personality characteristics and develop virtual friendships.

In sum, we don't know how much influence new media have in the socialization process. This effect of mass media has never been completely clear. Socialization is difficult to study, and determining if parents, media, communities, schools, or affiliations matter more in a particular individual's life at a moment in time is nearly impossible to discern. It is clear, however, that we spend a lot of time engaged with new media and that digital technology change how parents and children interact. In a connected world, parents find it more difficult to turn off their mobile phones and laptops and engage with their children. This is something that teens notice and complain about. In the next section, we will look at how this obsession with being connected changes how teens interact with one another and what this might mean for their relationships and their construction of self.

DIGITAL RELATIONSHIPS

The quality of our connections with family affects how we navigate our relationships. When our family life is stable and secure and we know we are loved, we feel more confident going out into the world, meeting new people, and trying new things. We can use the ideas of sociologist Anthony Giddens to begin to understand the importance of our relationships in the digital age. Giddens argues that the modern world is characterized by blurred boundaries between globalism, or networks of connections that bridge space and time, and individuality, or the characteristics that distinguish us from one another, which affect how we connect with one another.

This may seem a bit confusing. So let's use social media to understand the relationship between new media and ourselves. Social media

CASE STUDY

The Curated Life Online

Commemorating the twenty-fifth anniversary of the World Wide Web, the *Guardian*, a British newspaper, put together an interactive website on how we've been affected by the information revolution. The website, which is called the Seven Digital Deadly Sins, explores how the internet affects us socially, morally, and personally. For this exercise, take a look at the website and watch the short video titled "Envy." In it, Mary Walsh talks about how going on social media sites such as Facebook makes her feel bad about herself. She feels as though everyone looks better and has a more interesting life than she does. After you watch the video, think about the following questions:

- How much time do you spend curating your life on social media?
- Who are the audiences of your profiles?
- What are the goals of your performances?
- Do you feel pressure to post content that will be popular? Why or why not?
- Can we use Goffman to understand our performances on social media? Where do his ideas work? Where do they fall short?

platforms such as Facebook, Twitter, and Instagram primarily are tools for connecting people with one another around the world. However, as previously discussed, we also use social media to construct and convey our identities to our friends, coworkers, and other audiences through these sites. For example, who and what we "like" on Facebook gives people information about our tastes and preferences against a global backdrop. If you like Justin Bieber and a local environmental group, this indicates who you are and what you care about relative to all the other global interests and international concerns.

Of course, as we already discussed, we can use different accounts or social media platforms to construct different identities for different audiences. We may, for instance, have a fondness for celebrity culture and a desire to keep our interest in Kim Kardashian's latest exploits to ourselves. Social media platforms such as Twitter make it relatively easy to set up a private account, use a random user name, and connect with others who share our interest in the Kardashian's dramatic life. In the virtual world, we can literally participate in global conversations on celebrities, soccer, and feminism—all of which say something about who we are. New media, in short, give us a way to display our tastes and preferences publicly and assess how these identities are perceived by others in a potentially global network.

So far, Giddens's ideas might not seem too different from those of Goffman. They are. Why? Because Giddens considers how our close relationships with family and friends affect our behavior in the digital world. Specifically, Giddens argues that in order to operate fully in the modern world, where so much of our lives are virtual, individuals must possess a sense of *ontological security*, or an existential sense of self. Ontological security, according to Giddens, comes from our relationships with family members and friends and is achieved when we experience the positive and stable emotions that ground us in the "real" world. Giddens contends that this security is paramount because it contributes to our positive sense of self and helps us deal with events (such as a bad breakup or an economic recession) that are beyond our control. Individuals who are ontologically insecure, in other words, lack these important connections and experience frequent anxiety as a result. Given that new media change how parents and children interact with one another, it is easy to imagine that new media also affect how teens and young adults maintain a sense of ontological security.

Remember how Turkle found that we are constantly turning to our devices so that we feel connected? Teens report that being connected to one another through their smartphones and computers makes them feel ontologically secure. However, as mentioned above, Turkle also found that teens noted that the need to connect with others was compulsive. One teen, who Turkle calls Maury, explained that he ends phone calls with friends and family when an "unknown" call comes in because he has to know who it is and why they are calling him. It doesn't matter that it is probably a telemarketer. Maury reported that he simply *had* to take the call. As he and other teens described it, they need to connect, and resisting the urge to make new connections is futile. They simply cannot help but look at their phones to see who has texted or liked a comment or post on social media.

The problem with this, of course, is that teens sometimes focus on the number of connections they have in the form of "friends" and "likes" rather than the quality of their connections. In fact, as you can see in the chart based on Pew Research Center data below (figure 1.3), many teens feel obligated to post content that is attractive and will get them more connections on social media. According to Pew's survey, 40 percent of teens reported that they felt pressured to post only content that makes them look good to others and 39 percent said they felt pressured to post content that will be popular and get lots of comments or likes. The phenomenon of posting content that will attract "likes" is taken to its extreme in the Netflix show *Black Mirror*. In the episode titled "Nosedive," an individual's status, as well as her access to a nice apartment and decent service, is literally determined by her social media ranking.

Given the focus on being "connected" and "liked," it is easy to question how ontologically secure teens really feel in the digital age. The research suggests that the effects of new media on the ontological security of teenagers are complicated. On the one hand, new media create a safety buffer among teens, which makes them less willing to interact with one another face-to-face and over the phone. In the chart based on the Pew Research Center's surveys on teens, technology, and friendships (figure 1.4), you will notice that text messaging is teens' favorite way to contact their friends daily. Up to 55 percent of teens, in fact, stay in contact with their friends via text. While teens generally report that they believe their friends are very busy and they don't want to bother them with a visit or phone call, teens also noted that they prefer communicating via text because it allows them to control the conversation. Specifically, teens worry that they will either say something stupid or be made to look stupid in "real-time" interactions. Text messaging is better because they can edit what they say. One teen, who was interviewed by

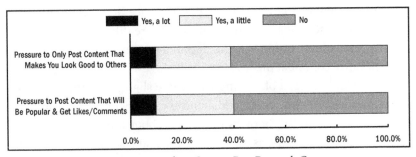

Figure 1.3. Pressures Teens Face Online. Source: Pew Research Center.

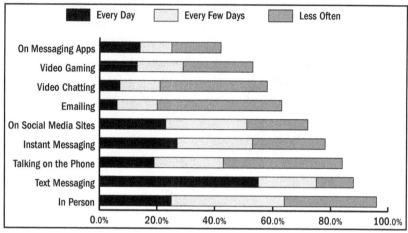

Figure 1.4. How Teens Communicate with Their Friends. Source: Pew Research Center.

Turkle during the course of her research, explained that she likes texting because it protects her from awkward and embarrassing interactions. She said, "Nothing will get spat at you. You have time to think and prepare what you are going to say, to make you appear like that's just the way you are. There's planning involved so you can control how you're portrayed to this person, because you're choosing these words, editing it before you send it. . . . A phone conversation is a lot of pressure. You're always expected to uphold it, to keep it going, and that's so much pressure." The young woman goes on to explain that she feels more in control over texts. She can communicate her main points and decide when the conversation begins and ends. The risk of saying too much or saying something stupid is much lower.

Social scientists have found that there are at least two problems with teens using new media to create digital distance between themselves and others. First, teens sometimes have a more difficult time dealing with interpersonal conflict. In the digital age, teens are very aware of every negative comment made about them and every party to which they are not invited. Instead of dealing with these slights face-to-face, teens sometimes lash out on social media and the conflict grows. A negative comment posted on Facebook by one friend about another, for example, can quickly grow in scope as others weigh in and take sides on the issue.

These online conflicts, which could be resolved with a quick face-to-face conversation, can be quite drawn out and end with "unfriending." Teenage drama online is probably more widespread than you think. The Pew Research Center found that 53 percent of teens who use social media have seen people post about events to which they were not invited and 68 percent of teen social media users say they've had experienced drama among their friends on sites such as Facebook and Instagram.

Second, and related, teens consistently note that they are much meaner to others online than they are face-to-face. Again, new media create a distance in interaction and this distance makes it easy for some individuals to say and do things that they may not otherwise. Teens are not alone in this regard, of course. There are plenty of adults who go online for the sole purpose of being mean to others for their own amusement (which is called "lulz"). Trolling is an excellent example of individuals engaging in intentionally mean interactions online, typically through social media. Let's talk about a couple of examples. The first involves Lindy West, a feminist writer. In an episode of *This American Life*, West talks to her worst troll and asks him what he was thinking when he tweeted nasty things about her. West is familiar with trolling. She, in fact, has lots of trolls. What made this troll different was that he impersonated her recently deceased father and made repeated and explicit rape threats. As you can imagine, this was very upsetting. West responded by writing an article about her dad and about how this particular troll's efforts were working. She felt devastated. The day after the post went up, West received the following email from her troll, which she posted online and reprinted in an article for the *Guardian*. The troll wrote,

Hey Lindy,
I don't know why or even when I started trolling you. It wasn't because of your stance on rape jokes. I don't find them funny either. I think my anger towards you stems from your happiness with your own being. It offended me because it served to highlight my unhappiness with my own self.
I have emailed you through two other Gmail accounts just to send you idiotic insults.
I apologize for that.

I created the paulwestdonezo@gmail.com account and Twitter account. (I have deleted both.)

I can't say sorry enough.

It was the lowest thing I had ever done. When you included it in your latest Jezebel article, it finally hit me. There is a living, breathing human being who's reading this shit. I'm attacking someone who never harmed me in any way and for no reason whatsoever.

I'm done being a troll.

Again, I apologize.

I made a donation in memory to your dad.

I wish you the best.

The troll attached a receipt for a fifty-dollar donation to the Seattle Cancer Care Alliance, where her father was treated for cancer, designated in her dad's memory. While West's follow-up conversation with her troll is quite memorable (check out the link at the end of the chapter), it is clear that the troll had not really thought of West as a person with feelings. The distance stripped her of a personality and their interaction of a context, which made it much easier for him to be mean.

West is not the only target of trolls. Female athletes, particularly those who are at the top of their game, often are the target of trolls. Serena Williams, who is arguably the world's most dominant female athlete, with, at the time of this writing, nearly two dozen Grand Slam tennis titles, often comes under attack. Trolls typically focus on Williams's body, accusing her of either looking too masculine or for drawing too much attention to her body. In 2016, when Williams was just one win away from her twenty-second Grand Slam win, people took to Twitter so that they could criticize her white tennis outfit, which, they charged, was too tight and revealing. Many individuals strangely focused on Williams's nipples, claiming that they were a distraction from the match. For example, one woman tweeted that "Serena Williams [sic] nipples are literally in HD like can u [sic] put them away I'm trying to watch the match." Another woman commented, "Just to let you know @serenawilliams we can see your nipples through your top! Whoops! #Wimbledon2016 #SerenaWilliams #WimbledonshouldbePG." Another asked, "What is it about Serena Williams nipples this Wimbledon?" It is worth noting that, in this case, many of the trolls were other women.

Unlike Lindy West, Serena Williams did not engage her detractors online, although she was frequently asked about them by reporters. In an interview with Elena Bergeron from the magazine *Fader* after her Wimbledon win, Williams noted, "People are entitled to have their opinions, but what matters most is how I feel about me, because that's what's going to permeate the room I'm sitting in. It's going to make you feel that I have confidence in myself whether you like me or not, or you like the way I look or not." Similarly, when asked about trolls by *Self* magazine, Williams responded, "I love my body, and I would never change anything about it. I'm not asking you to like my body. I'm just asking you to let me be me." While Williams continues to rise above the petty snipes of trolls, it is easy to see how this distance created among people in the digital world could translate into ontological insecurity.

On the other hand, it is clear that new media are not all bad for teens' relationships. Individuals can make meaningful connections online, and these connections legitimately make teens feel more ontologically secure. In its survey of teens, technology, and friendship, the Pew Research Center found that 57 percent of teens have connected with someone on social media or through online games that they wouldn't have necessarily met in real life. While the vast majority of these friendships remain online, 20 percent of teens reported that they meet their digital friends in the "real" world. Communicating online, Pew found, is particularly important for boys, who use gaming as a way to cultivate and maintain friendships. In fact, Pew found that boys often share their gaming handle with others with whom they would like to develop friendships and that 71 percent of boys use voice connections so that they can collaborate, chat, and trash talk with others while they play. These connections seem to be good for ontological security. You can see in the chart based on the Pew Research Center data below (figure 1.5) that gamers feel more connected with the friends that they game with (a total of 78 percent) and feel more relaxed and happy while gaming (a total of 82 percent). Only 30 percent of gamers reported that gaming made them more angry and frustrated. New media, in other words, provide forums where teens can connect with one another and cultivate meaningful, positive relationships.

New media also provide forums where teens can explore aspects of their personality, find support, and practice intimacy. Online forums

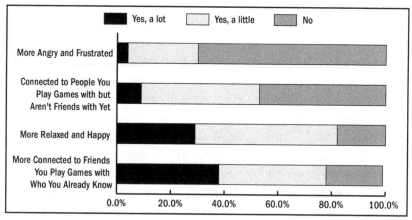

Figure 1.5. Feelings of Gamers Regarding Friendship. Source: Pew Research Center.

such as *Second Life* and *World of Warcraft* provide places where teens can interact with others and in contexts that are not unlike the real world. In *Second Life*, for instance, you can take classes, launch a business, buy land or products, build a home, and interact with friends, lovers, and community members. In this virtual space, the stages described by Goffman are clear. We choose the setting (school, library, church, store), and we know how we are supposed to perform in the setting. A space such as *Second Life*—one that mimics the "real world" in a lot of ways—is ideal for teens working on their identities. Teens report that they use these spaces to experiment with different aspects of their personalities. They practice everything from being more assertive with their friends to flirting and relationships. Teens also experiment with gender. Sociologists find that girls between thirteen and fifteen use social media, chat rooms, and role-playing games to switch genders, express emotions that feel taboo offline (such as sexual desire and aggression), and challenge norms around acting feminine. Teenage girls even go online to push back against sexual harassment and sexist behavior. Not surprisingly, teens describe their experiences in online forums as meaningful and positive, which suggests they can help teens feel ontologically secure.

REPRODUCING INEQUALITY
Racial Inequality Online

If you've taken a few sociology courses, you might have read "White Privilege: Unpacking the Invisible Knapsack" by Peggy McIntosh. If you are unfamiliar with the essay, McIntosh reflects on privilege, or the invisible and unearned advantages that individuals cash in on daily but do not necessarily see. She argues that once we recognize privilege, we are responsible for addressing it. For many students, the most powerful part of the essay is a list of conditions that McIntosh finds are givens in her life but not the lives of nonwhite individuals. Some of the conditions she discusses include the following:

- I can go shopping alone most of the time, pretty well assured that I will not be followed or harassed.
- I am never asked to speak for all the people of my racial group.
- If a traffic cop pulls me over, or if the IRS audits my tax return, I can be sure I haven't been singled out because of my race.
- I can choose blemish cover or bandages in "flesh" color that more or less match my skin.

While some of this may seem obvious to you, have you ever thought about how white privilege is reinforced online? Consider the following:

- Early versions of *Second Life* made it virtually impossible to create a nonwhite avatar. While *Second Life* has expanded the range of skin tones, or "skins," available to players, many of them are light. Additionally, *Second Life* players cannot adjust their avatars' facial features to mirror their own.
- The lack of diversity in virtual spaces such as *Second Life* affects the willingness of nonwhite users to create avatars that reveal their racial identity. Research conducted by social scientist Roselyn Jong-Eun Lee found that people of color who did chose nonwhite skins felt like "tokens" in the virtual space. One respondent noted, "One of the strangest things that I felt going through Second Life was that I was really one of the only black avatars pretty much everywhere I went . . . As I started to realize that I was literally one of the only black people on Second Life, I started to wonder what everybody else thought about the only token black guy walking around by himself."

- **White individuals who created nonwhite avatars in *Second Life* experience racism. Many of these individuals are called racial epithets and have difficulty making friends.**

Racial inequality is reinforced online in virtual spaces, and this is something that we participate in every time we create an avatar. When we choose a black, white, or brown avatar we make race part of the online space, and we signal what physical characteristics we value. The answer, however, is not as simple as to ask white users to create nonwhite avatars. Asking whites to be "identity tourists," or to take on a racialized identity, in online spaces when they do not understand the cause and consequences of these social statuses does not address inequality. It only reinforces it.

Finally, social scientists find that new media can help teens create new networks as they transition to adulthood. College students, for example, frequently go online and find the virtual chat rooms and forums associated with their new colleges and universities. These general forums help new students find the networks of people—gamers, dentists in training, young entrepreneurs, feminists, lacrosse enthusiasts, and more—they want to connect with. These networks, even if they are only online, are important because students can get advice and support from one another as they weather the trials of adulthood and higher education. In fact, social scientists find that college students who had made friends online were more likely to stay in school, even when the going got tough.

New media, in sum, can undermine and strengthen teens' relationships with one another and their ontological security. New media can undermine ontological security by focusing teens' attention on the number of connections that they have rather than the quality of these friendships. The problem with this focus is that these connections can be superficial and distant. Consequently, teens are sometimes meaner and less thoughtful about what they do and say in virtual contexts. However, it is difficult to deny that these connections can make teens more ontologically secure. Teens can use new media to make new friends, deepen existing friendships, and explore their feelings, insecurities, and interests. These virtual spaces can be important insofar as they allow us to make new friends who share our interests and can make us feel more secure about who we are in the real world.

CASE STUDY

Living Life Online

Watch the documentary *Life 2.0* on YouTube (there is a link at the end of the chapter). The film features individuals who spend most of their lives interacting and working online in the game *Second Life*. After you view the film, answer the following questions:

- What did you think about the people featured in the film? Were you sympathetic or unsympathetic to their stories? Why?
- Do you think you can find meaningful relationships entirely online?
- What do you think Giddens would say about the people featured in the film? Would he say that they are ontologically insecure? Why or why not?

CONCLUSION

In this chapter, we discussed the self and our relationships in the digital age. We learned that the self is different from identity. The self refers to the relatively stable set of perceptions we have about who we are relative to others. Our sense of self is shaped through interaction with others in different settings—some virtual, such as *Second Life*, and some real, such as school. Identity refers to the behaviors we perform in a setting that are related to the self. We perform many identities throughout the day including student, sibling, child, friend, worker, and partner, and new media allow us to explore or experiment with aspects of our identity. As discussed above, we can be Kim Kardashian lovers on Twitter and flirty on *Second Life*. Erving Goffman uses the theatre analogy in order to help us better understand the relationship between the self and identity and the importance of interaction and audience to our performances. He introduces the idea of the "back stage" so that we remember that all the identities we perform are authentic, related, and help constitute the self.

Then we talked about the family and its importance to establishing our sense of self. Our families socialize us into a larger community, provide a critical source of practical and emotional support, and give us a basic sense of self. Our interactions with our family at an early age help us understand our strengths, our flaws, and our place in the world. In this section of the chapter, we discussed concerns regarding the role of mass media and new media in socialization and outlined how inter-actions between parents and children have changed in the digital age. Teens, we learned, want to connect with their parents more often in the real world.

We concluded the chapter by outlining what new media mean for teens' ontological security and relationships. It is clear that new media are not simply good or bad for teens. Deriving ontological security from feeling connected is negative insofar as it can mean that teens primarily post and text content that they think will be liked by others and result in additional connections. These connections, however, may be superficial and conflict-ridden and create problems for teens in the "real" world. That said, teens can use new media to make meaningful connections with others. As we discussed, virtual spaces such as *Second Life*, Twitter, and Facebook can help teens connect with one another, experiment with aspects of their identity, and feel supported as they transition into adult-hood. In short, there is still much for sociologists to learn about the self and our relationships in the digital world.

CHAPTER LINKS

"The Merchants of Cool." 2001. *PBS Frontline*. Last modified February 27, 2001. http://www.pbs.org.

"Doom 1 (1993)." 2010. YouTube. Last modified August 13, 2010. http://www.youtube.com.

Manson, Marilyn. 1999. "Columbine: Whose Fault Is It? In the Aftermath of the Colorado School Shooting, Marilyn Manson Speaks Out." *Rolling Stone*. Last modified June 24, 1999. http://www.rollingstone.com.

"Seven Digital Deadly Sins." n.d. *Guardian*. http://www.theguardian.com. "Envy" is one of the short films on the site.

"U.S. Sexting Laws and Regulations." 2011. Mobile Media Guard. http://www.mobilemediaguard.com.

West, Lindy. 2015. "Ask Not for Whom the Bell Trolls; It Trolls for Thee." *This American Life*. Last modified January 23, 2015. http://www.thisamericanlife.org.

West, Lindy. 2015. "What Happened When I Confronted My Cruelest Troll." *Guardian*. Last modified February 2, 2015. http://www.theguardian.com.

Bergeron, Elena. 2016. "How Serena Williams Became the G.O.A.T." *Fader*. Last modified October 4, 2016. http://www.thefader.com.

Kahn, Howie. 2016. "Serena Williams, Wonder Woman, Is Our September Cover Star." *Self*. Last modified August 1, 2016. http://www.self.com.

"Home Page." 2018. Second Life. http://www.secondlife.com.

McIntosh, Peggy. 1989. "White Privilege: Unpacking the Invisible Knapsack." *Peace and Freedom*. http://www.nationalseedproject.org.

"Life 2.0" YouTube. http://www.youtube.com.

CHAPTER REVIEW QUESTIONS

1. What is the difference between the self and identity? Why does the distinction matter?
2. Do social scientists argue that mass media affect socialization? Why or why not?
3. How do new media affect the interactions between parents and their children?
4. What is ontological security and why does it matter?
5. Do new media negatively or positively affect the ontological security of teens?

LEARN MORE

"The Common Sense Census: Media Use by Tweens and Teens." 2015. Common Sense Media. http://www.commonsensemedia.org.

Dakin, Pauline. 2014. "Social Media Affecting Teen's Concepts of Friendship, Intimacy." *CBC News*. Last modified February 24, 2014. http://www.cbc.ca.

DeRosa, Denise Lisi. 2015. "Practical Advice for Raising Kids in the Digital Age." *Huffington Post*. Last modified November 4, 2016. http://www.huffingtonpost.com.

Dockterman, Eliana. 2014. "Kim Stolz: How Social Media Is Ruining Our Relationships." *Time*. Last modified June 24, 2014. http://www.time.com.

Fowlkes, Jasmine. 2012. "Viewpoint: Why Social Media Is Destroying Our Social Skills." *USA Today*. Last modified October 11, 2012. http://www.usatoday.com.

Gross, Terry. 2016. "The Twitter Paradox: How a Platform Designed for Free Speech Enables Internet Trolls." *Fresh Air*. Last modified October 26, 2016. http://www.npr.org.

"The Lawsuits: A Summary of the Civil Lawsuits Being Filed in School Shootings, as of January 2000." 2000. *PBS Frontline*. Last modified January 2000. http://www.pbs.org.

Moore, David, and Bill Manville. 2009. "What Role Might Video Game Addiction Have Played in the Columbine Shooting." *Daily News*. Last modified April 23, 2009. http://www.dailynews.com.

"Rage: A Look at a Teen Killer." 1999. *CBS News*. Last modified August 17, 1999. http://www.cbsnews.com.

Smith, Aaron, and Monica Anderson. 2016. "5 Facts about Online Dating." Last modified February 29, 2016. http://www.pewresearch.org.

Stout, Hilary. 2010. "Antisocial Networking?" *New York Times*. Last modified April 30, 2010. http://www.nytimes.com.

Ward, Mark. 2001. "Columbine Families Sue Computer Game Makers." *BBC News*. Last modified May 1, 2001. http://www.bbc.co.uk.

VIDEOS AND MOVIES

Black Mirror. 2017. Season 3, episode 1, "Nosedive." Netflix.

Cox, Courteney, dir. 2012. *TalHotBlond*. Lasky Productions. TV Movie.

Fisher, Helen. 2016. "Technology Hasn't Changed Love. Here's Why." *TED*. Last modified June 2016. http://www.ted.com.

Futerman, Samantha, and Ryan Miyamoto. 2015. *Twinsters*. Small Package Films. DVD.

"Generation Like." 2014. *PBS Frontline*. Last modified February 18, 2014. http://www.pbs.org.

Jonze, Spike. 2013. *Her*. Annapurna Pictures. DVD.

"The Merchants of Cool." 2001. *PBS Frontline*. Last modified February 27, 2001. http://www.pbs.org.

Yorkey, Brian. 2017. *13 Reasons Why*. Netflix. TV series.

CHAPTER REFERENCES

boyd, danah. 2014. *It's Complicated: The Social Lives of Networked Teens*. New Haven, CT: Yale University Press.

DeAndrea, David C., Nicole B. Ellison, Robert LaRose, Charles Steinfield, and Andrew Fiore. 2012. "Serious Social Media: On the Use of Social Media for Improving Students' Adjustment to College." *The Internet and Higher Education* 15 (1): 15–23.

Giddens, Anthony. 1991. *Modernity and Self-Identity: Self and Society in the Late Modern Age*. Palo Alto, CA: Stanford University Press.

Goffman, Erving. 1959. *The Presentation of Self in Everyday Life*. New York: Anchor.

Gray, Rebecca, Jessica Vitak, Emily W. Easton, and Nicole B. Ellison. 2013. "Examining Social Adjustment to College in the Age of Social Media: Factors Influencing Successful Transitions and Persistence." *Computers & Education* 67:93–207.

Greenfield, Patricia. 2014. *Mind and Media: The Effects of Television, Video Games, and Computers*. New York: Psychology Press.

Hasinoff, Amy Adele. 2013. "Sexting as Media Production: Rethinking Social Media and Sexuality." *New Media & Society* 15 (4): 449–65.

Hogan, Bernie. 2010. "The Presentation of Self in the Age of Social Media: Distinguishing Performances and Exhibitions Online." *Bulletin of Science, Technology & Society* 30 (6). https://doi.org/10.1177/0270467610385893.

Kelly, Deirdre, Shauna Pomerantz, and Dawn Currie. 2006. "'No Boundaries? Girls' Interactive, Online Learning about Femininities." *Youth & Society* 38 (1): 3–28.

Lee, Jong-Eun Roselyn. 2014. "Does Virtual Diversity Matter? Effects of Avatar-Based Diversity Representation on Willingness to Express Offline Racial Identity and Avatar Customization." *Computers in Human Behavior* 36:190–97.

Marwick, Alice E. 2011. "I Tweet Honestly, I Tweet Passionately: Twitter Users, Context Collapse, and the Imagined Audience." *New Media & Society* 13 (1): 114–33.

McGlotten, Shaka. 2013. *Virtual Intimacies: Media, Affect, and Queer Sociality*. Albany, NY: State University Press of New York.

Meyrowitz, Joshua. 1986. *No Sense of Place: The Impact of Electronic Media on Social Behavior.* New York: Oxford University Press.

Nakamura, Lisa. 2002. *Cybertypes: Race, Ethnicity, and Identity on the Internet.* London: Routledge.

Phillips, Whitney. 2015. *This Is Why We Can't Have Nice Things: Mapping the Relationship between Online Trolling and Mainstream Culture.* Cambridge, MA: MIT Press.

Robinson, Laura. 2007. "The Cyberself: The Self-ing Project Goes Online, Symbolic Interaction in the Digital Age." *New Media & Society* 9 (1): 93–110.

Rochadiat, Annisa M. P., Stephanie Tom Tong, and Julie M. Novak. 2017. "Online Dating and Courtship among Muslim American Women: Negotiating Technology, Religious Identity, and Culture." *New Media & Society* 20 (4). https://doi.org/10.1177/1461444817702396.

Schilt, Kristen, and Laurel Westbrook. 2009. "Doing Gender, Doing Heteronormativity." *Gender & Society* 23 (4): 440–64.

Shapiro, Eve. 2015. *Gender Circuits: Bodies and Identities in a Technological Age.* New York: Routledge.

Stets, Jan, and Peter James Burke. 2000. "Identity Theory and Social Identity Theory." *Social Psychological Quarterly* 60:185–217.

Strasburger, Victor C., Marjorie J. Hogan, Deborah Ann Mulligan, Nusheen Ameenuddin, Dimitri A. Christakis, Corinn Cross, Daniel B. Fagbuyi, David L. Hill, Alanna Estin Levine, Claire McCarthy, Megan A. Moreno, and Wendy Sue Lewis Swanson. 2013. "Children, Adolescents, and the Media." *Pediatrics* 132 (5): 958–61.

Strohmaier, Heidi, Megan Murphy, and David DeMatteo. 2014. "Youth Sexting: Prevalence Rates, Driving Motivations, and the Deterrent Effect of Legal Consequences." *Sexuality Research and Social Policy* 11 (3): 245–55.

Stryker, Sheldon, and Peter James Burke. 2000. "The Past, Present, and Future of an Identity Theory." *Social Psychological Quarterly* 63:284–97.

Su, Hua. 2016. "Constant Connection as the Media Condition of Love: Where Bonds Become Bondage." *Media Culture & Society* 38 (2): 232–47.

Turkle, Sherry. 2012. *Alone Together: Why We Expect More from Technology and Less from Each Other.* New York: Basic Books.

Watson, Brendan R. 2016. "'A Window into Shock, Pain, and Attempted Recovery': A Decade of Blogging as a Coping Strategy in New Orleans." *New Media & Society* 20 (3). https://doi.org/10.1177/1461444816681523.

2

Education in the Digital Age

KEY CONCEPTS

Functionalism, or functionalist perspective, refers to sociological theories that emphasize how social institutions help create consensus and cooperation in a society. Education, for instance, passes basic knowledge and skills to the next generation, teaches young people what is (and is not) acceptable behavior in society, and prepares them for the workforce.

Conflict theory describes sociological theories that focus on contention, power, and inequality in America. As the name suggests, these perspectives highlight how competition for scarce resources brings different groups into conflict with one another in ways that may not be immediately visible. The education system, for example, perpetuates income inequality in the United States by training students in poor schools to accept their position as lower-income-earning members of American society.

Symbolic interaction refers to sociological theories that examine how individuals use words, body language, and symbols to create a shared understanding with others. Like conflict theorists, sociologists who study interactions think about how power affects the ways in which people relate to one another. In school, for instance, teachers and professors run the classroom and determine whether and how students will be allowed to participate in class discussions.

Self-fulfilling prophecy describes the phenomena where a false assumption occurs because someone else predicted it. In the classroom, this happens when a student performs well (or poorly) because the student met the expectations of his teacher. If a teacher believes that a student can improve his performance or grade, the student picks up on this positive expectation and improves his performance or grade.

Early in our lives, we are told that education is critical to success in America. We are told that it doesn't matter if you are poor. Individuals who take education seriously can excel in the United States. Education is the path to the "American Dream" and economic success. We hear this message from a lot of different sources over our lives. Parents, teachers, politicians, and commentators all remind us that education will lead to financial security. In fact, the Brookings Institute (a think tank located in Washington, DC) recently released a report titled "Opportunity, Responsibility, and Security: A Consensus Plan for Reducing Poverty and Restoring the American Dream" reinforcing the widely held belief that education moves people from poverty to prosperity (there is a link to the report at the end of the chapter). Their 2015 report outlines the median family income by education level and shows that the more educated Americans are, the higher their family income. For example, individuals with an advanced degree such as a master's degree make substantially more than those with less than a high school education ($119,714 compared to $32,171). Even individuals with some college make quite a bit less than those with a bachelor's degree ($57,550 compared to $89,261).

This is by no means the only lesson we learn about education. We also know that the education system is failing. Politicians and pundits point their fingers in a lot of different directions when they discuss what's to blame for the shortcomings in the American education system. Social promotion, decreased funding, poor teacher training, and mass media are all identified as problems with education. Complaints about the deleterious effects of mass media on education have been around for a long time. In the 1980s, for example, social scientists such as Neil Postman argued that television's focus on entertainment was infecting America's social institutions like a malicious virus and dumbing down Americans. He argued that Americans' obsession with entertainment was making it difficult for there to be serious discussion and debate about pressing political issues and social problems. This, Postman warned, would have dire consequences for American society. More recently, a group of Canadian researchers outlined in detail the consequences of mass media on our youth. In their 2013 study, the researchers found that kids who watch more TV are less prepared academically and socially for kindergarten. Specifically, they found that for every additional hour of television that a child twenty-nine months of age watches, his vocabulary, mathematical knowledge, and motor skills are reduced.

Why are social scientists so concerned about the effects of mass media on education? One reason is that there are TV programs and entire channels dedicated to "educating" kids. The controversy over "educational" programming is not new. For example, the child-focused educational program *Sesame Street*, which premiered on November 10, 1969, was very controversial because it used commercial television techniques such as quick shots and short vignettes for educational purposes. The show, which was initially funded by government and private foundations, was a collaboration of producers, writers, educators, and researchers called the Children's Television Workshop (CTW), who shared the belief that producers could harness the "addicting" aspects of television for educational purposes. Specifically, the CTW used fast-moving action, humor, and music to teach kids everything from hygiene to their *ABCs*—and like commercial television, children often get more than one message at a time.

If you watch the first ten minutes of *Sesame Street*'s premiere, you will see that after introducing some of the main characters (Gordon; his wife, Susan; Mr. Hooper; Bert and Ernie; and Big Bird), the show does three short vignettes featuring hygiene. The first vignette introduces Ernie, who is in a bath, and Bert. The scene is interrupted by an animated cartoon featuring Solomon Grundy, who washes a body part on each day of the week. Each day of the week lights up as several children repeat a rhyme in the background. The cartoon fades to black and a live action movie begins. The movie features a young girl talking about all the things we can clean including ourselves, our clothing, and our driveways. The show cuts back to Bert and Ernie's bathroom where Ernie breaks into a song about washing yourself. The scene cuts between Ernie and the other residents of Sesame Street, who demonstrate how to wash their ears, hands, chest, and everything else (there is a link to the first episode at the end of the chapter). The show was a hit, and with research, television producers and social scientists learned that with a few adjustments they could capture children's attention and teach them new concepts and skills.

As you can probably guess, critics wondered if that was the only thing that kids learned from the show. Most relevant to our discussion is critics' concerns that programs such as *Sesame Street* teach kids that education should be entertaining and fun. The assumption, of course, is that education is hard and boring, and the only way to deal with the unpleasantness of education is through the use of upbeat music and colorful, animated characters. This concern has intensified in the digital age as the proliferation of educational software has made its way into the classroom. Some pundits and scholars continue to argue that the gamification of education—or the use of game thinking and game mechanics to stimulate learning—is problematic. Most educational games, after all, focus superficially on getting enough points to earn badges or build characters rather than whether students truly understand a concept. Of course, some of the concerns over mass media have fallen by the wayside in the digital age. The jobs of the future will involve new media and, consequently, Americans believe that students need to learn how to use digital tools in the classroom. In fact, a poll conducted by Harts Research Associates in 2012 found that the vast majority of teachers (79 percent) and parents (80 percent) believe that schools need to invest in and use technology more in the classroom because most of the nation's jobs in the future will rely heavily on technological skills. More important, the poll found that the majority of teachers and parents believe that America's schools are behind the curve in their use of technology and in teaching technological skills. In other words, how we understand the role of new media in education has changed dramatically over the last forty years.

In this chapter, we examine how new media have changed education. This chapter is organized around three kinds of theories that sociologists use to analyze social institutions like education. These theories are referred to as functionalism, or the functionalist perspective; conflict theory; and symbolic interaction. Briefly, *functionalism* describes sociological theories that emphasize how social institutions help create consensus and cooperation in a society. *Conflict theory* highlights how competition for scarce resources brings different groups into conflict with one another, sometimes in ways that may not be immediately visible to us. *Symbolic interaction* examines how individuals use words, body language, and symbols to create a shared understanding with others. Each is discussed in the sections that follow.

FUNCTIONALIST APPROACHES TO EDUCATION

Some sociologists adopt a *functionalist perspective*, which emphasizes how social institutions help create consensus and cooperation in a society. Universal education, for example, is intended to pass basic knowledge and skills to the next generation as well as to socialize young people. Education brings people from diverse backgrounds together and teaches them core values as well as what is (and is not) acceptable behavior in society. Sociologists distinguish manifest functions of social institutions from latent functions of social institutions. Manifest functions refer to the intended consequences of a social institution or phenomena. A manifest function of education is to help young people prepare for meaningful employment once they are older. This is why students are required to do homework, put together projects, and take tests and why teachers reward students who follow directions, obey authority, and meet the deadlines they are given. These are skills we need in order to get—and keep—a job. Latent functions refer to the unintended consequences of a social institution. A latent function of education is that it serves as a dating pool and, sometimes, a marriage pool. As you probably remember, most high schoolers date someone from the school they attend. This isn't surprising, since students have the opportunity to interact with one another most days of the week at a place they are required to be. Similarly, even though women and men get married later (the average age of a first marriage is 27 for women and 29 for men), more than a quarter of married couples attended the same college. Schools, in short, provide us with a social network and pool of potential romantic partners.

Some of education's functions have become controversial, causing parents to question whether the education system is doing its job. For example, not all parents are happy that schools are involved in child care and sexual education—tasks that used to fall squarely in the domain of the family. It is important to remember that schools have taken on more functions of the family in response to changes in American society. As more women have entered the work force, for instance, schools have taken on the task of watching kids before and after school as well as feeding them breakfast and snacks. Below you can see a chart created using data from the Bureau of Labor Statistics that shows the labor force participation of men and women over time (figure 2.1). Notice that

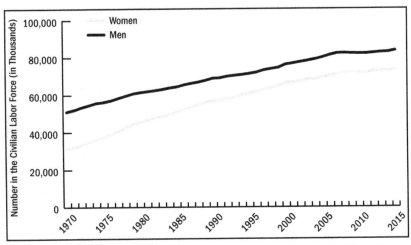

Figure 2.1. Men and Women's Labor Force Participation in America over Time. Source: The Bureau of Labor Statistics.

women's participation in the workforce has increased steadily. This shift matters because women typically were in charge of staying home and raising children, which included providing children a moral education and lessons about sex. As more and more women found employment outside of the home desirable and necessary, schools developed programs to help fill the gaps.

Women's labor force participation, of course, is not the only reason parents are unhappy with the education system. During this same time frame (from the 1970s to the 2010s), Americans increasingly became suspicious of government and its ability to pass legislation and come up with ideas that would improve the country's economic and social prospects. This is a big shift in public opinion. When public education was standardized and made compulsory through elementary school in the early 1900s, citizens and educators had a great deal of trust in the ability of the federal government to create policies that would improve the education of America's children. Although the federal government's role in education was contested during the social upheavals of the 1960s and 1970s, as you can see in the Gallup Poll chart below (figure 2.2), it wasn't until the 1980s that more than half of the citizens polled agreed that "big government," which refers to the federal government's regulation of social institutions such as education, was the biggest threat to the United

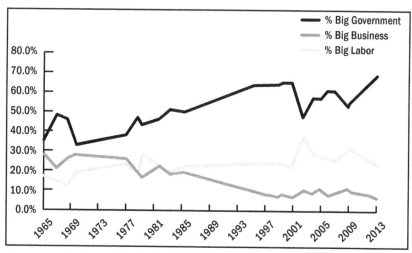

Figure 2.2. Views of Biggest Threat to the United States in Future, 1965–2013. Source: Gallup.

States. Notice in 2013, 72 percent of the individuals surveyed identified big government as the biggest threat to America's future.

The suspicion of big government extends to America's schools. Figure 2.3 shows that individuals polled by Gallup between 2000 and 2012 increasingly wanted the federal government to stay out of the classroom. Specifically, in 2000, 50 percent of parents believed that the government should be more involved in education, while 26 percent believed the government should be less involved in education. You can see that this has changed over time. In 2012, only 42 percent of parents felt the government should be more involved in education, while 35 percent believed the government should be less involved in education.

New media give parents options in terms of how they can respond to unwanted changes in the education system. For example, new media make it easier for parents to homeschool their children. If you are unfamiliar with homeschooling, which refers to parents educating their children at home, it has been around for a long time. It increased in popularity during the 1970s, in part, as a response to several books criticizing public education. Advocates of homeschooling argued that children were sent to school too early and that schools were too rigid in terms of how they educated children. John Holt, who wrote several books supporting homeschooling, believed that children shouldn't be

In terms of public education in this country, do you think the federal government should be more involved in education than it currently is, should keep its involvement about the same, or should be less involved in education than it currently is?

	More Involved (%)	Keep the Same (%)	Less Involved (%)	No opinion (%)
National adults				
2012 Aug 9–12	39	24	36	1
2010 Aug 5–8	43	20	35	1
2000 Apr 7–9	46	22	29	3
K-12 parents				
2012 Aug 9–12	42	22	35	*
2010 Aug 5–8	56	16	27	1
2000 Apr 7–9	50	22	26	2

* Less than 0.5%

Figure 2.3. How Americans Feel about the Federal Government's Involvement in Education. Source: Gallup.

forced to learn skills such as reading and math. He believed that children would learn these skills on their own if they were provided a stimulating environment. Since Holt saw the education system as beyond repair, he advocated that parents educate their children at home.

Plenty of parents have decided to homeschool because they believe that American schools neither have the staff and skills nor provide the kind of environment necessary to properly educate their children. In 2007, the United States Department of Education estimated that approximately 3 percent of students were educated at home—a number that according to the National Home Education Research Institute has increased dramatically over the last decade as parents become more convinced that America's education system is not functioning properly. In its survey, the United States Department of Education found that parents decided to homeschool largely due to their concerns about the school environment (85 percent), their desire to provide their children religious or moral instruction (72 percent), and their dissatisfaction with academic instruction at schools (68 percent).

More important, learning how to homeschool is easy in the digital age. Parents can go to a wiki and learn how to homeschool in several easy steps. If you visit the wiki "How to Homeschool Your Children," the page informs parents and guardians that their first step is to learn the laws regarding homeschooling in their state. The wiki even provides a link so that parents can quickly see what is and is not allowed in their state when it comes to home education. Parents can also go to websites such as Homeschool.com and Homeschoollife.com to find other homeschoolers in their area and learn about activities for homeschooled kids. In fact, many cities have art, theatre, music, and fitness classes targeting homeschooling parents who want to enhance the educational experiences of their children. Even if parents want to go it alone, they can go online and find plenty of free educational resources. Sites like Clickschooling.com offer parents web-based curriculum for math, science, language arts, social sciences, music, art, and language as well as virtual tours of places such as the Smithsonian museum. Alternatively, parents who are homeschooling can go to websites such as Khanacademy.org and have their children explore lessons in math, computing, science and engineering, arts and humanities, and economics and finance. For example, Disney sponsors a "course" on computer animation, where students can learn how Pixar Animation Studios makes its films and even create their own projects.

Parents who homeschool their children argue that they can achieve the manifest functions of education, which are to give children a shared basis of knowledge and the skills to succeed in the workforce. Likewise, homeschooling parents assert that they do a better job of educating their children than public schools and that this is clear in testing results. There is some evidence supporting these claims. Sandra Martin-Chang, a social scientist in Canada, found homeschooled students between the ages of five and ten whose parents followed a clear curriculum, tested a half grade higher in math and more than two grades higher in reading. This was not true for homeschooled students whose parents took an unstructured approach to learning. These students were behind and tested between one and four grades lower than students in public schools. Additionally, social scientists find that homeschooled students generally are well socialized and do not have trouble accepting differences and integrating with others as young adults. It is unclear, however, why this may be the case and when differences exist. For example, it is possible that parents who use new media to connect their children with other homeschooled kids are better socialized than parents who do not.

In sum, as with other social institutions, education plays an important function in our society by contributing to its stability. Sociologists who adopt a functionalist perspective focus on how social institutions like education create consensus and cooperation in society. It is clear, however, that as society has changed and we have become more reliant on schools to do some of the work of family, such as childcare and sexual education, parents increasingly question the ability of schools to effectively provide students a common base of knowledge and prepare them for the workforce. New media make it easier for parents to opt out of the traditional public education and come up with alternative curriculums that reflect their values and are attentive to their children's educational needs. While it is unclear what role new media play in homeschooling success, research suggests that when done correctly homeschooling can be an effective way to educate America's children.

CASE STUDY

Who's Responsible for Cyberbullying?

In 2013, debate erupted over a Southern California school district's controversial move. The district paid a private firm forty thousand dollars to comb through the social media of its fourteen thousand middle and high school students, looking for cyberbullying and threats of self-harm. Some have defended the district's actions, which became public a week after a twelve-year-old in Lakeland, Florida, killed herself after being cyberbullied by other kids.

In a *New York Times* article about the incident, the twelve-year-old's mother recounted how she had her daughter change schools and phone numbers to no avail. She believes that the school should have done more to help her daughter deal with the online bullying.

Read the following two articles and look at the stats on cyberbullying below (the links are at the end of the chapter):

- "We Aren't Doing Enough to Stop Bullying" by Kumaran Chanthrakumar for the *Huffington Post*
- "Teens and Social Media: How Do Schools Fit In?" by Joseph Palmisano for *Law Street*

TABLE 2.1. Cyberbullying Statistics

Percent of students who report being cyberbullied	52%
Percent of teens who have experienced cyberthreats online	33%
Percent of teens who have been bullied repeatedly through their mobile phones or the internet	25%
Percent of teens who do not tell their parents when cyberbullying occurs	52%
Percent of teens who have had embarrassing or damaging pictures taken of themselves without permission	11%

TABLE 2.2. Cyberbullying by Gender

	Male (%)	Female (%)
I have been cyberbullied.	16.6	25.1
Someone posted mean or hurtful comments online.	10.5	18.2
Someone posted a mean video about me online.	3.6	2.3
I have cyberbullied others.	17.5	21.3
I spread rumors online about others.	6.3	7.4
I posted a mean/hurtful picture online.	4.6	3.1

Statistical Verification

Source: Bureau of Justice Statistics, US Department of Health and Human Services, Cyberbullying Research Center.

Research Date: February 19, 2016.

Questions: Statistics on cyberbullying? Total percentage of children who are cyberbullied? What is the most common social network for cyberbullying? What percentage of teens have been bullied? Statistics on cyberbullying? What percentage of victims report being bullied in school?

See more at "Cyberbullying / Bullying Statistics—Statistic Brain." 2017 Statistic Brain Research Institute, publishing as Statistic Brain. May 24, 2017.

In a small group, discuss the following questions:

- Do you think cyberbullying is significantly disrupting students' education? Why or why not?
- Who do you think is responsible for addressing cyberbullying? Parents? Schools? Both?
- What problems do you see with the solutions discussed? Are there ways to resolve these problems?

CONFLICT THEORY: CAN TECHNOLOGY FIX THE
EDUCATIONAL INEQUALITY GAP?

Some sociologists focus on contention, power, and inequality in America. In particular, these sociologists highlight how competition for scarce resources brings different groups into conflict with one another. Conflict, however, doesn't mean you will necessarily see people fighting with one another over resources. Conflict, in fact, sometimes is not visible because those with power distribute resources in ways that ensure that they stay on top. Sociologists who use *conflict theory* when analyzing education argue that schools help perpetuate income inequality in the United States because they train students in resource-poor schools to accept their position as low-income-earning members of society. Essentially, schools teach poor students that they do not have what it takes to get into college and encourage them to focus their attention on jobs that they can get with a high school degree, such as employment in the fast food industry or at Walmart. Sociologists refer to this as the "hidden curriculum." Students in poor school districts are taught that they should not expect to achieve greatness and to accept their position in society.

Sociologists who use conflict theory point to dramatic differences in school funding as evidence that the education system intentionally reproduces inequality in America. Local property taxes are used to support public schools and, as you probably know, property values vary dramatically by county. This means that where children live affects how much is spent on their education. Not surprisingly, richer communities have more to spend on education, which means that they can offer teachers higher salaries; afford the latest textbooks, computers, and software; offer a range of field trips (sometimes to expensive destinations such as Washington, DC); and provide students with courses in music, foreign languages, and art. Poorer communities, particularly ones where the state government does not help fill the funding gap, find that their schools cannot afford to make basic repairs (such as fixing broken toilets) and have to share school nurses and teachers with other schools in the district. Teacher pay is lower in poorer districts, which makes it difficult to attract and keep good teachers. Some districts try to find creative ways to cut costs in order to increase teacher pay. Coolidge Unified

School District, a school district south of Phoenix, Arizona, shortened the school week to save money on utilities so that it could try to keep its teachers from commuting to wealthier districts in the area.

Let's take a closer look at the differences in educational spending across the country. The 2013 Annual Survey of School System Finances by the United States Census Bureau found that the states spending the most per pupil in 2013 were Alaska, Arizona, Connecticut, New Jersey, New York, and the District of Columbia. Idaho, Mississippi, Oklahoma, and Utah spent the least amount per pupil. In April 2016, National Public Radio (NPR) did a series of stories on school spending. If you go to NPR's website (the link is at the end of the chapter), you will see that how much is spent on each student can vary dramatically within a state. The state of Florida is a good example. In North Florida (near the state's capital), Leon county spent close to the United States' average per student, which is $11,841. The majority of Florida's school districts, however, spent 10 percent to 33 percent less than the United States' average. What counties spent the most on students in America? Those situated in the northeastern section of the United States. These districts spend well above the national average on each student—sometimes 33 percent more.

If you find this information surprising, check out the *New York Times*'s "The Upshot," which put together an interactive map on the relationship between money, race, and educational success (the link is provided at the end of the chapter). You will see that, just as conflict theorists argue, there is a relationship between resources and how well students do on standardized testing. The highest performing districts are predominantly wealthy and white. The highest performing school district is in Lexington, Massachusetts, where students are 3.8 grade levels above average. In Lexington, the median family income is $163,000 per year and the community is 59 percent white, 33 percent Asian/other, 4 percent black, and 4 percent Hispanic. One of the lowest performing school district is in Muskegon Heights, Michigan. Students who live here are 3.3 grade levels below average. The median family income in the area is $20,000 per year, which is quite low. In fact, a family of three is considered to be poor when the family income is less than $20,090 per year. Ninety-three percent of the families in the district are African American.

In the previous section on functionalism, we saw that new media offered parents a way to address the problems they saw with public education. Individuals and organizations that understand educational inequality as a result of unequal resources often herald new media as the solution. One popular argument is that if we can get schools on high-speed broadband and laptops or tablets into poor school districts, students will have the necessary tools for educational success. There are a lot of people and organizations that believe new media can solve our educational woes. Nonprofit organizations such as Education Superhighway, which was funded in part by Mark Zuckerberg's Startup:Education and the Gates Foundation, argue that high-speed broadband is key to restoring America's reputation for educational excellence in the world. These groups spend a lot of time trying to get the Federal Communications Committee to cap how much companies can charge schools for internet services.

Education Superhighway, for example, believes that digital learning will level the educational playing field and that to make this educational aspiration a reality, every school needs high-speed broadband. On its website, Education Superhighway states that its mission is to "upgrade the Internet access in every public school classroom in America so that every student has the opportunity to take advantage of the promise of digital learning. . . . We believe that digital learning has the potential to provide all students with equal access to educational opportunity and that every school requires high-speed broadband to make that opportunity a reality." If you go to Education Superhighway's website (www.educationsuperhighway.org), you will see why advocates think this is the best approach. On the website, they argue that high-speed broadband does the following:

- Increases the curriculum a school can offer. High-speed broadband will allow students to use teleconferencing, such as FaceTime and Skype, to connect with and learn from other teachers and other students from across the country. This, the organization argues, will broaden the range of educational materials available to students and their educational experiences.
- Enables teachers to offer the students different ways to learn course materials. Students don't just have to rely on a book or lecture to learn

concepts. They have access to games, films, and interactive programs, which helps reinforce the lessons they are learning.

- Allows parents to better monitor what their children are learning in the classroom and help them at home. New technology makes it so teachers can quickly update grades and post notes for parents to review at home. Parents can follow up with their kids and even assign additional homework.
- Increases test scores and graduation rates. High-speed broadband creates educational opportunities and improves the outcomes that are measured and influence school funding and teacher pay.

In other words, the assumption is that new media will make education better in poorer districts because students will have access to the same kinds of technological resources as students in richer districts.

Getting high-speed broadband in every school in America would be nice. Teachers working in poor districts complain that they have difficulty getting their students online. However, high-speed broadband alone is unlikely to fix educational inequality for several reasons. First, sociologists have found that teachers in poor school districts often have less technological training and, as a result, are not confident about using technological tools in the classroom. This lack of confidence is made worse by the lack of technological support at poor schools. Think about it. Schools that cannot afford to have a nurse on staff full-time certainly cannot afford to pay for tech support personnel regularly. This means teachers that use technology in the classroom have to be able to figure out everything from installation to troubleshooting on their own.

Second, even when teachers are confident in their technical skills, they often face other obstacles in the classroom. Teachers in poor school districts report that there are often not enough computers to go around and that there are other obstacles to using technology. Teachers who have large numbers of English-language learners or large numbers of students with limited computer experience, for instance, have a more difficult time integrating technology into their lessons. While teaching students basic computer skills may seem like the obvious solution, teachers are under a lot of pressure to increase student test scores, since this affects school funding and teacher pay.

HOW TEACHERS ARE USING TECHNOLOGY AT HOME AND IN THEIR CLASSROOMS
Survey conducted by the Pew Research Center

Pew found that teachers' experiences with using digital tools in the classroom varied according to the income status of the students they teach. Pew surveyed Advanced Placement and National Writing Project teachers in 2013, whose students would have more access to digital resources than the average student, particularly in poorer school districts. Here are some of the other findings from the survey taken from the Pew Research Center website:

- Seventy percent of teachers working in the highest-income areas say their school does a "good job" providing teachers the resources and support they need to incorporate digital tools in the classroom, compared with 50 percent of teachers working in the lowest-income areas.
- Seventy-three percent of teachers of high-income students receive formal training with digital tools, compared with 60 percent of teachers of low-income students.
- Fifty-six percent of teachers of students from higher-income households say they or their students use tablet computers in the learning process, compared with 37 percent of teachers of the lowest-income students.
- Fifty-five percent of teachers of higher-income students say they or their students use e-readers in the classroom, compared with 41 percent of those teaching in low-income areas.
- Fifty-two percent of teachers of upper- and upper-middle-income students say their students use cell phones to look up information in class, compared with 35 percent of teachers of the lowest-income students.
- Thirty-nine percent of teachers of low-income students say their school is "behind the curve" when it comes to effectively using digital tools in the learning process; just 15 percent of teachers of higher-income students rate their schools poorly in this area.
  See the link at the end of the chapter to read all of Pew's findings.

Finally, students in poor districts do not always have access to technology or the internet at home. A Pew Research Center survey, which interviewed 2,462 Advanced Placement and National Writing Project teachers in America in 2013, found that only 54 percent of teachers say that all or almost all their students have sufficient access to digital tools at school, and only 18 percent have access to the digital tools they need at home. As you can see in the summary of Pew's findings on the previous page, teachers in the poorest districts are the least likely to say that their students have sufficient access to the digital tools they need, both in school and at home. In fact, 56 percent of teachers working in lower income districts saw the lack of available digital resources to students as a "major challenge" to incorporating digital tools into the curriculum.

In sum, many individuals and groups agree with sociologists that the education system reproduces inequality in America. There is far less agreement, however, over the ability of new media to bridge this divide. Many politicians, entrepreneurs, and organizations believe that new media can be used to improve education and diminish inequality. They argue that high-speed broadband will open up the internet and educational opportunities to students in poor school districts. Sociologists find that internet access alone will not bridge the educational divide. Teachers working in poor school districts have fewer resources, less training with digital tools, and additional pressures that make it more difficult for them to use new media in the classroom. Additionally, poor students do not always have access to digital tools or the internet at home. All these factors make it clear that more than getting new media in poor schools is needed to address inequality in the education system.

SYMBOLIC INTERACTION: THE ROLE OF TEACHERS IN THE DIGITAL AGE

Some sociologists focus their attention on how people use shared symbols and reproduce society through their everyday interactions. Sociologists who analyze *symbolic interactions* examine how individuals use words, body language, and symbols to create a shared understanding with others. Like the conflict perspective, sociologists interested in symbolic interactions think about how power affects the ways in which people relate to one another. Generally speaking, people with more power

CASE STUDY

Massive Open Online Courses

You probably have heard a lot about massive open online courses (MOOCs) and their promise to bridge the divide in higher education. MOOCs were created in an effort to make knowledge more accessible to the general public. The idea is that any person can take a MOOC, learn about a topic, and engage an expert on the issues for free. The first MOOC was offered in 2008. The course, which was created by Stephen Downes and George Siemens at the University of Manitoba, Canada, was called "Connectivism and Connective Knowledge/2008." Approximately 2,200 people signed up for the course and 170 of them created their own blogs.

Four years later, two Stanford professors, Sebastian Thrun and Peter Norvig, offered a course called "Introduction to Artificial Intelligence" online for free. They designed the course to resemble a real classroom. More than 160,000 students in 190 countries signed up to take the class. It was the first truly massive online class.

There are critics and supporters of MOOCs. Supporters claim that MOOCs have the potential to change the face of higher education. By making college-level courses available for free, MOOCs provide individuals in developing countries an opportunity to build their skills and get jobs that were out of reach a decade ago. Critics are skeptical of this argument, particularly since researchers have found the following:

- Only a small percentage of individuals complete these courses.
- Almost 80 percent of individuals taking MOOCs already have a degree.
- Almost 60 percent of individuals taking MOOCs have full-time employment.
- Nearly 60 percent of individuals taking MOOCs came from developed countries such as the U.S.

Read the article at the *Harvard Business Review* titled "Who's Benefiting from MOOCs, and Why" and check out the information about the authors' survey data (the link is at the end of the chapter).

Think about the following:

- Given what we know about the survey data, what differences are there between Organisation for Economic Co-operation and Development (OECD) and non-OECD countries? Do these results uphold or challenge the conflict perspective?

are better able to influence how we understand reality by shaping how we interact. At school, for example, teachers and professors run the classroom and determine whether and how students will be allowed to participate in class discussions.

Social scientists have found that students' interactions with teachers are consequential. For example, in their 1968 study, Robert Rosenthal and Lenore Jacobson discovered that teachers can affect student performance. Rosenthal and Jacobson gave the students of Oak School an IQ test at the beginning of the school year. The researchers told Oak School teachers that the test was the "Harvard Test of Inflected Acquisition," which was designed to identify students who were about to "bloom" academically. Rosenthal and Jacobson then randomly identified some students with standard IQ tests as students who were likely to show marked improvement in their test scores over the coming year. They asked eighteen teachers at Oak School to keep an eye on these students to see if, in fact, the students did achieve their academic potential and improve their test scores over the year. Again, this was made up. An IQ test cannot predict whether a student is about to bloom academically. An IQ test measures your reasoning and problem-solving abilities. Nevertheless, when the researchers gave all the students the IQ test at the end of the year, the students who had been labeled as "ready to bloom" showed greater gains than those who had not been labeled in this way. Why? Rosenthal and Jacobson reasoned that students met the expectations of their teachers. The teachers believed that the students could improve, the students picked up on this positive expectation, and the students improved their scores. This phenomenon, where a false assumption occurs because someone else predicted it, is called a *self-fulfilling prophecy*.

Sociologist Ray Rist added to the research on self-fulfilling prophecy by showing that teachers' expectations of students varied by their social and economic status. In 1970, Rist conducted his research in a kindergarten classroom where both the students and the teacher were African American. Rist observed that after the eighth day of class, the teacher felt comfortable assigning students to tables based on their academic abilities even though she had not given them any sort of academic test. She assigned students who she believed were "fast learners" to the table closest to her, students she thought were "average learners" to the next table, and students she saw as "slow learners" to the table farthest away from her. Rist observed the students throughout the year and found that students closer to the teacher got the most attention and performed better academically. The farther a student sat from the teacher, the poorer his academic performance. Once again, we can see how teacher expectations shape interactions with students and affect their academic performance—self-fulfilling prophecy.

Rist made two additional important observations. First, the teacher labeled middle-class students as "fast learners" and poor students as "average" and "slow" learners. Rist wasn't able to say why the teacher did this, only that how she categorized students fell along social and economic lines. Second, since Rist followed the students through the next several years, he observed that the label assigned by the kindergarten teacher followed the student throughout their primary education. Students labeled "fast learners" were regarded as such throughout school and the same was true for students she branded as "slow learners." Rist concluded that the kindergarten teacher—for better or for worse—played a critical role in the kinds of interactions students had with their teachers, and this affected their long-term academic success.

As you can imagine, some politicians and pundits see new media as a potential solution to the problem of negative teacher-student interactions. New media change classroom dynamics and teachers' roles. Instead of teaching course material, teachers can simply draw on resources such as the American Federation of Teachers' Sharemylesson .com to find "playlists" of content related to the concepts they want to cover. Using this and other educational websites such as TES Connect and Teacherspayteachers.com, teachers can literally draw on thousands of online resources—tutorial videos, news clips, short articles, and PowerPoint presentations—to offer students different ways to learn course material. This changes student-teacher interactions because teachers are not experts imparting knowledge but are facilitators who simply provide students different tools so that they can essentially teach themselves the necessary material. Teachers are there to help students if they need it, but students choose the pace and style of their learning. "Fast learners" might read a short chapter on a topic and take an online quiz to make sure they understand the main concepts. "Slow learners," in contrast, might read a chapter, watch a video, and take virtual notes before completing the same quiz. Regardless of students' learning style, they get to the same point insofar as they learn the material well enough to pass an online quiz.

Online courses are also heralded as a way to change teacher-student interactions for the better. The most obvious way interactions are changing is that teachers and students no longer deal with one another face-to-face. Some social scientists argue that while the lack of face-to-face interaction means communication isn't immediate, it can be better because students reflect on course material and instructor feedback as opposed to simply responding to it emotionally. For example, a student who earns a "C" on a paper can't bombard his teacher after class demanding to know why he earned the grade he did. Instead, he would read the comments provided and contact his teacher if he needed additional guidance on how to improve his work. Additionally, as mentioned above, some social scientists point out that online classes broaden the range of people with which students interact. Students can talk to experts in other parts of the country and world as well as talk to one another. These online interactions are important for a couple of reasons. First, students who are shy or are slow learners may find it easier to share their experiences and express their opinions as it relates to course material. If you are a student who likes to really think things through before you speak, in-class discussions may be daunting. Once you feel you are ready to participate, the topic has moved on to something else. Online interactions are less bounded by time, which makes it easier for all students to participate. Second, and related, electronic spaces that encourage student interaction can foster a sense of community and cultural understanding among participants—an important goal of education.

Not all social scientists agree that new media are good for student-teacher interactions or education more generally. Some scholars show that the evidence is mixed on the effects of new media on education, while others argue that educators should be more careful before simply adopting new media in the classroom. For example, some social scientists argue that transforming teachers into facilitators whose primary job is to troubleshoot technology ignores the fact that teachers—as trained professionals—have an important role to play in the learning process. Teachers are experts on the material they teach and are trained not just to help students learn but to recognize how they learn and develop their skills. New media may make a broad range of educational resources available, but it is the collaboration between a teacher and a student that helps a student to grow intellectually. If teachers are little more than facilitators or if they only interact with anonymous students occasionally online, it is very difficult to help students develop or improve their critical thinking skills. Additionally, some sociologists point out that the structure of online classroom forums can actually reproduce inequality because those students with the technological know-how (which, as we know from the discussion above, tend to be wealthy, white students who live in resource-rich school districts) tend to dominate online discussions.

In sum, there is very little consensus on whether new media aid or undermine student-teacher interactions. Some scholars argue that new media will help address social inequality by making it more difficult for teachers to categorize students on factors other than their actual academic performance. Putting students in charge of their own education transforms the role of teachers from educators to facilitators of learning, which diminishes the role they play in evaluating students and their progress. Additionally, new media and online education provide more opportunities for shy students and slow learners to process information and participate in class discussions. Other scholars disagree with this assessment, noting that teaching is a profession that remains relevant in the digital age. Despite all the resources new media bring to education, teachers are needed to assess and encourage the intellectual development of their students—something that is very difficult to do in the virtual world.

CONCLUSION

In this chapter, we discussed how new media change debates over the quality of America's education system as well as how it might be improved. Specifically, we reviewed three central sociological perspectives and their relevance to education. We began with functionalism, or sociological theories that emphasize how social institutions help create consensus and cooperation in a society. We learned that the function of education is to pass on basic knowledge and skills to the next generation, teach young people what is (and is not) acceptable behavior in society, and prepare them for the workforce. Some parents do not believe that the education system is functioning properly and choose to

REPRODUCING INEQUALITY
For-Profit, Online Education

Have you ever seen an advertisement for a for-profit college such as the University of Phoenix? The advertisements make big promises. These institutions promise easy admission, ongoing registration, lots of online classes, and, of course, a big paycheck at the end. Attending a for-profit college, however, is very expensive. When I used the University of Phoenix website to estimate the costs for getting a bachelor of science in business, I was told that credits, tuition, and course-related materials and fees would run about $55,400. This estimate did not include books or other indirect expenses, which could run me another $23,000 to $49,000. According to the National Center for Education Statistics, this is significantly more than a public institution where four years of education will cost you $18,632. The website also encouraged me to apply for financial aid—noting that there were financial aid counselors on hand to assist me. The website noted that financial aid was the way to go, since the extra money would reduce my stress level as I invested in my future.

Consider the following:

- For-profit institutions recruit students—typically those who are eligible for the maximum amount of financial aid, which are the poorest in society—so that they can make money on tuition. In fact, the University of Phoenix gets nearly 85 percent of its funds from federally funded student-loan programs. As a result, tuition costs mirror the amount that students are allowed to borrow from the federal student aid program.
- The credentials offered at for-profit colleges are typically between 30 and 40 percent more expensive than the same degree from a nonprofit institution. For example, tuition and fees at for-profit colleges averaged $15,130 in the 2013–2014 academic year. Compare that with $3,264 at two-year public colleges and $8,893 at four-year public colleges for in-state students.
- Credits from for-profit institutions are notoriously difficult to transfer, and many for-profit colleges refuse to consider courses taken at other institutions.
- According to a 2014 report by the Institute for College Access and Success, a student at a for-profit college is nearly four times more likely to default on their student loans than a student from

a community college and more than three times more likely to default than a student from a four-year public or nonprofit college. Default is particularly high because students are expected to pay back private loans while they are in school.

- According to the National Bureau of Economic Research, students with degrees from for-profit schools are about 22 percent less likely to hear back from employers than applicants with similar degrees from community colleges. Additionally, individuals with degrees from for-profit schools often earn less than their peers. Part of this is because employers do not take degrees from many for-profit colleges seriously.

Although for-profit institutions are not universally bad, they certainly do not help most students achieve the "American Dream" by bringing them economic security and success—quite the contrary. For-profit institutions focus on making money, fold when their profits slip, and leave students with debt and no degree. Some students are fighting back. For example, fifteen students, including Mallory Heiney, refused to repay student loans to Everest Institute (a now-defunct college owned by Corinthian Colleges) in protest of its predatory lending practices and substandard education. Heiney noted that her instructors read material from books and several months into the twelve-month program quit coming altogether. Heiney and organizations like the Debt Collective are pushing back against the high costs of education.

---

educate their children differently. We focused on the example of homeschooling and discussed how parents can use new media for everything from learning more about homeschooling to finding a complete curriculum for their children.

Then we discussed conflict theory, which highlights how competition for scarce resources brings different groups into conflict with one another in ways that may not be immediately visible. The educational system perpetuates income inequality by training students in poor schools to accept their position as lower-income-earning members of American society. We talked about how individuals and groups, such as Education Superhighway and Startup:Education, believe that getting broadband into poor school districts will fix inequities in the education system. They assume that broadband will level the playing field because poor schools will have access to the same technological resources that rich schools have. Using social science research, we outlined some of the problems with this point of view. Schools that do not have money to fix their bathrooms or pay their teachers decently cannot afford technological support. This means that teachers have to be willing and able to install and troubleshoot software they use in the classroom. Even when teachers are willing to serve as their own technological support staff, teachers report that students rarely have access to new media at home.

We concluded the chapter with symbolic interaction, which are sociological theories that examine how individuals use words, body language, and symbols to create a shared understanding with others. Like conflict theorists, symbolic interactionists consider how power affects the ways in which people relate to one another. We discussed the most important relationship in education, that between teacher and student. We learned that teachers play a crucial role in the educational journey of students and that they also make assumptions about how fast a learner a student is based on her social and economic status. Teachers, in other words, reinforce inequality by interacting with students in ways that support the belief that children from higher-income-earning families are smarter than children from lower-income-earning families. As we discussed above, students live up to the expectations of their teacher; a phenomena known as a self-fulfilling prophecy. It is not clear if new media can completely address these problems. Some social scientists find that shy students and slow learners benefit from taking courses online. Others, however, find that online classes make it almost impossible for teachers to assess and encourage the intellectual development of their students.

CHAPTER LINKS

"Opportunity, Responsibility, and Security: A Consensus Plan for Reducing Poverty and Restoring the American Dream." 2015. Brookings Institute. http://www
.brookings.edu.
"Sesame Street Debut-Monday, November 10, 1969." 2015. YouTube. Last modified July 6, 2015. https://www.youtube.com.
Alvarz, Lizette. 2013. "Girl's Suicide Points to Rise in Apps Used by Cyberbullies." *New York Times*. Last modified September 14, 2013. http://www.nytimes.com.
Rich, Motoko, Amanda Cox, and Matthew Bloch. 2016. "Money, Race and Success: How Your School District Compares." *New York Times*. Last modified April 29, 2016. http://www.nytimes.com.

Chanthrakumar, Kumaran. 2014. "We Aren't Doing Enough to Stop Bullying." *Huffington Post*. Last modified October 29, 2014. http://www.huffingtonpost.com.

Palmisano, Joseph. 2014. "Teens and Social Media: How Do Schools Fit In?" *Law Street*. Last modified September 10, 2014. http://www.lawstreetmedia.com.

"Cyberbullying / Bullying Statistics." 2017. *Statistic Brain Research Institute*. Last modified August 24, 2017. http://www.statisticbrain.com.

Turner, Cory, Reema Khrais, Tim Lloyd, Alexandra Olgin, Laura Isensee, Beck Vevea, and Dan Carsen. 2016. "Why America's Schools Have a Money Problem." *National Public Radio*. Last modified April 18, 2016. http://www.npr.org.

Purcell, Kristen, Alan Heaps, Judy Buchanan, and Linda Friedrich. 2013. "How Teachers Are Using Technology at Home and in Their Classrooms." Pew Research Center. Last modified February 28, 2013. http://www.pewinternet.org.

Zhenghao, Chen, Brandon Alcorn, Gayle Christensen, Nicholas Eriksson, Daphne Koller, and Ezekiel Emanuel. 2015. "Who's Benefiting from MOOCs, and Why." *Harvard Business Review*. Last modified September 22, 2015. http://www.hbr.org. Be sure to check out the information about the authors' survey data.

Heiney, Mallory. 2015. "Students Like Me Don't Want a Handout. Merely Justice for Students Ensnared in a Debt Trap." *Washington Post*. Last modified March 16, 2015. http://www.washingtonpost.com.

Vara, Vauhini. 2015. "A Student-Debt Revolt Begins." *New Yorker*. Last modified February 23, 2015. http://www.newyorker.com.

CHAPTER REVIEW QUESTIONS

1. Why were scholars so concerned about the effects of mass media, excluding new media, on education?
2. What are the similarities and differences between functionalism, conflict theory, and symbolic interaction?
3. What are two changes that help us understand why some parents think America's education system no longer functions well? How have they responded?
4. Why won't broadband solve inequality in the education system?
5. How do new media potentially improve teacher and student interactions? How might new media make them worse?

LEARN MORE

Bielick, Stacey. 2008. "1.5 Million Homeschooled Students in the United States in 2007." National Center for Educational Statistics. Last modified December 2008. http://www.nces.ed.gov.

Coughlan, Sean. 2015. "Too Much Technology 'Could Lower School Results.'" *BBC*. Last modified September 15, 2015. http://www.bbc.com.

Dynarski, Susan. 2016. "Why Talented Black and Hispanic Students Can Go Undiscovered." *New York Times*. Last modified April 8, 2016. http://www.nytimes.com.

Edsall, Thomas. 2016. "How the Other Fifth Lives." *New York Times*. Last modified April 27, 2016. http://www.nytimes.com.

"Emerging and Developing Economies Much More Optimistic than Rich Countries about the Future." 2014. Pew Research Center. Last modified October 9, 2014. http://www.pewglobal.org.

Godsey, Michael. 2015. "The Deconstruction of the K-12 Teacher." *Atlantic*. Last modified March 25, 2015. http://www.theatlantic.com.

Henny, Christiaan. 2016. "Self-Fulfilling Prophecy in eLearning." eLearning Industry. Last modified March 23, 2016. http://www.elearningindustry.com.

Jankowski, Stephanie. 2015. "Online Teaching: The Good, the Bad and the Ugly." We Are Teachers. Last modified March 3, 2015. http://www.weareteachers.com.

Jeffries, Stuart. 2004. "Is Television Destroying Our Children's Minds?" *Guardian*. Last modified July 21, 2004. http://www.theguardian.com.

Knee, Jonathan. 2016. "Why For-Profit Education Fails." *Atlantic Monthly*. Last modified November 2016. http://www.theatlantic.com.

Kokalitcheva, Kia. 2015. "Facebook's Sheryl Sandberg Has a Few Ideas about Improving Education." *Fortune*. Last modified November 3, 2015. http://www.fortune.com.

Postal, Leslie. 2015. "Orange School Starts Monitoring Students' Social Media." *Orlando Sentinel*. Last modified May 28, 2015. http://www.orlandosentinel.com.

Quillen, Ian. 2012. "Teachers Report Mixed Impact of Digital Media." *Education Week*. Last modified November 6, 2012. http://www.edweek.org.

Rohde, David, Kristina Cooke, and Himanshi Ojha. 2012. "Special Report: The Unequal State of America—Why Education Is No Longer the 'Great Equalizer.'" *Reuters*. Last modified December 19, 2012. http://www.reuters.com.

Ross, Terrance. 2015. "When Students Can't Go Online." *Atlantic*. Last modified March 13, 2015. http://www.theatlantic.com.

Semensa, Gregory. 2015. "Online Teaching, It Turns Out, Isn't Impersonal." *Vitae*. Last modified December 11, 2015. http://www.chroniclevitae.com.

Shannon, Salley. 2005. "The Homeschool Revolution." *Parents*. Last modified February 2005. http://www.parents.com.

Tankersley, Jim. 2015. "Study: Kids Can Learn as Much from 'Sesame Street' as from Preschool." *Washington Post*. Last modified June 7, 2015. http://www.washingtonpost.com.

"Testing Our Schools." 2002. *PBS Frontline*. Last modified March 2002. http://www.pbs.org.

Walker, Tim. 2015. "Technology in the Classroom: Don't Believe the Hype." *NEAToday*. Last modified January 8, 2015. http://www.neatoday.org.

Wong, Alia. 2015. "The *Sesame Street* Effect." *Atlantic*. Last modified June 17, 2015. http://www.theatlantic.com.

VIDEOS AND MOVIES

Dhingra, Raj. 2012. "Can Technology Change Education? Yes!" *TEDxBend*. Last modified June 15, 2012. http://www.youtube.com.

Dyer, Harry. 2016. "Incorporating & Accounting for Social Media in Education." *TEDxNorwichED*. Last modified March 28, 2016. http://www.youtube.com.

Declining by Degrees: Higher Education at Risk. 2005. PBS. DVD.

Guggenheim, Davis. 2010. *Waiting for "Superman."* Electric Kinney Films. DVD.

Gosier, Jon. 2014. "The Problem with 'Trickle-Down Techonomics.'" *TED*. Last modified October 2014. http://www.ted.com.

Mitra, Sugata. 2013. "Build a School in the Cloud." *TED*. Last modified February 2013. http://www.ted.com.

Mondale, Sarah. 2004. *School, the Story of American Public Education*. Films for Humanities & Sciences. DVD.

Moyers, Bill. 1992. "Unequal Education." Moyers & Company. Last modified September 8, 1992. http://www.billmoyers.com.

Ward, William. 2013. "Incorporating Social Media in the Classroom." *TEDxKalamazoo*. Last modified October 7, 2013. http://www.youtube.com.

CHAPTER REFERENCES

Aagaard, Jesper. 2016. "Breaking Down Barriers: The Ambivalent Nature of Technologies in the Classroom." *New Media & Society* 19 (7): 1127–43. https://doi.org/10.1177/1461444816631505.

Bernard, Robert, Philip Abrami, Yiping Lou, Evgueni Borokhovski, Anne Wade, Lori Wozney, Peter Andrew Wallet, Manon Fiset, and Binru Huang. 2004. "How Does Distance Education Compare with Classroom Instruction? A Meta-analysis of the Empirical Literature." *Review of Educational Research* 74 (3): 379–439.

Binder, Amy. 2002. *Contentious Curricula: Afrocentrism and Creationism in American Public Schools*. Princeton: Princeton University Press.

Blumer, Herbert. 1968. *Symbolic Interactionism: Perspective and Method*. New York: Prentice-Hall.

Bowles, Samuel, and Herbert Gintis. 1976. *Schooling in Capitalistic America: Educational Reforms and the Contradictions of Economic Life*. New York: Basic Books.

Brown, David. 2001. "The Social Sources of Educational Credentialism: Status Cultures, Labor Markets, and Organizations." Extra issue, *Sociology of Education* 74:19–34.

Calarco, Jessica McCrory. 2014. "Coached for the Classroom: Parents' Cultural Transmission and Children's Reproduction of Educational Inequalities." *American Sociological Review* 79 (5): 1015–37.

Chapman, Lauren, Jessica Masters, and Joseph Pedulla. 2010. "Do Digital Divisions Still Persist in Schools? Access to Technology and Technical Skills of Teachers in High Needs Schools in the United States of America." *Journal of Education for Research* 36 (2): 239–49.

Collins, Randall. 1975. *Conflict Sociology: Toward an Explanatory Sociology*. New York: Academic.

Cottom, Tressie McMillan. 2017. *Lower Ed: The Troubling Rise of For-Profit Colleges in the New Economy*. New York: New Press.

Edmundson, Mark. 2008. *Why Read?* New York: Bloomsbury.

Gerber, Hannah. 2015. "Problems and Possibilities of Gamifying Learning: A Conceptual Review." *Internet Learning* 3 (2): 46–54.

Giroux, Henry. 1988. *Schooling and the Struggle for Public Life: Critical Pedagogy in the Modern Age*. Minneapolis: University of Minnesota Press.

Goode, Joanna. 2010. "The Digital Identity Divide: How Technology Knowledge Impacts College Students." *New Media & Society* 12 (3): 497–513.

Hansen, John, and Justin Reich. 2015. "Democratizing Education? Examining Access and Usage Patterns in Massive Open Online Courses." *Science* 350 (6265): 1245–48.

Hughes, Gwyneth. 2009. "Social Software: New Opportunities for Challenging Social Inequalities in Learning?" *Learning, Media and Technology* 34 (4): 291–305.

Journell, Wayne. 2007. "The Inequities of the Digital Divide: Is E-learning a Solution?" *E-Learning and Digital Media* 4 (2): 138–49.

Martin-Chang, Sandra, Odette N. Gould, and Reanne E. Meuse. 2011. "The Impact of Schooling on Academic Achievement: Evidence from Homeschooled and Traditionally Schooled Students." *Canadian Journal of Behavioural Science/Revue Canadienne des Sciences du Comportement* 43 (3): 195–202.

Medlin, Richard. 2013. "Homeschooling and the Question of Socialization Revisited." *Peabody Journal of Education* 88 (3): 284–97.

Nguyen, Tuan. 2015. "The Effectiveness of Online Learning: Beyond No Significant Difference and Future Horizons." *MERLOT Journal of Online Learning and Teaching* 11 (2): 309–19.

Palloff, Rena, and Keith Pratt. 2013. *Lessons from the Virtual Classroom: The Realities of Online Teaching*. New York: John Wiley & Sons.

Postman, Neil. 1985. *Amusing Ourselves to Death: Public Discourse in the Age of Show-Business*. New York: Penguin.

Rosenthal, Robert, and Lenore Jacobson. 1968. *Pygmalion in the Classroom*. New York: Holt, Rinehart and Winston.

Sims, Christo. 2017. *Disruptive Fixation: School Reform and the Pitfalls of Techno-Idealism*. Princeton: Princeton University Press.

Uecker, Jeremy. 2008. "Alternative Schooling Strategies and the Religious Lives of American Adolescents." *Journal for the Scientific Study of Religion* 47 (4): 563–84.

Warschauer, Mark, Michele Knobel, and Leeann Stone. 2004. "Technology and Equity in Schooling: Deconstructing the Digital Divide." *Educational Policy* 18 (4): 562–88.

Warschauer, Mark, and Tina Matuchniak. 2010. "New Technology and Digital Worlds: Analyzing Evidence of Equity in Access, Use, and Outcomes." *Review of Research in Education* 34 (1): 179–225.

3

Religion.com

KEY CONCEPTS

Media logic refers to how the structure of the medium and the format of the content affect communication. Medium structure determines the content we receive. Format refers to how information is presented to the audience.

Religion is a unified system of beliefs in which some things are identified as sacred and set apart from everyday items.

Religious practices are the rituals around the things that are considered sacred. For example, Muslims pray facing Mecca as a sign of unity and respect, and Jews recognize the transition to adulthood with a bar mitzvah or bat mitzvah.

Religious community refers to a group of people who are united by their shared beliefs and practices.

Religious dysfunction refers to the harmful effects of religion. Social scientists discuss two harmful effects of religious dysfunction: (1) persecution and (2) war and terrorism.

Media have always played an important role in our religious lives. While you may think of TV when you hear the word media, humans have been writing and reading for centuries. Religious texts including the Sutras (Buddhist sacred texts), the Bible (Christian sacred text), the Vedas (Hindu sacred texts), the Quran and Hadith (Islamic sacred texts), and the Tanach, Mishnah, Talmud, and Midrash (Jewish sacred texts) all were written with the purpose of informing how we think about this life and the next. Religious texts were designed to engage us intellectually and to get us to think about the meaning of our lives relative to something bigger than ourselves. Not surprisingly, as media have changed so have the ways religious leaders try to engage us.

Let's take the example of Jimmy Swaggart, who is an American evangelist. Swaggart began evangelizing, or bringing the gospel, to the American South in 1955. He quite literally traveled across the South preaching from a flatbed trailer that was donated to him. By 1960, he was recording and selling gospel music albums, and in 1961, he began spreading gospel on the radio. Before long, Swaggart was on TV and preaching the "good word" into living rooms across the country. Swaggart's show was wildly popular. If you watch his program (there is a link at the end of the chapter), you will see that he plays the piano, sings, and paces across the stage as he dramatically delivers his sermon. His show was very entertaining. By 1983, Swaggart's daily telecast, which featured Bible study and gospel music, was carried by more than 250 television stations in the United States.

As you can imagine, Swaggart and other TV evangelists had their fair share of critics. Generally speaking, TV evangelism is criticized for three related reasons, all of which are related to *media logic*. Media logic refers to the ways the structure of the medium and the format of the content affect communication. Medium structure is straightforward. Different mediums have different structures, and this shapes the information we receive. For example, we know that television is different from Twitter, which is different from a website. As such, we do not expect the news we get from *The Daily Show with Trevor Noah* to be the same as the news we find when we search for a hashtag on Twitter or go to the *New York Times* webpage. When we go to the *New York Times* online, we expect in-depth coverage on an issue or event, complete with graphics and additional links. We do not expect this from Twitter, which limits the news to dramatic headlines conveyed in 280 characters or less, or *The Daily Show*, which we expect to entertain us while recapping the news of the day.

Format refers to how the content is arranged for presentation. Producers determine what content will be presented as well as how it will be presented. Many social scientists, including Neil Postman, whom we discussed last chapter, have argued that our media formats primarily focus on entertainment, meaning the language, pace, and rhetoric of entertainment influences the content we receive. The widespread influence of entertainment on media formats, scholars argue, creates an overarching media logic that emphasizes dramatic, humorous, and thematic storytelling over critical and thoughtful commentary. This, in turn, affects how we understand institutional life and our experiences in it. Remember, Postman suggested that the emphasis on entertaining content would ultimately undermine our ability to have meaningful debate regarding social and political problems.

Religious content is not exempt from media logic. In fact, critics believe that media logic pollutes religious experiences in three ways. First, and most obvious, TV evangelism provides viewers entertainment rather than a meaningful religious experience. TV evangelists such as Jimmy Swaggart host shows that include thematic storytelling, drama, music, and occasionally humor—all the necessary ingredients for the audience to feel good once the program has ended—and lack depth when it comes to interpreting religious texts. Second, and related, TV evangelists are celebrities, who, critics argue, are more worried about their "brand" and selling products during commercial breaks than teaching the gospel. Swaggart, for example, sells the books, Bibles, and gospel music CDs that he features on his program. This makes his show seem more like a long commercial than a religious service. Critics believe that it is difficult to have a religious experience with Swaggart constantly pitching his products. Finally, TV evangelism fails to provide a religious community. Personal interactions and connections are key to meaningful religious experiences and growth, and neither can happen through the TV screen. TV evangelists don't have personal relationships with audience members so they cannot answer their questions or nurture their spiritual growth. TV evangelism, in short, is religion wrapped in a feel-good, entertaining package.

Of course, supporters of TV evangelism and evangelists themselves disagree with this assessment. They point out that weekly church attendance has declined since the 1990s. You can see this trend in the Gallup poll (figure 3.1). Notice that 34 percent of respondents went to church or synagogue weekly in 1992; a number that has declined over time. By 2015, only 25 percent of respondents reported attending services weekly. When another polling agency, the Pew Research Center, asked survey respondents why they do not go to weekly service more, individuals cited personal priorities (e.g., they are too busy) and practical difficulties (e.g., they don't have transportation). Supporters of TV evangelism argue that the decline in weekly attendance require religious

How often do you attend church or synagogue—every week, almost every week, about once a month, seldom, or never?

	Every Week (%)	Almost Every Week (%)	About Once a Month (%)	Seldom (%)	Never (%)
2016	26	12	13	28	20
2015	25	13	13	27	22
2014	29	9	13	31	17
2013	28	11	15	26	19
2012	31	11	15	25	18
2011	29	9	16	30	15
2010	30	12	13	28	16
2009	31	11	13	29	15
2008	30	12	15	27	16
2007	30	12	13	28	16
2006	31	12	15	28	14
2005	35	11	15	25	14
2004	34	10	15	27	14
2003	32	13	13	30	11
2002	32	13	15	29	10
2001	32	11	15	29	13
2000	35	11	14	29	10
1999	32	12	15	27	13
1998	32	13	17	28	10
1997	29	13	17	29	11
1996	29	12	15	32	11
1995	31	12	16	30	10
1994	32	13	16	28	10
1993	n/a	n/a	n/a	n/a	n/a
1992	34	10	14	27	14

2000–2015 based on yearly aggregates; 1992–1999 based on two polls in which full religion module was asked; * Less than 0.5%.

Figure 3.1. Religious Service Attendance. Source: Gallup.

leaders to "think outside the box" and deliver sermons in accessible and engaging ways. In the case of TV evangelism, the potential to bring the word of God (e.g., the Bible) into every household with a working television and allow those who otherwise would not be able to be a part of a religious service, greatly outweigh nuisances such as commercials.

TV evangelists are still around. New media, however, have changed how religious leaders reach their flock. Spiritual advisors have gone virtual, making their sermons accessible online and, sometimes, available as a podcast. In fact, in an effort to make religious doctrine accessible, thousands of churches worldwide turned to "Godcasting," or creating religious podcasts that could be downloaded to mobile devices and streaming videos to spread their message. Reasonabletheology.org offers site visitors a "Big List of Christian Podcasts." The now-defunct website Godcast1000.com also listed and ranked the top Godcasts. On June 6, 2017, Father Al Lauer held the top spot on the site with his daily Catholic scripture readings, followed by The Wired Homeschool and Ruidoso Baptist Church (See table 3.1). Each of these Godcasts gets hundreds of listeners daily. This practice of making sermons available online challenges how we, as a society, think about religious spaces and our experiences in them. Instead of sitting somberly in a church pew or even in the comfort of our homes, we can listen to religious leaders interpret religious texts while we are in our cars or on the treadmill at the gym.

Again, some religious leaders consider this a negative trend, arguing that we cannot have sacred experiences or build religious communities

TABLE 3.1. Top Three Godcasts from Godcast1000.com. Source: Christian Podcasts, www.godcast1000.com

Rank	Name	Denomination	Description
1	Father Al Lauer	Catholic	Inspired teaching on the daily Scripture readings.
2	The Wired Homeschool	Not provided	The Wired Homeschool provides practical advice for homeschooling parents who use technology as part of their homeschool curriculum. Topics include internet safety, responsible computer use, smartphones, tablets, e-readers, educational apps, and social media.
3	Ruidoso Baptist Church	Baptist	The latest feed from Ruidoso Baptist Church.

if we are on a treadmill. Likewise, critics point out that new media allow anyone to claim religious authority, even those without any formal spiritual training. There are lots of religious video bloggers, or vloggers, who are willing to play down scripture and reveal more and more about their lives to attract followers, gain celebrity, and earn money. Just look at video-sharing websites such as YouTube. Religious vloggers let viewers into their daily lives and earn money from the ads shown on their videos. Take the example of Sam and Nia Rader, Christian vloggers, who grabbed the attention of the online community in 2014 with a video of them lip-synching the film *Frozen's* "Love Is an Open Door" in their car with their children in the backseat (the link is at the end of the chapter). The couple who shares all aspects of their lives with their YouTube followers, consider the vlogs part of their "mission for God." They argue that by showing others how fulfilling their lives are, others will accept Christ into their lives. The couple took heat in 2015 when Sam surprised Nia on the vlog with the results of her pregnancy test. Sam took some of Nia's urine from the toilet, tested it, and gave Nia the news on the vlog. As of June 2017, the video had more than eighteen million views. Two days later, Sam and Nia announced her miscarriage on the vlog. The drama attracted millions of new viewers to their channel and additional revenue for the Rader family. Sam soon announced that he was quitting his job as an ER nurse to make the vlog and his family his full-time job. While you may be skeptical, it is not impossible to live off of the ad revenue associated with YouTube. According to BuzzFeed, Sam and Nia make approximately $9.60 per thousand ad views, which means they are making a six-figure salary from their YouTube channel.

While examples of Jimmy Swaggart and the Rader family clearly illustrate that media can be used in ways that bring financial benefits to some individuals, it is not clear how we might evaluate the effects of new media on religion. As a first step, we need a sociological framework for understanding religion and its role in American society.

DURKHEIM AND RELIGION

In 1912, French sociologist, Émile Durkheim, published an influential book on religion titled *The Elementary Forms of Religious Life* in which he tried to identify common elements of different religions. As a functionalist, Durkheim believed that religion was critical because it helped maintain balance and order within society. Since Durkheim surveyed religions from around the world, he recognized that they were very different. In fact, he tried to find at least one belief or practice shared by different religions but couldn't find one. He did find that religions share three basic and related elements. First, *religion* is a unified system of beliefs in which some things are identified as sacred and set apart from everyday items. For example, some Hindu denominations consider Tulsi, or basil, sacred because it's believed to be an incarnation of the Goddess Tulsi, who was turned into a basil bush by the God Vishnu so that she could be worshipped in the morning and evening by every person in the world. Similarly, Catholics consider the rosary sacred and put this string of prayer beads in a special place.

Second, all religions have *practices* or rituals around the things that they consider sacred. Muslims, for instance, pray facing Mecca, which is the holy city of Islam, five times daily—at dawn, noon, midafternoon, sunset, and nightfall—as a sign of unity. Praying facing Mecca gives Muslims a common focus and sense of purpose regardless of whether or not they are in a temple. Some religious practices are less frequent. For example, Jews recognize the transition into adulthood through bar mitzvahs (for boys) and bat mitzvahs (for girls). The purpose of the religious coming-of-age ceremony is to officially recognize that childhood is over and that the young adults are accountable for their decisions and actions under Jewish law. Finally, all religions are united by their shared beliefs and practices into a single *religious community*. Muslims praying to Mecca around the world are part of a religious community and so are the Catholics that attend mass and celebrate the Eucharist, which is to share the "body" and "blood" of Christ.

In sum, religion is composed of religious practices and religious communities. In this chapter, we will focus on each of these and specifically explore the role of new media in religious practices and religious communities. We also will discuss religious dysfunction. As you may have guessed from the last chapter, functionalists are not just interested in how social institutions make society cohesive and stable. They also are concerned with the failure of social institutions. In this case, functionalists pay attention to when religion harms—rather than helps—society.

CHANGING RELIGIOUS PRACTICES IN THE DIGITAL AGE

Individuals regularly gather together to practice their faith. Christians, Jews, and Muslims all set aside one day of the week on which they typically gather for worship. They are Sunday for Christians, Saturday for Jews, and Friday for Muslims. Typically, *religious practice* is something that is done in the "real" world in a scared space, such as a church or temple, with a <u>religious leader</u>, or individual who has recognized authority within a religion. Religious leaders, which include priests, preachers, ministers, reverends, rabbis, imams, and swamis, among others, interpret sacred texts to practitioners. Social scientists who study religion analyze how new media influence religious practices.

Let's start with what we know about how individuals use new media to learn more about religion. First, individuals use new media to learn more about churches and temples as well as particular religions themselves. In 2012, Beliefnet.com reported on a survey conducted by Grey Matter Research that found that in the last six months

- nineteen percent of those surveyed visited the website of a place of worship they are currently attending,
- seventeen percent of those surveyed visited the website of a place of worship they were not attending,
- nineteen percent of those surveyed visited a religious instruction website, and
- seventeen percent of those surveyed read religious-oriented blogs.

Second, individuals use new media to connect with religious leaders and their churches and temples. The Beliefnet.com story titled "Are Americans Finding God in Cyberspace?" also reported that in the last six months

- fourteen percent of those surveyed have a religious leader as a "friend" on a social media platform like Facebook,
- one out of ten of those surveyed "liked" a place of worship on a social media site,
- eight percent of those surveyed participated in religious-oriented discussions online,

- two percent of those surveyed follow a place of worship on Twitter, and
- two percent of those surveyed follow a religious leader on Twitter.

Finally, most of the individuals using new media for these purposes are young. Beliefnet.com reports that 57 percent of adults who are online and under the age of thirty-five use the internet for religious purposes.

Given these realities, it makes sense that there are so many churches and temples with an online presence. Want to learn more about Tibetan Buddhism? Go to the Foundation for the Preservation of the Mahayana Tradition website and take a free online course on Buddhist meditation. Don't remember all the words to the Catholic prayer "Hail Mary"? Navigate over to the Catholic Online website and search this, and hundreds of other prayers, in the prayer resource center. If you watch the Hail Mary video (the link is at the end of the chapter), you'll see that the prayer is accompanied by inspirational images and that the prayer is also read to you. If you want to catch a Muslim prayer service, you can head over to the Virtual Mosque and scroll through the list of topics. There are dozens of videos covering everything from Ramadan, where Muslims observe a month of intense prayer and dawn-to-dusk fasting, to the Muslim vote. You can even get closer to God during your lunch break using an application on your mobile phone. The Virtual Hindu Temple Worship allows individuals to pray while listening to meditation music. These sites suggest that new media are changing the way individuals practice their faith.

While these efforts may seem like little more than religious advertisements, new media change how we think about sacred spaces. Digital technology decouples religious practice from physical space. We don't have to go to a physical church, temple, or synagogue at a specific time to practice our faith. We can go online and watch a sermon or simply run an app that offers motivation and music for our meditation. In other words, we no longer have to share a physical space to practice our faith together, and this changes where and how we engage in religion.

Social scientists find that new media are particularly important for individuals who want to practice a faith that is considered outside of the mainstream. A good example is Wicca, whose practitioners generally believe in a god and goddess who take the form of deities familiar to us (e.g., from mythology). Wiccans generally celebrate eight holidays, or Sabbats, which are tied to the seasons and the Earth's natural rhythms. Sabbats celebrate the Earth's journey around the sun, which Wiccans call the Wheel of the Year, and Wiccans commemorate each Sabbat. Wiccan ceremonies, however, can vary dramatically. Some Wiccans publicly celebrate each Sabbat in an effort to educate the broader public about their religion. For example, they might put on a play that outlines the importance of a particular Sabbat. Other Wiccans prefer private celebrations that only include other practitioners. In short, while Wiccans may celebrate common holidays, their practices are very different.

Some of you may be asking yourself, "Is she talking about witches and witchcraft?" It turns out that Wicca and witchcraft are quite different. Witchcraft is not a religion, and witches focus on practicing magic. But, as you can imagine our general lack of knowledge regarding Wicca—not to mention the countless movies and TV series that dramatize events such as the Salem Witch Trials, where two hundred people were accused of witchcraft and twenty people were executed for this crime—means that many people assume Wicca and witchcraft are one and the same. Because of this association, many Wiccans practice their religion outside the view of the public. Before new media, learning more about Wicca or attending a Sabbat might have been quite difficult. If you didn't know anyone Wiccan, then you would have had to start asking around to see if you could find any Wiccans in your community—something you may or may not have felt comfortable doing. New media, however, make it possible for individuals curious about alternative religions like Wicca to go online and learn more about and even practice their faith. Specifically, individuals can use virtual forums like chat rooms to discuss religious ideas, hold online services, and even try to find other practitioners in their communities so that they can meet up in the real world. Websites like Wiccan Together offer a number of ways—discussion forums, groups, and chat rooms—for members to connect with one another and discuss various aspects of their faith. New media, simply put, offer individuals new ways to practice their faith.

New media also change how we connect with religious leaders. Again, when you think about religious leaders, you probably think about a pastor, minister, priest, imam, pujari, or umze—the individual who has authoritative knowledge about God or a deity and provides guidance regarding how believers should think and behave. Before new media, your contact with religious authorities may have been limited to before or after the service, or possibly nonexistent. Many Catholics, for instance, only see their priest once a week at church and most Catholics have never met the Pope, who is the leader of all the Catholic churches in the world. If you are Catholic, these religious leaders may seem intimidating and unapproachable. It can be difficult for some to imagine having a conversation with a priest about religious doctrine and its application to a situation in your life.

This is exactly why new media can be a powerful tool for religious leaders. Priests, reverends, ministers, rabbis, and imams can use websites, blogs, and social media to show us how they live their faith and communicate with us in a more direct way. Some religious leaders even encourage this. Read the following excerpt from the statement Pope Francis released on the Forty-Eighth World Communications Day. Notice that he asks the priest and pastoral ministry to think about the internet as "a gift from God," and to use new media for authentic encounters with others. He urges the priest and pastoral ministry to view the digital revolution as a "thrilling challenge" and to use online tools to "share with others the beauty of God." Does it matter if religious leaders use new media to connect with their flock? Yes, new media does seem to break down the walls between religious leaders and believers by making them more accessible, which, research shows, helps keep practitioners engaged with religion over time.

Let's stay with the Catholic example to get a sense of how a religious leader might use social media to communicate with his congregants. I did a quick search for Catholic churches in North Florida and found a church where the priest publicly shares gospel, thoughts, and information about himself. His "friends" on Facebook can "like," comment on, and share his posts. This particular priest shares personal details about his life, such as the fact that he is a twin, along with religious information. In one of his posts, his "friends" learn that the feast of the apostle St. Thomas, who, like the priest, was a twin, is on July 3. This, arguably, is an authentic attempt to make Catholicism more accessible to the broader public. While the priest doesn't go into great detail about St. Thomas's life—it turns out he is the "doubting Thomas" we hear about every now and then because he refused to believe that a resurrected Jesus had appeared to the ten other apostles until he saw it

MESSAGE OF POPE FRANCIS FOR THE 48TH WORLD COMMUNICATIONS DAY

Communication at the Service of an Authentic Culture of Encounter

POSTED SUNDAY, 1 JUNE 2014

In a world like this, media can help us to feel closer to one another, creating a sense of the unity of the human family which can in turn inspire solidarity and serious efforts to ensure a more dignified life for all. Good communication helps us to grow closer, to know one another better and ultimately, and to grow in unity. The walls which divide us can be broken down only if we are prepared to listen and learn from one another. We need to resolve our differences through forms of dialogue which help us grow in understanding and mutual respect. A culture of encounter demands that we be ready not only to give, but also to receive. Media can help us greatly in this, especially nowadays, when the networks of human communication have made unprecedented advances. The Internet, in particular, offers immense possibilities for encounter and solidarity. This is something truly good, a gift from God. . . .

It is not enough to be passersby on the digital highways, simply "connected"; connections need to grow into true encounters. We cannot live apart, closed in on ourselves. We need to love and to be loved. We need tenderness. Media strategies do not ensure beauty, goodness and truth in communication. The world of media also has to be concerned with humanity; it too is called to show tenderness. The digital world can be an environment rich in humanity; a network not of wires but of people. The impartiality of media is merely an appearance; only those who go out of themselves in their communication can become a true point of reference for others. Personal engagement is the basis of the trustworthiness of a communicator. Christian witness, thanks to the Internet, can thereby reach the peripheries of human existence.

As I have frequently observed, if a choice has to be made between a bruised Church which goes out to the streets and a Church suffering from self-absorption, I certainly prefer the first. Those "streets" are the world where people live and where they can be reached, both effectively and affectively. The digital highway is one of them, a street teeming with people who are often hurting, men and women looking for salvation or hope. By means of the Internet, the Christian message can reach "to the ends of the earth" (*Acts* 1:8). Keeping the doors of our churches open also means keeping them open in the digital environment so that people, whatever their situation in life, can enter, and so that the Gospel can go out to reach everyone. We are called to show that the Church is the home of all. Are we capable of communicating the image of such a Church? Communication is a means of expressing the missionary vocation of the entire Church; today the social networks are one way to experience this call to discover the beauty of faith, the beauty of encountering Christ. In the area of communications too, we need a Church capable of bringing warmth and of stirring hearts. . . .

The Church needs to be concerned for, and present in, the world of communication, in order to dialogue with people today and to help them encounter Christ. She needs to be a Church at the side of others, capable of accompanying everyone along the way. The revolution taking place in communications media and in information technologies represents a great and thrilling challenge; may we respond to that challenge with fresh energy and imagination as we seek to share with others the beauty of God.

---

for himself—he humanizes the apostle and himself by sharing authentic details about his life. This kind of sharing makes him more accessible. This priest is not the only one using social media to try to connect with Catholics. As you may have guessed from his statement above, Pope Francis, leader of the Catholic Church, tweets daily and as of May 2018 had more than seventeen million followers. In the tweets below (figure 3.2) you can see that Pope Francis urges his followers to reflect on their faith and to take care of our natural environment. While you might not get a reply from the Pope if you tried to engage him, it is clear that these social media efforts are intended to make religious leaders more accessible to their parishioners.

Recognized religious leaders such as the Pope are not the only ones who can use new media to try to make religious ideas more accessible. There are thousands of individuals online who explicitly draw on religious texts and the ideas of religious authorities to discuss the relevance of religious teaching in our lives. Take Christian blogger Priscilla Shirer, for example. Shirer is a wife and a mother of three boys, who also has a

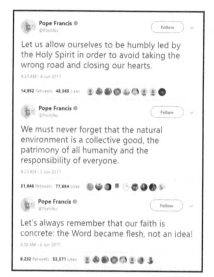

Figure 3.2. Tweets from Pope Francis. Source: Twitter, @Pontifex.

master's degree in biblical studies. She is the author of several Christian books for women and, recently, started publishing children's fare. On her blog, she uses a mix of metaphors, personal experiences, and Bible verses to help individuals recognize God's work in their lives. For instance, in one of her blogs, Shirer outlines how even seemingly menial tasks such as doing dishes can be done in the service of God. She recounts the story of Sandra, who took pride in tending her house and family but who also hated doing dishes. The saving grace of performing this loathsome task was that she washed dishes in front of a window and, every morning, watched the teenagers on the corner wait for the school bus.

Sandra, however, has a transformative moment. As Shirer describes it,

> Her gloved hands fell limp when she heard the hushed tones of God's Spirit burn in her heart. She had been asking God to reveal why He'd created her and what He could do through her to minister to others, while she was elbow-deep in these ordinary, mundane tasks of motherhood. She wanted an audience of lives to impact, but didn't know how it could fit in with the regular rhythms of daily living. Yet somehow, in this moment, it was clear. Her audience was right outside her window. Had been all along.

And if she had neglected the undesirable task of doing these dishes, she'd never have seen her brand new discipleship group. The next morning, she padded out to that street corner armed with doughnuts and a sheet of selected and prayed-over Scripture verses, handing them out one-by-one to each student. For more than *ten years*, she faithfully met dozens of them there—three times a week, fifteen minutes a day, claiming that corner as her consecrated mission field, right outside her kitchen window.

Shirer argues that Sandra's experience was destiny and is comparable to Biblical figures including Saul (who finds God while looking for his father's donkeys) and David (who slays Goliath while delivering food to his brother). She concludes by noting that, "For by God's providence, every earthly assignment is intertwined and interconnected with a heavenly one. Even your most ordinary task, done with eyes and ears wide open, can beckon you to brand new, eternally significant opportunities."

In sum, new media can play an important role in American religious practices. New media allow individuals to practice their faith during lunch breaks and in virtual spaces. For individuals whose religions fall outside of the mainstream, religious websites, chat rooms, and discussion boards provide a critical link to religious leaders and other practitioners. This, we learned, is true for followers of Wicca, who often find it difficult to overcome stereotypes and find others who celebrate Sabbats. New media makes it easier for Wiccans to find one another in the virtual and real worlds. New media are important to religious leaders as well. The digital era offers religious leaders new opportunities to connect with parishioners and the broader public outside of weekly services. We saw that Pope Francis encourages the priest and pastoral ministry to use social media to connect with others and share the word of God; something he does himself on Twitter. Of course, you don't have to be the Pope to spread religious messages online. Pricilla Shirer uses new media to help her followers find Christ in their daily lives.

RELIGIOUS COMMUNITY ONLINE

We live in a network-based society. Our friends may live all over the world, but new media allow us to stay connected to one another. Not surprisingly, new media have altered how individuals experience

REPRODUCING INEQUALITY
Death in the Digital Age

April 1945, President Franklin D. Roosevelt died from a stroke. Since he was in Georgia at the time of his death, a funeral train, accompanied by a procession of two thousand American soldiers, took his body to Washington, DC, for burial. All along the train tracks between Georgia and Washington, DC, Americans gathered day and night to grieve and pay their respects to their fallen president.

April 2016, the artist Prince died from a drug overdose. While people gathered in Prince's hometown (Minneapolis, MN) to grieve (and dance), thousands of people took to Twitter so that they could share their thoughts about the musician. On Facebook, community pages memorializing the artist and his music popped up.

When we lose someone we admire or care deeply about, we grieve. Before the internet, we would grieve together in the "real" world. When someone famous died, such as a well-loved president, people would gather together in order to grieve and pay their respects. In the digital age, we do not have to attend a memorial or service. We can simply go online. In fact, it is not uncommon for us to announce the deaths of parents, spouses, and pets on Facebook or to post tributes on memorial pages.

There are benefits associated with digital grieving. New media provide a place for us to come together and give meaning to death and the dead. Engaging with other mourners or just reading their online tributes can help us accept the deaths of loved ones.

New media also have created new companies and products associated with grieving and death. Internet memorials are sold with funeral packages and promoted as a way to keep loved ones involved in the grief process, even when they cannot be physically present. There are countless memorial websites (like Legacy.com and Nevergone.com) where you can pay to create an everlasting presence for your loved ones. There are even companies that allow you to make a "second self" while you're alive so that your memories and personality are eternal. Lifenaut, for example, uses uploaded reflections, online utterances, social media posts, and emails to create a "mind clone" that can interact with as well as offer information and advice to family and friends after your death.

These new industries remind us that inequality affects us even in death. Consider the following:

- Internet memorials typically cost money. Given that standard memorials run between seven thousand dollars and ten thousand dollars, for many mourners, internet memorials are out of financial reach.
- Internet access varies by income. These companies assume internet access.
- Internet access varies by geography. Individuals living in rural areas have less access to internet services, which make everything from grieving online to constructing a "second self" more difficult.

religious community. Recall that *religious community* refers to a strong sense of belonging that is based on individuals' shared faith. Communities have a common way of thinking about, talking about, and practicing religion. In other words, religious practices and religious communities often are related to one another. Before new media, religious communities were primarily built through face-to-face interactions at places of worship. Individuals might attend church services and church-related activities such as youth groups and bake sales and, over time, develop a sense of religious community. New media make it possible for religious communities to transcend geographic borders. An online church can be run by a person on one continent while attendees are from several others. Additionally, outside of online services, new media provide a space where individuals can formally or informally interpret religious ideas, make friends, and ask for advice when they need it.

Building a religious community online can take some effort. Let's look at the example of St. Pixels. St. Pixels began in 2004 as an online experiment of the group, Ship of Fools, whose aim is to "help Christians be self-critical and honest about the failings of Christianity, as we believe honesty can only strengthen faith." St. Pixels was a 3D church that individuals could attend. Using avatars, individuals would enter the church and participate in the service. According to the website, the 3D church attracted a lot of new members. The creators of St. Pixels recognized new media's community-building potential and put together a website that used a bulletin board and chat room as their major meeting points. The purpose of their meetings was to build a sacred space online. According to the St. Pixels website, this is when much of the community-building work took place. It wasn't easy. The creators of St. Pixels had to figure not only what their religious practices would look like online but also how they understood religious texts. This wasn't something that they could do by themselves and dictate to others, not if they wanted St. Pixels to be an open and welcoming space. A lot of people participated in the conversations regarding what St. Pixels should be. Apparently, their community-building efforts were often heated. However, participants spent hours talking through their religious views and, over time, grew to care about one another and pray for one another even when they disagreed. This process went on for more than two years and represented a critical step in the church's efforts to build meaningful religious community online.

While the 3D format for church services was very innovative, it was too expensive to maintain. So in 2011, St. Pixels held its first interactive service on Facebook and officially moved the church to Facebook and Twitter in 2012. When asked about this move to social media, St. Pixels pioneer Mark Howe explained, "Love it or hate it, Facebook is where people are. . . . If the Gospel is for today's connected culture, it has to find a distinctive but culturally-appropriate place within social networking." St. Pixels is still around. The services mostly take the form of a slideshow, which you can watch. Individuals can also participate in group prayer sessions and talk with one another in a chat room. St. Pixels has made an effort to broaden its religious community. It now links to i-church, an online Christian community, where followers and visitors can attend weekly services in the virtual world or debate religious topics in a chat room.

Of course, Christians are not the only ones trying to find creative ways to build religious communities online. You can visit a Buddhist or Hindu temple in the virtual reality game *Second Life*, or use the hashtag #openpractice on Twitter to find other Buddhists with whom you can practice your meditation. While you may be skeptical of these online religious communities, they seem to work for the people who participate in them. In a post for the *Lion's Roar*, a Buddhist magazine, Nate DeMontigny describes his experience meditating in a temple in *Second Life*. Notice that he mentions that he lives in an "isolated place" and hasn't "met many Buddhists in the real world." For DeMontigny, *Second Life* provided him a religious community of people he came to trust to answer his questions and "give good advice." It doesn't matter what your religion may be, there likely is a community online in which you can participate and find like-minded others to discuss matters of faith.

A PRECIOUS "SECOND LIFE" ONLINE?

Lion's Roar

BY NATE DEMONTIGNY
FEBRUARY 25, 2010

. . . One of the first things I did was to search out Buddhist places. I was blown away to find how many there were. There weren't as many as there are today, but there were meditation groups meeting and discussion groups as well. I began by sitting and chatting with the "Skeptical Buddhists"—their name says it all. The talk was peer-led and discussion was well maintained. I think there were 20+ people at this particular discussion.

For me this was great: I hadn't met many Buddhists in the real world so it had been hard to discuss things I was curious about. With this "Second Sangha" I was able to engage not only in the discussions but start an actual meditation routine. How does one meditate in a "game," you ask? It's actually just a simple as meditation in real life.

Groups of meditators get together, sit on virtual cushions, and a peer who leads the meditation hits a virtual gong (or Tibetan singing bowl, or what have you). The idea is that while your avatar is engaging in this meditation you are supposed to do the same in real life. The gong is struck and meditation begins. Then after the sitting session has ended, it's hit again and meditation is over. . . .

Being a "lone practitioner" it's sometimes difficult to keep a constant practice going. I need that extra nudge from time to time. By logging in to Second Life and attending a meditation session or a dharma talk, I get virtual nudge that I can transfer to my real life. That stale feeling I had before is replaced with a commitment to get back on track. I know it's more "involved" than that to get back into a practice, but with a lack of folks to meet with here in the real world (I live in a fairly isolated place), Second Life is a great fallback when I need to get back to my real-life practice. And I've built relationships with people I've come to trust to answer my questions and give good advice.

There are two additional points we need to consider about religious community in the digital age. First, some individuals participate in religious communities both online and offline. Social scientists find that many individuals who engage in religious communities online attend a local church or temple as well. These individuals report that they participate in both in order to deepen their religious lives. In fact, respondents who participate in religious communities online and offline describe their religious lives as multilayered and very satisfying. Second, not all of these religious communities are constructed around ideas American society sanctions. Let's use the Branch Davidians, which began as a sect that split away from the Seventh-day Adventist church, as an example. Under the leadership of David Koresh, the Branch Davidians became a doomsday cult in the 1980s. The Branch Davidians lived together outside Waco, Texas, in a compound, where members grew their own food and studied the Bible. Koresh believed that the final, encompassing battle of Armageddon, which is mentioned in the Bible, would begin at his compound. In preparation for this battle, the Branch Davidians began to assemble large numbers of guns and antitank rifles. One source estimates that there were eleven tons of weapons in the compound.

In the spring of 1993, the Bureau of Alcohol, Tobacco, and Firearms and Explosives (ATF), a governmental agency, decided to arrest Koresh on firearm violations. A group of seventy-six agents entered the compound in order to serve Koresh a warrant, and a shot was fired. This shot started a gunfight between the Branch Davidians and the ATF in which ten people died and more than two dozen were injured. The ATF withdrew from the compound and a fifty-one-day siege followed. The Federal Bureau of Investigation ended the siege by storming the compound. Koresh and more than seventy of his followers died. In the years that followed, survivors of the Branch Davidian Waco tragedy went online to share their stories, offer their views on their experiences with Koresh, and use new media to spread the Branch Davidian message to a new generation.

In sum, new media provides tools that groups and individuals can use to create religious communities online. As we saw with the example of St. Pixels, it can take a lot of time and effort to build religious communities. Members can spend years debating the religious values and beliefs that will hold them together. Individuals, however, clearly benefit from these efforts. People like Nate DeMontigny, who are geographically isolated and lacking a religious community in the real world, can find others whose religious guidance they trust online. For these individuals, new media offer them a way to practice and discuss matters of faith. We should not think about religious communities as something individuals participate in either online or in the real world. Social scientists find that many individuals do both and report that online and offline religious communities enhance their religious lives. Of course, not all religious communities are good for a society. This is the topic of our next section.

CASE STUDY

Extremist Religious Communities

America is known for its freedom of speech and religious freedom. While these freedoms are important, we have also noted that not all religions are mainstream. For example, Wicca, which is discussed above, may be a religion with which you are unfamiliar and, perhaps, uncomfortable. Regardless, Wiccans are allowed to practice their religion because the US Constitution protects the freedom of all citizens to do so unless the practice harms others or undermines other compelling societal interests.

The exclusion of religions whose practices harm others is often hotly debated by religious communities that feel as though the US government unfairly monitors them and their practices in an effort to try to "catch" them breaking the law. One such religious community is the Christian Identity community, whose belief system is built on racism. Followers of Christian Identity believe that Christianity is for whites only and that whites of European descent can be traced back to the "Lost Tribes of Israel." They also believe that Jews are the Satanic offspring of Eve and the Serpent and nonwhite people are "mud peoples" created before Adam and Eve. The Ku Klux Klan (KKK) and Aryan Nation both are based on Christian Identity doctrine.

Here are a few of their beliefs, which appear on the Christian Identity website (www.thechristianidentityforum.net):

- The white European people, Britons, Americans, Germans, Australians, and others are the Hebrews/Israelites of the Bible and are the biological sons and daughters of the living God.

- The people known today as Jews are imposters masquerading as God's chosen people and are the biological children of the Devil.
- Christianity is a religion for racially pure whites exclusively. Christ said that He came only for the lost sheep of the House of Israel, all of the members of which were and are white. There is no epistle in the New Testament written to any group of non-white people.
- The Bible was written to members of the Adamic race and to Israelites in particular, so when it uses language like every creature and all men, it means "every white person" and "all white men," not every man and woman on earth. Universalism, which teaches that the promises and covenants in the Bible apply to all races and is embraced by most nominally Christian churches, is a false doctrine.

As with other religions, new media makes it easier for followers of Christian Identity to find each other, organize, and practice their faith. In fact, sociologists who study Christian Identity groups find that new media have contributed to their strength because forums, chat rooms, and blogs provide believers a place to express themselves and a religious community.

Extremist religious communities don't post direct threats against people or groups. Leaders and followers know that to do so would violate the Constitution and get them in a lot of trouble. Instead, the threats are veiled. Extremist religious communities note what individuals they are keeping an eye on and frequently share the information and location of those being "watched." This is permitted because being "watched" doesn't mean that individuals are targets for beatings or death.

Read the Christian Identity Statement of Faith (the link is at the end of the chapter) and discuss the following questions in a small group:

- Should the government disband religious communities that are racist? Why or why not?
- Should extreme religious communities be monitored by the US government? Why or why not?
- How important do you think extremist religious communities are to religious diversity in the United States?

RELIGIOUS DYSFUNCTION ONLINE

Functionalists also examine the ways in which religion is *dysfunctional*, or how it can bring about harmful results. There are two common dysfunctions that result from religion: religious persecution as well as war and terrorism. Religion can be used for persecution, or used to rationalize rejecting, harming, and even killing people based on their religious beliefs. Adolf Hitler, for example, blamed Jews for Germany's defeat in World War I, the subsequent revolution that overthrew the monarchy, and the country's economic crisis that followed. Hitler used this hatred toward a religious population to rise to power and systematically imprison and murder millions of Jews.

There are countless examples of religious persecution throughout history, and of course, religious persecution still exists today. The group Open Doors, which tracks the religious persecution of Christians worldwide, compiles a yearly watch list that details the top fifty countries with the highest levels of persecution. In 2016, the organization found that North Korea, Afghanistan, Pakistan, Iran, Iraq, Syria, Sudan, and Somalia severely persecuted Christians. Open Doors also found that Christians were killed at record high rates in sub-Saharan Africa (Nigeria, Central African Republic, Chad, Democratic Republic of Congo, Kenya, and Cameroon) for practicing their faith. In fact, of the 7,100 reported deaths due to religious persecution, 4,028 were in sub-Saharan Africa. The point here is that religious persecution is not a new phenomenon.

New media can aid in religious persecution, particularly in America. Since individuals have the constitutionally protected right to free speech, they can create websites and social media accounts that offer outrageous accounts of a religious doctrine with which they do not agree. A good example of this kind of website is Jihad Watch, an anti-Muslim site that is "dedicated to bringing public attention to the role that jihad theology and ideology play in the modern world and to correcting popular misconceptions about the role of jihad and religion in modern-day conflicts." Jihad Watch believes that Islam is inherently violent and poses a threat to the American way of life. On its website, Jihad Watch incorrectly argues that Islam requires all Muslims to "impose" their religion and Islamic law on other societies, using violence if necessary. A central concern of Jihad Watch is that American laws will be replaced by Sharia law, which is an Islamic framework that guides some aspects of public and private life. Jihad Watch warns that Sharia law will deny Americans basic rights and dignity. This concern, however, is unfounded, since, like Christianity, Islamic denominations are diverse and because Sharia law in its entirety has not been implemented in any country of the world, including Muslim countries.

The potential effects of such websites cannot be ignored because Jihad Watch cultivates suspicion and even hatred toward Muslims through the spread of misinformation. In fact, the American Defamation League, Council on American-Islamic Relations, and the Southern Poverty Law Center all have classified Jihad Watch as a hate group that advocates and practices hatred, hostility, or violence toward Islam and Muslims. The Southern Poverty Law Center, which tracks and maps hate groups in America, identified 954 hate groups in operation in May 2018. If you look at the map (there is a link at the end of the chapter), you will notice that most of these are in the eastern half of the country and all of them have an online presence. While issues of race are central to most of these groups (e.g., white power and neo-Nazi organizations), anti-Muslim groups are on the rise. According to the Southern Poverty Law Center, since 2015, there has been an uptick in the number of Muslim hate groups in America. In 2015, there were 34 anti-Muslim groups. This rose to 101 in 2016. The Southern Poverty Law Center attributes some of this growth to Donald Trump's candidacy and ascendance to the White House. Trump's advisors, including Steve Bannon, who promoted Islamophobia as the executive chairman of the Alt Right outlet Breitbart, urged him to label Muslims as the source of terrorism. Trump took their advice. On the election trail, Trump made anti-Muslim comments and vowed to ban Muslims from entering the United States. In March 2017, Executive Order 13780, titled "Protecting the Nation from Foreign Terrorist Entry into the United States," suspended most travel from several Muslim countries for ninety days. This order was replaced in September 2017 by another, which indefinitely banned most travel to the United States from Iran, Libya, Syria, Yemen, Somalia, Chad, and North Korea. While both of these orders were blocked by lower courts, the Supreme Court upheld Trump's ban in June 2018.

The other dysfunction that results from religion is war and terrorism. Again, there are countless examples of religious wars throughout human history. The Crusades, for example, refers to a series of bloody battles between Christians and Muslims. Beginning in the eleventh century, Christian popes launched attacks on Muslims in an effort to take possession of Jerusalem (their Holy Land). More recently, Islamic extremists used religion as a reason for the September 11, 2001, attacks on the Pentagon and the World Trade Center towers. New media make it easier for religious-based terrorists to communicate with one another. For example, ISIS (an extreme Muslim faction, which is also known as ISIL or the Islamic state, that advocates violence in the name of religion) uses new media to find recruits. Sheera Frenkel, a reporter for BuzzFeed, studied how ISIS used the internet for six months. She learned that ISIS doesn't simply use the "dark web" to meet up in clandestine virtual spaces or just send one another messages through the secret end-to-end encryption service Telegram, which, like Snapchat, includes a self-destruct timer. ISIS members try to engage people in chat rooms and find new recruits on dating websites. For example, Frenkel reported that ISIS members try to attract women recruits by promising them wealth and luxury once they journey to Syria.

The scariest part of religious extremists' use of new media is that they can use the internet to spread their ideas without ever having direct contact with individuals who act violently on their behalf. ISIS, for instance, sends out its radical messages through social media such as Twitter and uploads recruitment and execution videos to YouTube, which makes it easy for individuals to go online, learn extremist religious positions, and then act on them. Unfortunately, there have been several examples of new media contributing to religious-based terrorism worldwide. On April 15, 2013, two men detonated two pressure cooker bombs near the finish line of the Boston Marathon. One of the terrorists admitted that they were motivated by extremist Islamic beliefs and had learned how to make the bombs from materials published by a religious extremist group online. More recently, twenty-nine-year-old Sayfullo Saipov, who was inspired by ISIS propaganda he found online, killed eight and injured twelve in Manhattan, New York, when he purposely ran a rented truck into a bike lane and targeted bikers and pedestrians.

While it is unclear whether new media make the dysfunctional aspects of religion worse, it is clear that new media make it easier for extremists of all kinds to spread their ideas to those looking for them. Extremists promoting religious persecution as well as those promoting violence in the name of religion can quickly set up a website that endorses their positions and use social media such as Facebook, Tumblr, Twitter, and Instagram to make sure that they have a widespread, virtual presence. Likewise, new media make it much easier for individuals to self-radicalize, or adopt an extreme position and act on it. Extremist groups provide not only a doctrine but, often, how-to manuals that offer instructions on how to forward a particular cause.

CASE STUDY

Countering Extremism Online

Extremist groups are not the only ones using new media to spread their messages. Websites like Islamicity.com and Twitter accounts such as @islamicthought, @Islam, and @IslamSpeaks try to educate the general public about Muslim practices and Islamic faith. There are also efforts to make fun of and discredit extremist religious groups like ISIS. The group Anonymous, which is an international network of activists and hackers, has targeted ISIS, using illegal methods to find and share information about the religious terrorist organization. In March 2015, Anonymous released 9,200 names of Twitter accounts suspected of ISIS affiliation. Anonymous hoped releasing the names would force Twitter to take action against individuals using the platform to spread extremist ideology and propaganda. It is not clear how many (if any) accounts were removed.

 Check out the following websites:
- IslamiCity: www.islamicity.com
- Islamic Broadcast Network: www.ibn.net
- Islam-USA: www.islam-usa.com
- Muslim Women's League: www.mwlusa.org
 Discuss the following questions:
- Do you think these websites help counter misinformation about Islam and Muslims? If so, how? If not, what do you think would work?

CONCLUSION

In this chapter, we discussed how new media are changing religion. We began by outlining Durkheim's definition of religion and identifying two related aspects of religion: religious practice and religious community. We learned that new media change how we think about sacred spaces. Digital technology decouples religious practice from a physical space, meaning we don't have to go to a physical church, temple, or synagogue at a specific time to practice our faith. We simply can go online and watch a sermon or run an app that offers motivation and music for our meditation. This is an important shift because it changes where and how we engage religion. We can create sacred spaces in our offices, cars, and online, and practice alone or together. Then we outlined two other consequences of new media on religious practices. First, we learned that digital technology makes it easier for individuals who practice alternative religions such as Wicca to find and connect with one another around their shared faith. Second, we discussed how religious leaders use social media in an effort to make religious doctrine and themselves more accessible to practitioners.

After our discussion of religious practice, we turned our attention to the effects of new media on religious community, or a group of people united by their shared beliefs and practices. We discussed the example of St. Pixels and the many years of work its founders put into cultivating a religious community online. The church started out as an expensive 3D experiment that was a success. Over time, the creators and members hashed out their values and beliefs, and the religious community still exists today on Twitter and Facebook. Religious communities can use new media in lots of different ways. Individuals or religious leaders can build virtual churches, temples, mosques, and synagogues in games such as *Second Life*, connect via hashtag on Twitter, or create private spaces where only members can chat with one another. We also learned that many individuals participate in religious communities online and offline, and that religious communities do not always represent the values of mainstream society.

We concluded the chapter by exploring the harmful effects of religion, or religious dysfunction. Social scientists typically discuss two harmful effects of religious dysfunction—religious persecution and war and terrorism—and we outlined how new media influence both. In the United States, our liberal free speech laws make it easier for groups to spread misinformation about a religion. Jihad Watch, for example, falsely claims that Muslims are violent and Islam is a threat to an American way of life. This is not the only organization that uses new media to spread hate. The Southern Poverty Law Center found that Muslim hate groups are on the rise in the United States and that these groups advocate violence against Muslims. One reason groups such as Jihad Watch have supporters is because there are extremist groups such as ISIS that advocate violence in the name of religion. As we discussed, it is much easier for extremist groups such as ISIS to spread their ideas in the digital age. They don't have to direct contact with the public to recruit them. They simply use new media to spread their messages of extremism and destruction.

CHAPTER LINKS

"Faulty Fire, Faulty Worship Jimmy Swaggart Preaching on Holiness" 2013. YouTube. Last modified June 24, 1993. http://www.youtube.com.
"Good Looking Parents Sing Disney's Frozen (Love Is an Open Door)." 2014. YouTube. Last modified March 10, 2014. http://www.youtube.com.
McNeal, Stephanie, and Rachel Zarrell. 2015. "Doctors Cast Doubt on Viral Video Stars Sam and Nia's Pregnancy Claims." *BuzzFeed*. Last modified August 12, 2015. http://www.buzzfeed.com.
"Are Americans Finding God in Cyberspace?" n.d. Beliefnet. http://www.beliefnet.com.
"Home Page." n.d. FPMT. http://www.fpmt.org.
"Hail Mary." 2015. Catholic Online. Last modified September 15, 2015. http://www.catholic.org.
"Virtual Hindu Temple Worship." 2015. Hobbypoint.in. Last modified January 26, 2015. http://www.play.google.com.
"Home Page." n.d. Wiccan Together. http://www.wiccantogether.com.
Pope Francis. 2014. "Communication at the Service of an Authentic Culture of Encounter." The Vatican. Last modified June 1, 2014. http://w2.vatican.va.
Shrirer, Priscilla. 2017. "A Dish. A Donkey. A Destiny." Going Beyond Ministries. Last modified October 1, 2017. http://www.goingbeyond.com.
"Home Page." n.d. Ship of Fools. http://www.shipoffools.com.
"Home Page." n.d. St. Pixel. http://www.stpixels.com.
"The Ganesh Temple & Gardens." n.d. Second Life. http://www.secondlife.com.

Demontigny, Nate. 2010. "A Precious 'Second Life' Online?" *Lion's Roar*. Last modified February 25, 2010. http://www.lionsroar.com.

"World Watch List." n.d. Open Door. http://www.opendoorsusa.org.

"Hate Map." n.d. Southern Poverty Law Center. http://www.splcenter.org.

"Hate Groups Increase for Second Consecutive Year as Trump Electrifies Radical Right." 2017. Southern Poverty Law Center. Last modified February 2, 2017. http://www.splcenter.org.

Frenkel, Sheera. 2016. "Everything You Ever Wanted to Know about How ISIS Uses the Internet." *BuzzFeed*. Last modified May 12, 2016. http://www.buzzfeed.com.

CHAPTER REVIEW QUESTIONS

1. What is media logic and why do some scholars think it is bad for religion?
2. How, according to Durkheim, can we define religion?
3. What are three ways that new media change religious practices?
4. Why are religious communities important?
5. Why do functionalists care about religious dysfunction? What does religious dysfunction look like online?

LEARN MORE

Ardalan, Davar. 2002. "Islam on the Internet." *National Public Radio*. Last modified March 16, 2002. http://www.npr.org.

Banerjee, Neela. 2007. "Wiccans Keep the Faith with a Religion Under Wraps." *New York Times*. Last modified May 16, 2007. http://www.nytimes.com.

Bardin, Jeff. 2015. "What It's like to Be Recruited by ISIS Online." *Business Insider*. Retrieved June 7, 2017. Last modified May 22, 2015. http://www.businessinsider.com.

Greene, Richard Allen, and Nick Thompson. 2016. "ISIS: Everything You Need to Know." *CNN*. Last modified August 11, 2016. http://www.cnn.com.

Kosoff, Maya. 2016. "Google and Facebook Quietly Escalate Their Cyber-War on ISIS." *Vanity Fair*. Last modified June 27, 2016. http://www.vanityfair.com.

Larsen, Elena. 2001. "CyberFaith: How Americans Pursue Religion Online." Pew Research Center. Last modified December 23, 2001. http://www.pewinternet.org.

Price, Rob. 2014. "Inside the World of Virtual Churches." *Kernel*. Last modified March 19, 2014. http://www.kernelmag.dailydot.com.

Ralli, Tania. 2005. "Missed Church? Download It to Your IPod." *New York Times*. Last modified August 29, 2008. http://www.nytimes.com.

"Robert Spencer." n.d. Southern Poverty Law Center. Retrieved June 7, 2017. http://www.splcenter.org.

Scott, Eric. 2016. "10 Things I Wish Everyone Knew about Wicca." OnFaith. Last modified September 24, 2016. http://www.onfaith.co.

Susman, Tina, and Matt Pearce. 2015. "On Web, White Supremacists Stir Up a Growing and Angry Audience." *Los Angeles Times.* Last modified June 24, 2015. http://www.latimes.com.

Wong, Kristina. 2016. "How the US Is Working to Defeat ISIS Online." *Hill.* Last modified June 25, 2016. http://thehill.com.

Wood, Graeme. 2015. "What ISIS Really Wants." *Atlantic.* Last modified March 2015. http://www.theatlantic.com.

VIDEOS AND MOVIES

Andrescik, Robert. 2011. "Religion & Social Media." YouTube. Last modified April 4, 2011. http://www.youtube.com.

BBC Trending. 2016. "The Mouse Messiah Bringing Salvation to India's Atheists." *BBC.* Last modified April 11, 2016. http://www.bbc.com.

Barlow, Rich. 2011. "Cutting-Edge Technology for an Ancient Religion." *BU Today.* Last modified July 5, 2011. http://www.bu.edu.

"Children of ISIS." 2015. *PBS Frontline.* Last modified November 23, 2015. http://www.youtube.com.

"Social Media Brings Religion to the Masses." 2012. *Fox News.* April 27, 2012. http://www.foxnews.com.

Stern, Melissa. 2015. "Muslims Condemn ISIS for Abusing the Name of Islam with Social Media Campaign." *Fox News.* Last modified December 4, 2015. http://www.fox4kc.com.

CHAPTER REFERENCES

Altheide, David, and Robert Snow. 1979. *Media Logic.* Thousand Oaks, CA: Sage.

Barzilai-Nahon, Karine, and Gad Barzilai. 2005. "Cultured Technology: The Internet and Religious Fundamentalism." *Information Society* 21 (1): 25–40.

Campbell, Heidi. 2007. "Who's Got the Power? Religious Authority and the Internet." *Journal of Computer-Mediated Communication* 12 (3): 1043–62.

———. 2010. "Religious Authority and the Blogosphere." *Journal of Computer-Mediated Communication* 15 (2): 251–76.

———. 2012 "Understanding the Relationship between Religion Online and Offline in a Networked Society." *Journal of the American Academy of Religion* 80 (1): 64–93.

Campbell, Heidi, and Antonio La Pastina. 2010. "How the iPhone Became Divine: New Media, Religion and the Intertextual Circulation of Meaning." *New Media & Society* 12 (7): 1191–207.

Campbell, Heidi, and Oren Golan. 2011. "Creating Digital Enclaves: Negotiation of the Internet among Bounded Religious Communities." *Media, Culture & Society* 33 (5): 709–24.

Cann, Candi. 2014. *Virtual Afterlives: Grieving the Dead in the Twenty-First Century.* Lexington: University of Kentucky Press.

Castells, Manuel. 2011. *The Rise of the Network Society: The Information Age: Economy, Society and Culture*. Hoboken, NJ: Wiley-Blackwell.

Cheong, Pauline Hope, Alexander Halavais, and Kyounghee Kwon. 2008. "The Chronicles of Me: Understanding Blogging as a Religious Practice." *Journal of Media and Religion* 7 (3): 107–31.

Cheong, Pauline Hope, Peter Fischer-Nielsen, Stefan Gelfgren, and Charles Ess, eds. 2012. *Digital Religion, Social Media and Culture: Perspectives, Practices and Futures*. New York: Peter Lang.

Cho, Kyong. 2011. "New Media and Religion: Observations on Research." *Communication Research Trends* 30 (1): 4–22.

Dawson, Lorne, and Douglas Cowan, eds. 2013. *Religion Online: Finding Faith on the Internet*. New York: Routledge.

Durkheim, Émile. 1995 [1912]. *The Elementary Forms of Religious Life*. New York: Free Press.

Højsgaard, Morten, and Margit Warburg. 2005. *Religion and Cyberspace*. New York: Routledge.

Jacobs, Stephen. 2007. "Virtually Sacred: The Performance of Asynchronous Cyber-Rituals in Online Spaces." *Journal of Computer-Mediated Communication* 12 (3): 1103–21.

Shaap, Julian, and Stef Aupers. 2016. "'Gods in World of Warcraft Exist': Religious Reflexivity and the Quest for Meaning in Online Computer Games." *New Media & Society* 19 (11): 1744–60. https://doi.org/10.1177/1461444816642421.

4

Is Big Brother Watching Us?

KEY CONCEPTS

Legal institutions refer to those organizations charged with enforcing laws and protecting the populace. The Federal Bureau of Investigation (FBI), Central Intelligence Agency (CIA), National Security Agency (NSA), law enforcement, and the court system are examples of legal institutions.

Legal actors are the individuals who work for and represent legal institutions, including police officers, FBI agents, NSA analysts, lawyers, and judges.

Bureaucratization refers to the adoption of clear organizational structure, protocols, and procedures. Max Weber observed that bureaucratization was a key feature of modern institutions and played an important role in maintaining power over the citizenry.

Authority refers to the power of an institution to give orders, make decisions, and force citizens to comply.

Rational-legal authority refers to the kind of power that bureaucracies use to maintain their legitimacy with a population. Legal institutions get their legitimacy from a system of rules that are obeyed because they are consistent with the values of a society and upheld by institutional actors.

Corporate legitimacy is a result of how people evaluate a company, its goals, and its appropriateness. Some of a corporation's legitimacy results from its compliance with the rules and regulations of a country. However, we also evaluate the legitimacy of a corporation based on the social values it represents.

The phrase "Big Brother is watching you" conjures either thoughts of CBS's popular reality TV show or an image of an unseen government force watching what you do, who you hang out with, and what you read, view, and listen to. The surveillance of citizens by *legal institutions*, or those organizations charged with enforcing laws and protecting the populace, has long been the subject of debate. There is a lot of disagreement among Americans regarding what kinds of information legal institutions should be allowed to access for national security, which refers to the idea that the government should protect itself and its citizens from threats. While some Americans believe legal institutions should be allowed to collect a wide range of information about individuals and groups to maintain national security, other Americans argue that legal institutions such as the Federal Bureau of Investigation (FBI) often overstep their bounds and violate our Fourth Amendment right against unreasonable searches and seizures.

As you can imagine, changes in mass media have dramatically shifted the debate over surveillance in America. Before the advent of new media, legal institutions had to clearly identify threats to national security and take steps to monitor individuals and organizations. For example, between 1956 and 1971, the Federal Bureau of Investigation (FBI) operated five counterintelligence programs designed to surveil groups it regarded as "subversive" and threatening to the stability of the US government. The massive surveillance program, called COINTELPRO, targeted political groups as diverse as the Ku Klux Klan (KKK), a hate organization designed to ensure the dominance of the "white race," and Students for a Democratic Society (SDS), a progressive group fighting for political representation and equality. While the groups were very different, the FBI sought to control both organizations. Mass media played an important role in the FBI's efforts.

The KKK is known for intimidating and committing violence against African Americans in order to maintain white supremacy. The FBI identified the KKK as a threat to national security because the KKK, particularly in the South, had the support of local law enforcement. Local police officers as well as county sheriffs and deputies would turn a blind eye to the KKK's illegal activities and, sometimes, the local lawmen were active leaders and members of the organization. Not surprisingly, the FBI did not want the broader public to know how widespread support for the

KKK was among Southern law enforcement, since it would cause citizens to question the ability of the US government to uphold its own laws and protect the populace. This, the FBI feared, might lead to violence in other parts of the country or revolution. To keep the KKK in check, the FBI infiltrated its groups, or klaverns, and used mass media to try to disrupt their regular activities.

In some cases, the FBI used letter writing campaigns to stir discontent in the KKK. The FBI reasoned that if KKK members were busy fighting among themselves, they would have time for little else. FBI agents, for example, sent an anonymous letter to the Imperial Wizard (basically the president of the KKK), Robert Shelton, to report that another KKK leader was talking behind his back. Shelton got angry and had the leader removed from the organization. The FBI tried to disrupt the daily activities of the organization using letters in other ways as well. The FBI used anonymous letters to affect the personal businesses of Klan members, to criticize the use of public funds that would make Klan activities easier (such as paving roads around and to KKK meeting places), and even to announce incorrect meeting dates and places. Not surprisingly, Shelton eventually became concerned that there were traitors in his midst and proposed that the group use lie detector tests and sodium pentothal (a.k.a. truth serum) on KKK members in order to flush informants out into the open. Worried that its surveillance would be exposed and its agents rooted out, the FBI sent a fake letter from a rival leader "exposing" the proposal to the membership. The letter denounced Shelton's lack of trust in Klan members and vigorously criticized his willingness to endanger their health. The FBI even pulled strings with newspapers to make sure the KKK did not get good press for its activities. For instance, FBI agents made sure that a story on a Klan-organized "Sportsman's Club" turkey shoot was never published in a community newspaper. While the FBI did not destroy the organization, it effectively sowed discord among KKK members and made it more difficult for the organization to operate.

The FBI did play a part in the destruction of Students for a Democratic Society (SDS). The organization used college and university campuses to engage students in political debate—particularly about the Vietnam

War—and challenge everything from <u>imperialism,</u> or the US practice of extending its power through policy and military force, to corporate domination of democratic participation. The FBI regarded SDS as a threat to national security because the organization challenged racial and income inequality; conscription, or involuntary service in the US military; and social norms regarding sexual behavior and drug use. The ideas of "free love" and "flower power" are still around today—only not how the SDS envisioned them. "Flower power," for example, was a symbol of passive resistance and nonviolent action. The idea was to make antiwar protests peaceful and positive (rather than violent) spectacles. As you can see in the image below, student protestors literally offered soldiers and military police flowers. The FBI, however, used mass media to characterize SDS members as dirty and sexually depraved. FBI agents circulated anti-SDS leaflets that featured unkempt demonstrators, planted negative articles about the group and their illicit use of drugs and sex in newspapers and magazines, and created and circulated cartoons ridiculing the organization. The FBI even wrote SDS members' parents to inform them of their children's "subversive" activities at school. Not surprisingly, the FBI's use of mass media helped destroy

Figure 4.1. Flower Power Photograph by Bernie Boston. Source: Electronic Frontier Foundation, CC BY 3.0 US.

SDS. The stereotypes about SDS, however, remain. Today, when we hear "flower power," we think about dirty, oversexed hippies who experiment with hallucinogenic drugs.

In the digital age, surveillance of the citizenry by legal institutions is more widespread. Legal institutions no longer have to identify specific targets of surveillance. Legal institutions have access to data on who we are (called demographics), where we are (called geo-demographics), and what we think and think about (called psychographics), which they "mine," or extract patterns from. The widespread surveillance of American citizens became the topic of international debate in 2013 when Edward Snowden famously disclosed the extent of the surveillance by releasing thousands of documents the National Security Agency (NSA) had gathered through its PRISM program. Launched in 2007, PRISM monitors the telecommunication and electronic messages of citizens, companies, and other governments. It is not completely clear how PRISM works. Lorenzo Franceschi-Bicchierai from Mashable created a hypothetical/working model of the program (there is a link to his graph at the end of the chapter). An NSA analyst requests user data, the FBI processes the request, and the analyst receives the data via PRISM. Requests from analysts are not denied because these requests are permitted under the USA PATRIOT (the Uniting and Strengthening America by Providing Appropriate Tools Required to Intercept and Obstruct Terrorism) Act of 2001, which allows law enforcement to search telephone, email, and financial records without a court order.

Surveillance, however, was not restricted to individuals alone. Snowden also revealed details about a secret court order requiring Verizon (and, it turns out, every other phone company) to hand over millions of Americans' phone records daily, uncovered the NSA's secret wiretapping into Google and Yahoo data centers, and exposed a program called XKeyScore that searches unfiltered internet traffic in real time. NSA analysts can use XKeyScore, which vacuums up individuals' emails, user names, passwords, search histories, social media activities, facsimiles, videos, and phone conversations with only a general justification for the search—one that is not reviewed by a court or a senior NSA official before it is processed. It is not clear how much data on American citizens were swept up by NSA analysts, or how these data were used. The NSA and Central Intelligence Agency (CIA) even used new media to monitor citizens in virtual worlds such as *World of Warcraft, Second Life*, and Xbox Live. Snowden found that the NSA and CIA spied on citizens as well as tried to recruit informants from these services.

The released documents sparked international controversy with some calling Snowden a traitor and others publicly thanking him for his efforts to preserve democracy. Interestingly, you can see that Americans' opinions on the debate over whether legal institutions go too far or not far enough when it comes to national security are in flux. Figure 4.2, which shows the percentage of Pew survey respondents who think the US government has either not gone far enough to protect the country or gone too far in restricting our civil liberties, illustrates the shifts in Americans' feelings on the debate. Notice that public opinion in the wake of Snowden's 2013 revelations about the NSA surveillance programs shifts and respondents express a belief that the government has gone too far restricting civil liberties. Otherwise, although there is fluctuation by year, Americans generally think that legal institutions have not done enough to protect the country. Snowden continues to defend his action publicly. In a statement from Moscow, where he has temporary asylum, Snowden stated, "I acted on my belief that the NSA's mass surveillance programs would not withstand a constitutional challenge, and that the American public deserved a chance to see these issues determined by open courts . . . today, a secret program authorized by a secret court was,

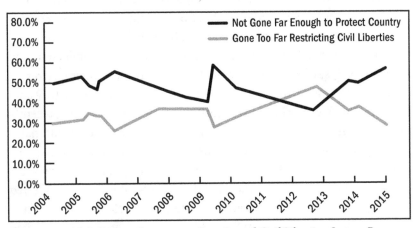

Figure 4.2. Public's Shifting Concerns on Security and Civil Liberties. Source: Pew Research Center, Survey Conducted Dec. 8–13, 2015. "Don't Know" Responses Not Shown.

when exposed to the light of day, found to violate Americans' rights. It is the first of many." Clearly, the debate over the line between legal institutions and individual rights is ongoing and complicated.

THE "LIVING" LAW

For some of you, the idea that laws are something that are argued over may be a new idea. Laws, we often think, are something that we have to follow, whether or not we agree with them. Sociologists make sense of these debates by thinking about the law as "living," which means that the law is created (and recreated) through the practices of the *legal actors*, such as police officers, FBI agents, NSA analysts, lawyers, and judges, working in legal institutions. For example, police officers, FBI agents, and NSA analysts all draw on their training and experiences when deciding who to target as potential perpetrators of crimes. While existing laws inform both their training and experiences, they are not the only thing that matter. Social acceptance, or whether the majority of citizens agree with a law, affect whether it is enforced. Here's a quick example. Do you know (or have you ever heard of) someone being arrested for cohabitation, or living with someone to whom he or she is not married? The idea of getting arrested and going to jail for cohabitation seems absurd given that this has been a common practice among Americans for decades. Yet in 2013, four states (Florida, Michigan, Mississippi, and Virginia) had laws on the books that made cohabitation among opposite-sex couples illegal. As you can imagine, legal actors in these states do not enforce cohabitation bans. These bans do not reflect our current understanding of relationships, making enforcement of such laws a problem. Arrested couples, for example, might sue that state for having discriminatory laws on the books. The Florida and Virginia Supreme Courts, in fact, recently threw out the states' cohabitation bans, calling them unconstitutional.

The law is also "living" because we create new laws (and, as we saw above, get rid of old ones) in response to the broader political environment and the social wants, or the claims and demands, of the people. Viewed this way, we have to contextualize our discussion of surveillance, civil rights, and legal institutions in light of the terrorist attacks on the United States on September 11, 2001. Islamic terrorists hijacked four commercial airplanes and crashed one into the Pentagon (where the Department of

Defense is housed); one into a field near Shanksville, Pennsylvania (it was headed to Washington, DC, but the passengers overpowered the hijackers); and two into the World Trade Center towers in New York City. The attacks paved the way for policy change, including the USA PATRIOT Act of 2001. This expanded the *authority*, or the power, of legal institutions. Organizations such as the NSA used their new legal authority to initiate the surveillance programs described above. There is debate over these surveillance programs because there is not a clear or consistent agreement among Americans that the authority of legal institutions is more important than the individual rights of citizens. As we discussed above in figure 4.2, public opinion on this debate shifts year to year.

Authority is an important sociological concept, particularly in the digital age. In fact, sociologists still refer to the work of Max Weber, who wrote about authority in institutions in the nineteenth century. Weber noticed that *bureaucratization*, or the adoption of clear organizational structure, protocols, and procedures, were a key feature of modern institutions, and he wrote about how bureaucracies maintained their power over the citizenry. Legal institutions, he observed, primarily maintain their power through *rational-legal authority*, meaning they get their legitimacy from a system of rules that are obeyed because they are consistent with the values of a society and upheld by institutional actors. Laws, in other words, are regarded as legitimate and justified by those leading institutions and by the citizenry. For example, Americans value their right to "life, liberty, and the pursuit of happiness." Legal institutions determine the rules by which we can achieve this goal; rules that we accept. We know that if we operate outside these rules (e.g., steal what we want or kill others for what they have), we will be arrested, tried, and imprisoned.

Legal institutions maintain their rational-legal authority in part because their authority extends only so far as the country's borders, and the rules of interaction between us (as citizens) and legal institutions in the real world are clear. Legal actors such as police officers, for instance, cannot search our vehicles or come into our homes without a search warrant issued by a judge or "probable cause," meaning there is enough information to cause a reasonable person to believe that either a crime was committed or evidence of a crime exists. The authority of legal institutions is less clear in the virtual era because cyberspace extends beyond the boundaries of any given nation and is not the domain of legal actors alone. Multinational corporations, for instance, also operate online and often provide the platforms for our interactions. AOL, Apple, LinkedIn, Microsoft, Facebook, Google, Twitter, and Yahoo are all examples of multinational corporations that offer American consumers products so that they can access virtual spaces and socialize, conduct business, and commit crimes.

While corporations do not want their products to be used for criminal activities, they do want to maintain a customer base so that they have a healthy bottom line. One way that corporations try to keep you interested in their products is through the use of "cookies," which are small files stored on your computer. When you visit a company's website, the website sends a cookie to your computer, which tracks your visits and activity on the site. This information is used for everything from keeping track of items in your shopping cart to suggesting other items you might want to purchase. Another way that multinational corporations try to maintain relationships with their customers is by protecting their personal information and, as we discuss in more detail below, butting heads with legal institutions over whether they are required to hand over customer data. In these battles, multinational corporations often point out that they are not simply accountable to US legal institutions but the legal institutions of other countries. Many multinational technology companies incorporate Article 12 of the United Nations Declaration of Human Rights, which declares that "no one shall be subjected to arbitrary interference with his privacy, family, home or correspondence, nor to attacks upon his honour and reputation. Everyone has the right to the protection of the law against such interference or attacks," into their business models and believe that their success in a global economy depends on their ability to protect their customers' data from threats, including intrusions by legal institutions such as the NSA. As you can see, the boundaries over who has authority in digital spaces get very complicated very fast.

This chapter takes a closer look at how new media provide the landscape for contemporary battles over authority. We begin by examining how individuals and groups use new media to challenge the authority of legal institutions and the practices of legal actors. Then we turn our attention to corporations, which also struggle to maintain their authority in the digital age. As we will see, authority is something that is contested, meaning different actors challenge who has power—as well as who is exploiting their power—in the digital age.

REPRODUCING INEQUALITY
"Big Data" and Policing

We hear a lot about "big data." You can barely listen to the news without someone mentioning how big data are being used to influence everything from a company's bottom line to a presidential election. What is big data?

Big data refers to how data are handled. A company, for example, starts with large data sets, it searches the data, and then it clusters the information based on the search results. Since the company has access to multiple data sets, it can cross-reference information and look for patterns. A company like Netflix would then use these results to suggest movies and TV shows that we might enjoy.

Legal institutions use big data to predict behavior and intervene before a crime is committed. Think about that for a minute. Big data has completely reversed how policing and intelligence are done. Legal actors used to identify individuals whom they thought were engaged in illegal activities and investigate them. In the digital age, all of us are potential criminals, and law enforcement tries to determine which of us is likely to commit a crime by collecting and cross-referencing data from airport Wi-Fi, license plate recognition software, mobile phones, and social media.

Chicago mayor Rahm Emanuel calls it "predictive policing" and uses it to identify neighborhoods likely to experience violent crimes, the likely perpetrators of those crimes, and the likely victims of those crimes. The idea is to send out officers to intervene before crimes happen. So what's the problem? Consider the following:

- Police data are not collected uniformly. This actually makes a lot of sense. Crime is largely a hidden social phenomenon, which means police databases consist of nonlawbreaking behavior such as calling 911.
- Police data are not objective. If we've learned anything from watching the recent push back against local law enforcement from the Black Lives Matter movement, it's that low-income communities and communities of color often feel repressed rather than protected by police. Arrests, warranted or not, go into the database and bias the results.
- Algorithms are not neutral. We like to think that removing people from the equation makes predictive policing better. Of course,

imperfect individuals design the algorithms and, as we know, they are not working with good data. Even programs that promise to be "race neutral," for example, fall short because the data they are working with is so flawed.

The result? Low-income neighborhoods and communities of color are targeted at disproportionately high rates by law enforcement. Worse, predictive policing is sometimes used to inform bail and sentencing decisions, reproducing racial inequality. Lots of counties in the United States, for example, use COMPAS (Correctional Offender Management Profiling for Alternative Sanctions), which is used to predict recidivism, or the likelihood of someone ending up back in jail. A study by ProPublica uncovered that the COMPAS system

- incorrectly found black defendants to be at a higher risk of recidivism than white defendants and
- incorrectly found black defendants to be at a much higher risk of committing a violent crime than white defendants.

NEW MEDIA AND CITIZEN CHALLENGES TO AUTHORITY

The terrorist attacks of September 11, 2001, were unprecedented. In twenty minutes, a handful of terrorists, who were allegedly retaliating for America's support of Israel, its involvement in the Persian Gulf War, and its military presence in the Middle East, effectively changed how Americans thought about national security and individual rights. After the attacks, citizens approved of ethnic profiling, or law enforcement using racial or ethnic characteristics to determine who was likely to commit a crime and prevent these crimes from occurring. One third of Americans supported internment, or removing Arab Americans from the community and placing them in camps until their innocence could be determined. Additionally, support for increased military spending skyrocketed to 50 percent, a level far exceeding the previous twenty-five years. Support for racial and ethnic profiling was still high three years after the attack. According to a Gallup poll (see figure 4.3), almost half of those surveyed thought that profiling at airport security checkpoints was justified. Compare this to other kinds profiling of which the same respondents largely disapproved.

Not surprisingly, in the months and years after the terrorist attacks, American Muslims felt as though they were living in a superpanopticon.

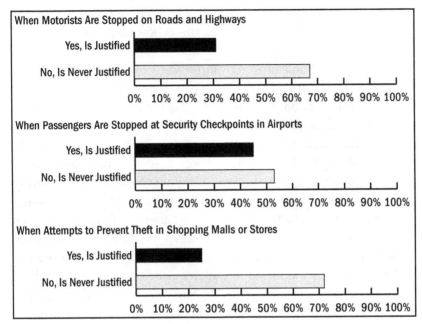

Figure 4.3. Is Racial Profiling Justified? Source: Gallup.

What's a panopticon? It is a model of an ideal prison that philosopher and social theorist Jeremy Bentham came up with in the eighteenth century. The distinguishing feature of the panopticon is that it is structured in such a way that all the cells are open to a central tower where there is a guard. Prisoners cannot interact with one another nor can they tell precisely when they are being watched by the guard in the tower. This affects prisoners' behaviors. The panopticon makes the prisoners feel as though their actions are always visible to an unseen guard and that they are always being watched, so they behave in ways that keep them out of trouble on the chance that they are, in fact, being watched. The *superpanopticon* refers to the hypersurveillance that is possible by institutions, such as legal institutions, in the digital age. Computer databases give legal actors the ability to retrieve and verify information about individuals without having to know who the individuals are. In the digital age, there are no guards or prisoners. There is information, there are institutional actors who retrieve the information that they want, and there is us—and either we fit their search criteria or we don't. The effect, however, is the same. We know that we are being observed, but we do not know when we are being watched, where we are being watched, or how often we are being watched. This affects how we behave online and offline.

Back to the example of American Muslims in the wake of September 11, American Muslims in New York City felt as though they were in the superpanopticon and consciously altered their behaviors in ways to keep themselves off the radar of legal institutions and out of trouble. A report published by the Creating Law Enforcement Accountability & Responsibility (CLEAR) Project as well as several American Muslim civil liberties groups in 2013 titled "Mapping Muslims: NYPD Spying and Its Impact on American Muslims" describes how Muslims censored their conversations, changed their event programs, and altered how they used the internet in an effort to keep themselves off the New York Police Department's (NYPD) radar. In the report, a Sunday school teacher explained that she was afraid to criticize policies directed at Muslims for fear that she might be targeted by law enforcement. To make sure that the NYPD did not show up on her door, she was very careful about what she said on social media sites such as Facebook. She explained, "I don't talk about the NYPD on Facebook. We'll put articles up, but we will never comment on them, put up our own words. Maximum we'll say, 'It's sad that this is happening.' But, we will never show our anger, that we're really, really angry."

They weren't wrong to be careful. In August 2011, the Associated Press began publishing stories on a surveillance program approved by then-mayor Michael Bloomberg that allowed the NYPD, in cooperation with the Central Intelligence Agency (CIA), to conduct surveillance on hundreds of Muslims hundreds of miles outside the city's border. The goal of the program was to "map" Muslims in communities. The NYPD used "rakers," or undercover officers, to monitor the daily lives of Muslims in bookstores, bars, cafes and nightclubs and "mosque crawlers," or informants, to monitor the content of sermons—even when there was no evidence of wrongdoing. In all, the program monitored more than 250 mosques and student groups in an effort to root out would-be terrorists. If you go to the Associated Press website, you can see what some of the "mapping" looks like (there is a link at the end of the chapter). You will see a map identifying businesses—primarily restaurants, bookstores, and grocery stores—Egyptians frequent in Brooklyn, New York. The NYPD program also kept careful tabs on individual and group websites as well as social media pages, looking for signs of threats.

Civil rights groups criticized the program for violating the rights and privacy of American Muslims. Linda Sarsour, who works for the Arab American Association of New York, noted, "Those documents, they showed where we live. That's the cafe where I eat. That's where I pray. That's where I buy my groceries. They were able to see their entire lives on those maps. And it completely messed with the psyche of the community." A senior FBI official agreed that the program had done more harm than good. He added that the program actually undermined national security because it sowed distrust of legal institutions within the Muslim community. New York City mayor Michael Bloomberg defended the program, arguing, "I believe we should do what we have to do to keep us safe. And we have to be consistent with the Constitution and with people's rights. We live in a dangerous world, and we have to be very proactive in making sure that we prevent terrorism." Bloomberg went on to compare the ethnic profiling done by the NYPD to screening kids for the measles. He noted, "If there is a community where the crime rate is very high, to not put more cops in that community is ridiculous. If you want to look for cases of measles, you'll find a lot more of them among young people. That's not targeting young people to go see whether they have measles or not." The NYPD's "Demographics Unit," which was the official name of the unit charged with spying on American Muslims, was disbanded in 2015.

American Muslims were not the only targets of surveillance while Bloomberg was in office. When the Republican National Committee announced that it would hold its 2004 convention in New York City, Bloomberg extended his surveillance efforts to include progressive activists in the United States, Canada, and Europe. The NYPD used "open source intelligence" (or "OSINT"); social media networks such as Twitter, Facebook, Instagram, and YouTube to track protest plans; and even online data as a rationale for infiltrating nonviolent activist groups and questioning protestors about their political activities. Bloomberg also approved a plan for arresting and processing large numbers of protestors during the event. More than 1,800 citizens—not all of whom were even protestors—were arrested in the days before and during the Republican National Convention. On average, an arrested citizen spent twenty-four hours in custody in what many considered substandard conditions. Individuals were confined in overcrowded metal cages at Pier 57, where they had limited access to food, water, medical care, and medication and were exposed to extreme temperature shifts, sleep deprivation, and hazardous chemicals. Many of the individuals arrested were charged with minor violations that did not require jail time. Lawyers and activists argued that the NYPD effectively punished protestors for exercising their First Amendment rights. This charge was echoed in civil lawsuits and a complaint filed by a coalition of environmental, human rights, housing rights, and animal rights activists, which accused the NYPD of targeting "First Amendment protected activities like political advocacy" that provide "vital nourishment to our democratic system of government and prevents its corruption and atrophy."

While the surveillance program, which extended beyond the convention, was revealed by media sources years after the Republican National Convention, activists documented the NYPD's behavior as it happened. It turns out that the NYPD did not like citizens recording their surveillance activities. An organizer for Picture the Homeless, who was filming the post office near Madison Square Garden where recipients of public assistance had reported difficulty picking up their checks, was grabbed by a police officer and dragged across the street. A police captain informed him that he was not allowed to film the police checkpoint outside the post office. He also told the organizer that he would delete anything from the camera he didn't like. According to a report compiled by the New York Civil Liberties Union in 2004, at least ten independent videographers were targeted by the NYPD. Seven of the videographers were arrested, and of these, the NYPD held their cameras as evidence even after they were released. One of the videographers reported that his camera was smashed by an officer.

There were many uses of new technology and media by citizens that the NYPD did not catch. Citizens and activists alike used mobile phones to report on the conditions at Pier 57 and their treatment. For example, a detained activist used a smuggled mobile phone to contact the news outlet *Democracy Now!* and report on the conditions. Detainees passed the phone around, and the show's producer, Mike Burke, interviewed detainees (a link to the report is provided at the end of the chapter). One woman, Emily, reported,

> I was arrested yesterday off of Union Square East, on East 15th Street in between Union Square East and Irvine. I was on the sidewalk, and I was never told that I would be arrested. I was just on the sidewalk. And no one ever read me my rights. They just took us all away. They trapped us and put us all into buses. We've been in jail for over 13 hours right now. In our first nine hours, the only food we received was an apple. In our first four hours here we weren't allowed to go to the bathroom or get water. So none of us were read our rights; we haven't been able to talk to any lawyers. A lot of people here that were arrested without even protesting, they were—just happened to be on the sidewalk where everyone was on that block—was arrested. And there are chemical warning signs all over this place that we're being held. A lot of people are forming rashes on their skin from the floor—from whatever it is that is on it. And I'm going to pass this on to someone else who has another story.

Another woman named Althea told her story, noting,

> I was—am a New York City public school teacher. I was out on Union Square on 16th Street between Irving and Union Square just walking, trying to enjoy the day, and I got swept up in a demonstration. I wasn't a part of the demonstration and I was arrested. I was arrested about 8:00 p.m., handcuffed and we've been sitting in the Chelsea piers in very crowded conditions. Right now some people are experiencing toxic reaction to the environment, itching in their skin, and we're very crowded. We have been given water and a sandwich, but they have not been giving us any information, and we've just been sitting here really penned in. . . . And no one knows where I am. Basically I feel like I've been 'disappeared.' Nobody knows in my family that I have been arrested. And I was out by myself shopping; so, you know, there's no one to—they haven't allowed me to contact anyone.

These two women were picked up in one of the NYPD's mass arrests—a common tactic used by the NYPD during the convention. Police would cordon off an area and arrest everyone in it.

Pedestrians were not the only ones caught in the crossfire. Several professional photographers and journalists were arrested during the demonstrations even though they were wearing NYPD-issued press credentials. Those who were able to leverage their connections and secure a quick release reported on the mass arrests and detentions. Photographer Robert Stolarik, for example, was taking pictures of an arrest when police tackled him, choked him, and tightly cuffed his hands behind his back. The cuffs were so tight that doctors believed that Stolarik's bones in his wrists were fractured and that he may have permanent nerve damage in his hands. Stolarik was not the only photographer wearing their NYPD-issued press credentials who was arrested and subjected to rough treatment. Six other professional photographers described being pushed to the ground or being hit by police and, like Stolarik, were quick to use news blogs, radio, and mass media to report what was happening on the streets of New York.

Some of the police monitoring efforts by citizens were coordinated. The National Lawyers Guild observed arrests and the New York Civil Liberties Union trained 154 observers to monitor the tactics being used by police during the convention. Monitors attended an intensive training session, where they learned how to observe police, learned how to use still and video cameras, and became familiar with guidelines governing how police and protesters are allowed to interact. As you can imagine, the efforts by individuals and organizations to report on the behavior of the NYPD resulted in more than just bad press and national outrage. The video taken by monitors helped overturn legal cases. For instance, a group called I-Witness, which recorded incidents of misconduct, helped overturn four hundred cases where the video evidence contradicted that of sworn statements by police officers. Additionally, the National Lawyers Guild in conjunction with several other organizations sued the NYPD for unlawful arrest and detainment of American citizens. The city of New York settled the case in 2014 and paid those wronged (1,638 individuals) a total of eighteen million dollars.

CASE STUDY

Law Enforcement and Body Cameras

Over the last few years, there has been a lot of talk about having police officers wear body cameras. Individuals who support the use of body cameras argue that their use increase transparency in police encounters, deter officers from abusing their authority, make citizens more respectful of police authority, and provide evidence to support arrests and prosecution of wrongdoers. Supporters note that there are hundreds of incidents involving police officers that show the time for body cameras has come.

Individuals who oppose the use of body cameras argue that they cost too much money and violate the privacy of both the citizen and the officer. Opponents point out that less than 1 percent of police-citizen contact involves force. Most of the time, police officers mediate disputes, help individuals in distress, and assist the mentally ill—none of which should be captured on film. More important, opponents of body cameras argue that their use undermines the authority of police officers because it signals that there is no trust between law enforcement officers and the communities they protect.

There is very little evidence to support either position. In fact, a study published in May 2016 by the University of Cambridge and RAND Europe found that officers wearing body cameras were 15 percent more likely to be assaulted. The researchers are not sure why this is the case. Potential reasons include the following: (1) officers are less assertive when they are wearing cameras, (2) citizens get aggressive when they learn they are being filmed, and (3) police are more likely to report assaults by citizens because they have video evidence.

There is no shortage of (sometimes graphic) videos on YouTube documenting police-citizen interactions. Go to YouTube and watch these very different videos. The links are provided at the end of the chapter.

- The first video, taken with a cell phone, shows officer Ben Fields flipping a South Carolina high school student to the ground and throwing her across a classroom. The incident received national media attention.
- The second video, created by the Denver Police Department, discusses the department's use of body cameras and why they think it is important.

- The third video, taken with a body camera, shows a man coming to a front door and stabbing an officer in his bulletproof vest.

Discuss the following questions:

- Do you think that police officers should use body cameras? Why or why not?
- Do body cameras diminish the authority of law enforcement? Why or why not?

What does all this mean for individuals' interactions with legal institutions? Legal institutions can surveil us without our knowledge and the frequency and scale of their monitoring are difficult to assess. As the examples of the PRISM program and the NYPD's surveillance of citizens before the Republican National Convention in 2004 illustrate, the September 11 terrorist attacks changed how many citizens viewed the responsibilities of legal institutions, and the USA PATRIOT Act gave legal institutions more authority when it came to national security. However, not all citizens approve of surveillance programs and, in fact, think that legal institutions sometimes abuse the authority they have been given. These citizens individually and collectively use new media to observe the behavior of legal actors to ensure that Americans are not subject to undue search and seizure or arrest. When they are, these citizens and groups report these violations and use them as evidence in civil and class-action lawsuits. So while the power between legal institutions and American citizens is unequal, new media make surveillance bidirectional. Law enforcement can surveil individuals, and individuals can surveil law enforcement. This is an important shift because it allows American citizens to better ensure that legal institutions do not abuse their authority.

CORPORATIONS VERSUS LEGAL INSTITUTIONS: WHO RULES VIRTUAL SPACE?

It is often observed that we live digital lives. We share our photos and videos on social network sites, activate location-aware apps on our mobile phones to find a way around a traffic jam, and log in to sites where we get our email, retrieve the documents we have stored, and check our search history. All these data are whizzing around the web in ways that we do not quite understand and much of it is maintained by corporations. While we often are aware that we are in corporate spaces when we share a picture via Instagram, tweet our opinions, or use a sponsored lens on Snapchat, we rarely think about what corporations do with our data, let alone whether legal actors have ever requested a company to hand it over. Yet as the discussions of the PRISM and other surveillance programs highlight above, these requests happen, and we almost never find out about them. Indeed, these data requests are so frequent that tech companies are challenging the authority of legal institutions to make them.

Let's consider a recent example. In April 2016, Microsoft sued the US government, alleging that forcing the company to keep access request secret violates the individual's constitutional rights against illegal searches and seizures of property. According to Microsoft's president and chief legal officer, legal institutions made 2,576 requests for data in the past eighteen months; 1,752 of these secrecy orders (or 68 percent of the total) contained no fixed end date, effectively prohibiting Microsoft from ever telling its customers that the government obtained their data. Microsoft's lawsuit accused the US government of exploiting "the transition to cloud computing as a means of expanding its power to conduct secret investigations" on American consumers and businesses. On the Official Microsoft Blog (posted April 14, 2016) Smith explained,

> We believe these actions violate two of the fundamental rights that have been part of this country since its founding. These lengthy and even permanent secrecy orders violate the Fourth Amendment, which gives people and businesses the right to know if the government searches or seizes their property. They also violate the First Amendment, which guarantees our right to talk to customers about how government action is affecting their data. The constitutional right to free speech is subject only to restraints narrowly tailored to serve compelling governmental interests, a standard that is neither required by the statute being applied nor met by the government in practice here.

The lawsuit, in part, is a response to existing public policy regulating government surveillance, which Microsoft argues needs to be revisited by Congress. Currently, surveillance is primarily regulated by the

Electronics Communication Privacy Act (ECPA) of 1986, which protects wire, oral, and electronic communications while those communications are being made, are in transit, and when they are stored on
computers. The ECPA has three specific provisions. First, it prohibits the
interception, use, and disclosure of communication and forbids illegally
obtained communications from being used as evidence. For example,
you cannot tape a phone conversation with your landlord without her
knowledge and permission and try to use it against her in a dispute over
your eviction. Second, the ECPA protects the privacy of the contents
stored by service providers (such as Yahoo) as well as the records the
service provider has about you, such as your name, billing records, and
IP address. Finally, the ECPA requires legal institutions to get a court
order before monitoring your communications. The ECPA, however,
was passed before the popularization of the internet and the advent of
tech companies such as Google and, therefore, does not apply to other
digital communications like email and messages you send through Facebook, Twitter, and Instagram. As we discussed above, many of the rules
regarding the ability of legal institutions to monitor you online have
been made easier by the USA PATRIOT Act.

The lawsuit also is an attempt to maintain *corporate legitimacy* with
a customer base. Some of a corporation's legitimacy results from its
compliance with the rules and regulations of a country. However, we
also evaluate the legitimacy of a corporation based on the social values
it represents. Corporations maintain their legitimacy by making sure
their customer base evaluates them positively. Let's unpack the definition of corporate legitimacy a bit more. First, corporations must comply
with the laws governing them in order to be legitimate. When we find
out that a company has violated US law in some way, we get upset and
withdraw our support for—and dollars from—them. This happened
recently to oil giant BP. In 2010, one of BP's oil rigs, Deepwater Horizon,
exploded in the Gulf of Mexico and sunk, killing eleven workers and
resulting in the worst oil spill in American history. A sea-floor oil gusher
flowed for eighty-seven days, dumping 210 million gallons of oil into the
ocean. An investigation by the US government found that a faulty well
and gross negligence were to blame for the spill. BP, in other words, violated a number of safety and labor laws. BP pled guilty to eleven counts
of manslaughter, two misdemeanors, and a felony count of lying to

Figure 4.4. Culture Jam of BP Logo. Source: Eric Hunsaker on Flickr, CC BY 2.0.

Congress. BP agreed to be monitored by the federal government and pay 4.5 billion in fines and payments to Americans whose livelihoods (e.g., fisherman and local businesses) were destroyed by the spill. Not surprisingly, American citizens were not happy with BP. Americans protested; marched on BP's headquarters in Houston, Texas; and used Facebook to organize consumer boycotts. Citizens defaced and reworked BP's logo to read "Boycott Polluters" (see figure 4.4). BP's sales plummeted.

Second, and related, corporations must represent some of the values of their consumers. We expect corporations to give back (or at least to care about) the world in which they operate. This is why most companies have a corporate social responsibility program detailing how the company uses some of its profits to address issues that we generally care about such as healthy communities and the environment. A number of companies including GAP and Coca-Cola highlight their efforts to make their businesses more sustainable. GAP, for instance, advertises that the company is doing its part to reduce climate emissions, use preferable raw materials such as organic cotton for some of its garments, and collaborate with organizations such as the Ethical Trading Initiative in order to improve the labor conditions in its supply chain. The purpose of these sustainability programs is to try to find ways for corporations to conduct business and make a profit while taking steps to protect the environment, our natural resources, and their workers.

So how does this relate to the Microsoft lawsuit? Microsoft wants to maintain its corporate legitimacy by showing us that it cares about our constitutionally protected rights. You can see this in the statement below by Brad Smith, which was posted on the Official Microsoft Blog in the wake of Snowden's revelations about the NSA's surveillance programs on December 4, 2013. Smith clearly positions Microsoft as the defenders of Americans' civil liberties and legal institutions (and the US government more generally) as a threat to our rights to privacy. He noted,

> Many of our customers have serious concerns about government surveillance of the Internet. We share their concerns. That's why we are taking steps to ensure governments use legal process rather than technological brute force to access customer data. Like many others, we are especially alarmed by recent allegations in the press of a broader and concerted effort by some governments to circumvent online security measures—and in

our view, legal processes and protections—in order to surreptitiously collect private customer data. In particular, recent press stories have reported allegations of governmental interception and collection—without search warrants or legal subpoenas—of customer data as it travels between customers and servers or between company data centers in our industry. If true, these efforts threaten to seriously undermine confidence in the security and privacy of online communications. Indeed, government snooping potentially now constitutes an "advanced persistent threat," alongside sophisticated malware and cyber attacks. In light of these allegations, we've decided to take immediate and coordinated action in three areas:

> We are expanding encryption across our services.
> We are reinforcing legal protections for our customers' data.
> We are enhancing the transparency of our software code, making it easier for customers to reassure themselves that our products do not contain back doors.

Notice that Smith compares the snooping done by the government to "sophisticated malware and cyber attacks" and suggests that Microsoft is making efforts to ensure the "legal protections" of its customers. The post makes clear that this is a voluntary effort designed to protect the privacy of American consumers.

Microsoft's actions against the government also divert consumer attention away from the fact that the company sells data mining tools to other businesses as well as mines its own users' data. Data mining refers to the practice of searching large stores of data in order to find trends and patterns in it. Companies engage in data mining so that they can forecast their sales, create profiles of the people who buy and use their products, and discover the best ways to market their products to consumers—among many other things. The summer before Microsoft filed its lawsuit, its new operating system, Windows 10, came under fire for collecting vast amounts of user data, which was then mined for information. According to Microsoft's privacy policy, Microsoft can

> access, disclose and preserve personal data, including your content (such as the content of your emails, other private communications or files in

private folders), when we have a good faith belief that doing so is neces-sary to: 1. comply with applicable law or respond to valid legal process, including from law enforcement or other government agencies; 2. pro-tect our customers, for example to prevent spam or attempts to defraud users of the services, or to help prevent the loss of life or serious injury of anyone; 3. operate and maintain the security of our services, includ-ing to prevent or stop an attack on our computer systems or networks; or 4. protect the rights or property of Microsoft, including enforcing the terms governing the use of the services—however, if we receive informa-tion indicating that someone is using our services to traffic in stolen intel-lectual or physical property of Microsoft, we will not inspect a customer's private content ourselves, but we may refer the matter to law enforcement (excerpted from the BGR webpage).

As you can imagine, some Windows 10 users became very angry and accused Microsoft of burying its data collection and mining in its twelve-thousand-word-long service agreement. The outrage over Micro-soft's practices grew and reached a fevered pitch in January 2016—just a few months before the lawsuit—when Yusuf Mehdi, corporate vice president of the Windows and Devices Group, shared some of the cor-poration's milestones, which included figures on how many hours users have spent using Microsoft devices, including Xbox One. Microsoft, of course, is not the only corporation to use data mining. Twitter, with about 5 percent equity in the company Dataminr, provides the com-pany access to public tweets in real time. These tweets are mined for trends and relevant information that is sold to a variety of companies (including newspapers, hedge funds, and investment banks), which use this information to advise their day-to-day decision-making. Likewise, Google gives away educational apps to schools (called Google Apps for Education) and mines students' emails for personal information that can be used to generate ad revenue.

You can see that part of the reason corporations take a strong stand on individuals' privacy rights is because they want to distract consum-ers from their own data mining activities and maintain their legiti-macy with consumers. Maintaining corporate legitimacy is increasingly important because consumers are less and less willing to trade their data for discounts and freebies. A 2015 survey conducted by Joseph Turow and his colleagues found the following:

- Ninety-one percent of respondents disagree (77 percent of them strongly) that "if companies give me a discount, it is a fair exchange for them to collect information about me without my knowing."
- Seventy-one percent of respondents disagree (53 percent of them strongly) that "it's fair for an online or physical store to monitor what I'm doing online when I'm there, in exchange for letting me use the store's wireless internet, or Wi-Fi, without charge."
- Fifty-five percent of respondents disagree (38 percent of them strongly) that "it's okay if a store where I shop uses information it has about me to create a picture of me that improves the services they provide for me."

In short, we are growing intolerant of the expectation that we should trade our data for product and service discounts.

What makes the battles over authority between legal institutions and corporations interesting is that they sometimes provide the startup funds for the same data mining companies. Dataminr, mentioned above, is a great example. In April 2016, online magazine the *Intercept* reported that the Central Intelligence Agency (CIA) has a venture capital firm, which is a firm that invests in businesses that are seen as risky, called In-Q-Tel. This venture capital firm has been investing in businesses that surveil and data mine social media platforms such as Twitter. In-Q-Tel and the CIA were interested in Dataminr because it identifies patterns and trends from real-time data from Twitter and other public sources. If you navigate to the Dataminr website, you will see that the company uses a variety of sources including location data, financial data, news wires, tweets, and even Wikipedia to identify breaking news, real-world events, "off the radar" perspectives, and emerging trends, which it sells to companies in the news industry, public sector, and financial sector.

In-Q-Tel also invested in companies making location-based tools. For example, In-Q-Tel invested in the company Geofeedia, which lets clients, which include a number of police departments, use a tool to draw a perimeter around an area of interest. Geofeedia displays all the geo-tagged social media posts from Twitter, Facebook, Instagram, YouTube,

CASE STUDY

Corporations and Dataveillance

Have you ever felt like you are being watched by invisible eyes as you walk down the grocery aisle? In some ways, you are being watched. The grocery store is monitoring what you buy and how often you buy it. It's called dataveillance, which refers to the monitoring of our actions online and through our communication devices. Lots of companies engage in dataveillance.

Let's use Disney's Magic Kingdom as an example. Disney monitors your actions a few different ways. Disney makes extensive use of video cameras and plain clothed security throughout its parks. This kind of surveillance has been around for a long time. However, if you downloaded Disney's app or used its "My Disney Experience" website while in the park, the company tracked your movements this way. The company's ability to know exactly what you were doing was greatly enhanced if you wore a MyMagic+ wristband, which let Disney know when you were stopping for a snack at a concession stand, getting advanced tickets for the next ride, or relaxing at one of the resorts. Disney even used biometrics—which refers to measuring parts of our biological data—in its parks. When you swiped your ticket to enter a Disney park, they scanned your fingerprint to authenticate your identity.

Dataveillance doesn't end when you exit the park. This Disney app—like many of the apps we download, including those for airlines and hotels—continue to work long after our trips are complete. In fact, if you don't close down many apps completely, they will track your location. Companies then sell the data for profit.

Listen to the Fresh Air segment called "'Aisles Have Eyes' Warns That Brick-and-Mortar Stores Are Watching You," which talks about all the ways companies monitor our behaviors. Then discuss the following:

• Why do we give corporations so much authority? Is it convenience? Ignorance? Something else?
• Should consumers be compensated when companies buy and sell their data? If so, how?
• Are there some kinds of data companies should not collect? What?

Flickr, Picasa, and Viddy and lets clients organize the social media content into a timeline so that they can monitor multiple locations at once in real time. Basically, a client highlights a geographic area of interest so that she can see all the geotagged social media posts in that area. Then she has the option of organizing the posts by date and time as well as the ability to monitor new posts.

The CIA venture capital firm In-Q-Tel, however, is not the only backer of businesses like Dataminr. Twitter also invested in Dataminr and, in fact, has a 5 percent stake in the company. While this is not a huge stake in monetary terms, Dataminr is the only outside company with full access to Twitter's real-time data and permission to sell that data. Without access to the raw feed of all Twitter data, which is called the Twitter firehose, Dataminr falls apart. Dataminr recently found itself in an awkward position. Twitter used its leverage to force Dataminr to stop selling data to legal institutions that want the data for surveillance purposes. This all came to a head because Dataminr had created a free pilot program for US intelligence agencies, which was used for surveillance purposes. In September 2015, the contract for the free program expired and Dataminr made an effort to transition the program into a paying contract. In May 2016, Twitter used a veto clause in its contract to prevent the company from doing so. A Twitter spokesperson told *Wired* magazine that "Dataminr uses public Tweets to sell breaking news alerts to media organizations such as Dow Jones and government agencies such as the World Health Organization, for nonsurveillance purposes. We have never authorized Dataminr or any third party to sell data to a government or intelligence agency for surveillance purposes. This is a longstanding Twitter policy, not a new development."

Authority is at the center of the battle over how Dataminr can be used. Legal institutions want to use Dataminr for a broad range of surveillance purposes and, given the USA PATRIOT Act, believe they have the authority to do so. Here are two quick examples of how legal institutions have used Dataminr in their surveillance efforts. After the 2013 bombing at the Boston Marathon, which killed 3 people and left 260 people wounded, local law enforcement used Dataminr to try to ensure that the event, which attracts thousands of people each year, was not attacked again. The FBI and police departments also use Dataminr to monitor activists and social change-oriented groups (such as Black Lives

CASE STUDY

Apple versus the FBI

On December 2, 2015, Syed Rizwan Farook and Tashfeen Malik entered the Inland Regional Center in San Bernardino, California, and opened fire, killing fourteen people and injuring another twenty-two. The day after the shootout, the FBI searched the married couple's townhouse and found, among other things, a cell phone. Since the couple perished in a shootout, the FBI could not ask Farook his password—and the phone was set to erase itself after ten wrong guesses. The FBI asked Apple, the maker of Farook's phone, for help. The FBI wanted Apple to trick Farook's phone into updating its software. The software would turn off the ten wrong guesses trigger and the FBI would be able to crack Farook's password. Apple gave the FBI some advice but refused its request to break into the phone to retrieve Farook's data.

The FBI obtained a court order requiring Apple to break into Farook's phone. Again, Apple refused. Tim Cook, Apple's CEO, argued that the company is concerned that the FBI will use this solution to access other iPhones as well, which would be a clear violation of individual privacy. Apple also took issue with the All Writs Act, which the FBI used to obtain its court order. The All Writs Act allows federal courts to issue "all writs necessary or appropriate in aid of their respective jurisdictions and agreeable to the usages and principles of law." Apple argued that forcing the company to write, test, debug, deploy, and document the necessary software to break into Farook's phone was burdensome and exceeded the bounds of the All Writs Act. Lots of other companies agree with Apple. AT&T, Airbnb, eBay, Kickstarter, LinkedIn, Reddit, Square, Twitter, Cisco, Snapchat, Amazon, Facebook, Google, and Microsoft have all publicly supported Apple's position.

Debate time!

Get into small groups (three to five people). Come up with arguments that either support or oppose the following statement: legal institutions have the right to monitor our communication to prevent terrorism and obtain access to the personal devices of those who have committed acts of terrorism. After you choose a side, come up with at least three solid arguments as to why your position is correct. You want to anticipate your opponents' arguments and have good rebuttals! No personal attacks allowed.

Matter) that use Twitter to discuss political issues and organize. The use of Dataminr for surveillance stands in opposition to Twitter's goal, which is to give people "the power to create and share ideas and information instantly, without barriers." Twitter, in other words, sees itself as a platform for democracy and free speech. People can speak their minds about a topic and even organize to affect change. If Twitter willfully gives legal institutions access to its firehose for surveillance purposes, people might quit using Twitter. Twitter, in short, is trying to maintain its corporate legitimacy.

In sum, new media and how digital tools are used can put legal institutions and corporations at odds with one another. Legal institutions need the cooperation and compliance of corporations in order to surveil individuals they feel are a threat to national security. Corporations may comply or they may challenge the authority of legal institutions. Corporations are likely to challenge legal institutions' authority if they feel like their legitimacy with the public is at risk. Given the debate over surveillance in America, it is not surprising that some companies decided to publicly challenge secret requests for personal information, such as the case of Microsoft, or refuse to let legal institutions have access to their data, such as the case of Twitter.

NAVIGATING A DIGITAL WORLD: DEALING WITH SURVEILLANCE

Because we live digital lives, we also contribute to our own surveillance. Every time we share a photo through Instagram and Snapchat or upload a picture to Flickr or Picasa, we provide a great deal of data about ourselves. Pictures often include, or are tagged with, information about where, when, and how they were taken, not to mention who is included in the photo. If you think about pictures on sites such as Flickr, you even get information about the camera the picture was taken with as well as its settings. We also like to use social media sites, such as Facebook and Instagram, to "check in" our location and let our friends and family know where we are and what we are up to. However, as we have learned in this chapter, our friends and family are not the only ones who are paying attention to where we are and what we're doing.

Opting out of the new media is very difficult to do. As we learned in the introduction, people use new media for a range of activities, including shopping, keeping up with friends, banking, work, and school. New media make our lives easier and more enjoyable. However, there are things you can do to reduce the information you make available about yourself. First, you can read the end user license agreements (EULAs) before you install new software on a device and peruse the terms and conditions before you set up a social media account. Admittedly, this is not an easy thing to do. These agreements are notoriously long. A study done by Lorrie Faith Cranor and Aleecia McDonald in 2008 found that the average privacy policy on just a website was 2,215 words. Apple's EULA is much longer; it is approximately twelve thousand words or more than fifty pages long. Window's EULA, discussed above, is just as long. EULAs also are filled with legalese and are easy to skip. There almost always is a button that you can click that says "I Agree," which most of us click without much thought. In fact, Jeff Sauro, who analyzed how much time 2,500 people spent reading EULAs found that on average users spent only six seconds on the page before clicking "I Agree."

A second, and much easier, way to reduce the information you make available about yourself is to find trustworthy organizations that analyze and summarize these agreements for you. Groups such as the Electronic Frontier Foundation (EFF), which is a nonprofit organization dedicated to protecting individual civil liberties in the digital world, research and report on companies and their privacy agreements. You can see a summary of the EFF's 2017 annual report above, which is titled "Who Has Your Back?" The summary provides an overview of several companies' privacy policies and specifically outlines which companies have pro-user policies, disclose their data retention policies to users, and disclose government requests for data or removal of content (table 4.1). You can see that companies such as Adobe, Dropbox, Pinterest, WordPress, and Uber do well on all five measures. Others, such as AT&T, Verizon, Amazon, T-Mobile, and WhatsApp do rather poorly. Using this information, we can decide whether to change providers or cancel our account. Alternatively, we can look to sources such as the *Intercept*, *Wired*, *PC World*, and *Technology Review* for guidance on what information the programs we use such as Siri, Cortana, and S Voice transmit to third parties and store.

TABLE 4.1. EFF's Who Has Your Back Ratings

Who Has Your Back?

Protecting Your Data from Government Requests

	Follows Industry-Wide Best Practices	Tells Users about Government Data Requests	Promises Not to Sell Out Users	Stands Up to NSL Gag Orders	Pro-User Public Policy
Adobe	✓	✓	✓	✓	✓
airbnb	✓			✓	✓
Amazon.com	✓				✓
Apple	✓	✓	✓	✓	
AT&T	✓				
Comcast	✓				
Credo Mobile	✓	✓	✓	✓	✓
Dropbox	✓	✓	✓	✓	✓
Facebook	✓	✓	✓		✓
Google	✓	✓	✓		✓
LinkedIn	✓	✓	✓		✓
Lyft	✓	✓	✓	✓	✓
Microsoft	✓	✓	✓		✓
Pinterest	✓	✓	✓	✓	✓
Slack	✓		✓	✓	✓
Snap Inc.	✓		✓		✓
Sonic	✓	✓	✓	✓	✓
T Mobile	✓				
Tumblr	✓	✓			✓
Twitter	✓		✓		✓
Uber	✓	✓	✓	✓	✓
Verizon	✓				
WhatsApp	✓				✓
Wickr	✓	✓	✓	✓	✓
WordPress.com	✓	✓	✓	✓	✓
Yahoo!	✓	✓	✓		✓

Third, you can hide your browsing data. More than anything we do online, what you search for and click on are used to create a profile of who you are and what you like. If you have ever been on Facebook, you know that ads are targeted to you based on your browsing habits. A fairly easy way to mask your browsing habits is to use a virtual private network (VPN). Typically, when we go online, our computers access the World Wide Web through our internet service providers (ISP), and we navigate to a website. If anyone is looking closely, he or she can see that connection. A VPN puts an intermediary server between us and the sites we are connecting to. So if someone is looking closely, he or she can only see a connection from the VPN server to the site on the other end. The VPN hides your identity. You can even download a TOR browser, which will route your connection through three separate servers before connecting you to a website. As you can imagine, it is very difficult for anyone to monitor your browsing data using TOR. If this sounds too difficult, you can install an extension to your browser that allows you to see what companies are tracking you. The extension Ghostery, for example, gives you more control over ads and tracking data on the websites you visit and anonymizes your personal data. If you just want to have a bit of fun at social media companies' expense, look for free extensions such as Go Rando, which automatically balances your emotional expression on Facebook in order to confuse the company's algorithms. Over time, Go Rando makes it seem as though you have perfectly balanced views, which makes your data more difficult to interpret. Using VPNs and TOR may become increasingly popular in the coming years, especially since Congress voted in March 2017 to roll back regulations on the ability of ISP to track, interact with, and sell our data.

CONCLUSION

We began the chapter with a discussion of surveillance in the digital age. We learned that legal institutions, or the organizations charged with enforcing laws and protecting the populace, use new media to watch the digital traffic of American citizens. Legal actors, or the individuals who work for and represent legal institutions, argue that this is necessary for national security. This, however, is not universally accepted by Americans. Approximately half of the citizens surveyed believe that legal institutions have overstepped their authority. In order to explain these debates over authority, sociologists think about the law as living. Legal institutions maintain their rational-legal authority in part because the laws we obey are consistent with the values of society more broadly. New media throw some of this authority into question.

Then we explored how citizens challenge authority directly. We discussed three different ways that citizens challenged police practices during the 2004 Republican National Convention. First, citizens who were falsely arrested called news programs such as *Democracy Now!* to report on the conditions at Pier 57. Second, citizens used new media to monitor the police tactics during the convention. Finally, and related, lawyers used these videos to file lawsuits against the NYPD and won. Of course, Americans are aware that legal actors can observe their behavior online and offline without their knowledge. Muslim Americans, for example, knew they were being surveilled by legal actors and did not express their anger online, fearing that their anger might be misunderstood as a threat of terrorism.

While legislation such as the USA PATRIOT Act gives legal institutions more authority to surveil our activities in the digital age, they are not the only ones vying for control over our data. Corporations, which create the programs, platforms, and technology we use daily also want to have a say over who has access to our data. In fact, corporations are vying for legitimacy and want us to view them positively. To do so, corporations must convince us that even though they collect, store, and sometimes share our data, they are the good guys in the battle for individual privacy. We can see these battles dramatically playing out with Microsoft and Twitter. The tug of war between legal institutions and corporations are quite complicated. This is particularly true, since corporations and legal institutions sometimes put financial resources into the same companies. Dataminr is a good example. Both the CIA and Twitter have a financial interest in Dataminr's future but disagree over how data from the Twitter firehose may be used. These issues are unlikely to be resolved quickly. As we see above, existing laws regarding what legal institutions can do, what corporations can do, and how privacy concerns fit into the relationship between the two are vague.

CHAPTER LINKS

Bicchierai-Franceschi, Lorenzo. 2013. "See How PRISM May Work—in This Infographic." *Mashable*. Last modified June 14, 2013. http://www.mashable.com.

Larson, Jeff, Surya Mattu, Lauren Kirchner, and Julia Angwin. 2016. "How We Analyzed the COMPAS Recidivism Algorithm." *ProPublica*. Last modified May 23, 2016. https://www.propublica.org.

"Egyptian Locations of Interest Report." 2006. *Associated Press*. Last modified July 7, 2006. http://www.ap.org.

"Cop Flips Black Student in Her Desk." 2015. YouTube. Last modified October 27, 2015. http://www.youtube.com.

"How It Works: Police Body Cameras." 2014. YouTube. Last modified August 27, 2014. http://www.youtube.com.

"Knife Attack against a Police Officer Caught on Body Camera." 2015. YouTube. Last modified April 24, 2015. http://www.youtube.com.

Smith, Brad. 2016. "Keeping Secrecy the Exception, Not the Rule: An Issue for Both Consumers and Businesses." Microsoft. Last modified April 14, 2016. http://www .blogs.microsoft.com.

Meisner, Jeffrey. 2013. "Protecting Customer Data from Government Snooping." Microsoft. Last modified December 4, 2013. http://www.blogs.microsoft.com.

Epstein, Zach. 2015. "Windows 10 is Spying on Almost Everything You Do—Here's How to Opt Out." BGR. Last modified July 31, 2015. http://www.bgr.com.

Turow, Joseph, Michael Hennessy, and Nora Draper. 2015. "The Tradeoff Fallacy: How Marketers Are Misrepresenting American Consumers and Opening Them Up to Exploitation." Annenberg School for Communication, June 2015. http://www.asc .upenn.edu.

Gross, Terry. 2017. "The Aisles Have Eyes Warns That Brick-And-Mortar Stores Are Watching You." *Fresh Air*. Last modified February 13, 2017. http://www.npr.org.

Fang, Lee. 2016. "The CIA Is Investing in Firms That Mine Your Tweets and Instagram Photos." *Intercept*. Last modified April 14, 2016. http://www.theintercept.com.

Barrett, Brian. 2016. "Twitter May Have Cut Spy Agencies Off from Its Flood of Data." *Wired*. Last modified May 9, 2016. http://www.wired.com.

Reitman, Rainey. 2017. "Who Has Your Back? Government Data Requests 2017." Electronic Frontier Foundation. Last modified July 10, 2017. http://www.eff.org.

CHAPTER REVIEW QUESTIONS

1. How have new media changed the ways in which legal institutions and actors conduct surveillance?
2. What does it mean when we say the law is living?
3. Is the super panopticon metaphor a good one or is it too simple? Why?
4. How do legal institutions maintain their authority? How is this similar to and different from corporations?

5. What is the USA PATRIOT Act and why is it so important to debates over surveillance?

LEARN MORE

Albright, Dann. 2015. "Avoiding Internet Surveillance: The Complete Guide." MakeUseOf. Last modified January 25, 2015. http://www.makeuseof.com.

Apuzzo, Matt, and Joseph Goldstein. 2014. "New York Drops Unit That Spied on Muslims." *New York Times*. Last modified April 15, 2014. http://www.nytimes.com.

Ball, James. 2013. "NSA's Prism Surveillance Program: How It Works and What It Can Do." *Guardian*. Last modified June 8, 2013. http://www.theguardian.com.

Belter, Cassandra. 2014. "Unconventional Arrests." Reporters Committee: For Freedom of the Press. http://www.rcfp.org.

Cole, David. 2015. "We've Used Racial and Ethnic Profiling for Centuries, and It Hasn't Worked Yet." *Nation*. Last modified November 25, 2015. http://www.thenation.com.

Conger, Kate, and Ingrid Lunden. 2016. "Dataminr Was in an Unpaid Pilot with Intel Agencies when Twitter Ended the Deal." *TechCrunch*. Last modified May 9, 2016. http://www.techcrunch.com.

Creating Law Enforcement Accountability & Responsibility (CLEAR). 2013. "Mapping Muslims: NYPD Spying and Its Impact on American Muslims." City University of New York School of Law. Last modified March 11, 2013. http://www.law.cuny.edu.

Friedersdorf, Conor. 2013. "The Horrifying Effects of NYPD Ethnic Profiling on Innocent Muslim Americans." *Atlantic*. Last modified March 28, 2013. http://www.theatlantic.com.

Greenwald, Glenn. 2013. "XKeyscore: NSA Tool Collects 'Nearly Everything a User Does on the Internet.'" *Guardian*. Last modified July 31, 2013. http://www.theguardian.com.

Grossman, Lev. 2016. "Inside Apple CEO Tim Cook's Fight with the FBI." *Time*. Last modified March 17, 2016. http://www.time.com.

Hatmaker, Taylor. 2017. "Congress Just Voted to Let Internet Providers Sell Your Browsing History." *TechCrunch*. Last modified March 28, 2017. http://www.techcrunch.com.

"Highlights of AP's Pulitzer Prize-Winning Probe into NYPD Intelligence Operation." *Associated Press*. Retrieved July 2017. http://www.ap.org.

"Human Rights after September 11." 2002. International Council on Human Rights Policy. http://www.ichrp.org.

Jouvenal, Justin. 2016. "The New Way Police Are Surveilling You: Calculating Your Threat 'Score.'" *Washington Post*. Last modified January 10, 2016. http://www.washingtonpost.com.

Kalir, Erez, and Elliot E. Maxwell. 2002. "Rethinking Boundaries in Cyberspace: A Report of the Aspen Institute Internet Policy Project." Aspen Institute. http://www.assets.aspeninstitute.org.

Khazan, Olga. 2013. "Actually, Most Countries Are Increasingly Spying on Their Citizens, the UN Says." *Atlantic*. Last modified June 6, 2013. http://www .theatlantic.com.

Lee, David. 2016. "Microsoft Sues US Government over Secret Data Requests." *BBC News*. Last modified April 14, 2016. http://www.bbc.com.

Lee, Micah, Glenn Greenwald, and Morgan Marquis-Boire. 2015. "Behind the Curtain: A Look at the Inner Workings of NSA'S XKEYSCORE." *Intercept*. Last modified July 2, 2015, http://www.theintercept.com.

Madrigal, Alexis C. 2012. "Reading the Privacy Policies You Encounter in a Year Would Take 7 Work Days." *Atlantic*. Last modified March 1, 2012. http://www.theatlantic.com.

Marquis-Boire, Morgan, Glenn Greenwald, and Micah Lee. 2015. "XKEYSCORE: NSA's Google for the World's Private Communications." *Intercept*. Last modified July 1, 2015. http://www.theintercept.com.

"Mayor Bloomberg Defends NYPD Anti-terror Surveillance." 2011. *CBS New York*. Last modified September 8, 2011. http://www.newyork.cbslocal.com.

"Report: Rights and Wrongs at the RNC (2005)." 2005. New York Civil Liberties Union. http://www.nyclu.org.

Rogers, Josh. 2004. "Photographers Describe Picture of Rough Treatment." *Villager*. Last modified September 8–14, 2004. http://www.thevillager.com.

Sauro, Jeff. 2011. "Do Users Read License Agreements?" MeasuringU. Last modified January 11, 2011. http://www.measuringu.com.

Schneier, Bruce. 2013. "The Battle for Power on the Internet." *Atlantic*. Last modified October 24, 2013. http://www.theatlantic.com.

"Top Ten Abuses of Power since 9/11." n.d. American Civil Liberties Union. Retrieved July 2017. http://www.aclu.org.

"Tor." n.d. TorProject. Retrieved July 2017. http://www.torproject.org/.

"Violation Tracker." n.d. Good Jobs First. Retrieved July 2017. http://www.goodjobsfirst .org.

Waddell, Kaveh. 2016. "How Big Data Harms Poor Communities." *Atlantic*. Last modified April 8, 2016. http://www.theatlantic.com.

Weiser, Benjamin. 2014. "New York City to Pay $18 Million over Convention Arrests." *New York Times*. Last modified January 15, 2014. http://www.nytimes.com.

VIDEOS AND MOVIES

"Bratton: NYPD Muslim Monitoring Program Never Accomplished Anything." 2015. *CBS New York*. Last modified November 19, 2015. http://www.newyork.cbslocal .com.

Brown, Heather. 2015. "Good Question: What Are Our Social Media Privacy Rights?" *CBS Minnesota*. Last modified September 29, 2015. http://www.minnesota.cbslocal.com.

"Clock Runs Down for Patriot Act Surveillance Programs." 2015. *CBS News*. Last modified May 31, 2015. http://www.cbsnews.com.

"Guantanamo on the Hudson: Detained RNC Protesters Describe Prison Conditions." 2004. Democracy Now! Last modified September 2, 2004. http://www.democracynow.org.

Husband, Andrew. 2015. "Funny or Die Sketch Offers 'Perfect Phone for Filming Police Brutality.'" *Mediaite*. Last modified October 1, 2015. http://www.mediaite.com.

Johnson, Kevin. 2013. "NSA Director: Surveillance Foiled 50 Terror Plots." *USA Today*. Last modified June 18, 2013. http://www.usatoday.com.

Klausner, Alexandra, Ollie Gillman, and J. Taylor. 2015. "'I Want Surveillance of Certain Mosques, OK?': Fans Cheer in Alabama as Trump Continues His Support for a Muslim Database Despite Thousands Protesting Worldwide." *Daily Mail*. Last modified November 21, 2015. http://www.dailymail.co.uk.

Lyon, David. 2013. "Social Media Surveillance: Who is Doing It?" *TEDxQueensU*. Last modified April 27, 2013. http://www.youtube.com/watch?v=_hX1r2Tbv5g.

Macaskill, Ewen, and Gabriel Dance. 2013. "NSA Files: Decoded: What the Revelations Mean for You." *Guardian*. Last modified November 1, 2013. http://www.theguardian.com.

Mayer, Andre, and Michael Pereira. 2014. "Digital Surveillance: How You're Being Tracked Every Day." *CBC News*. Last modified March 7, 2014. http://www.cbc.ca.

"Obama: Surveillance of Muslims 'Makes No Sense.'" 2016. *USA Today*. Last modified March 23, 2016. http://www.usatoday.com.

Oliver, John. 2015. "Government Surveillance: Last Week Tonight with John Oliver (HBO)." *Last Week Tonight*. Last modified April 5, 2015. http://www.youtube.com.

"Paul, Rubio Spar over Surveillance, Data Collection." 2015. *CNN*. Last modified December 16, 2015. http://www.cnn.com.

Poitras, Laura, and Glenn Greenwald. 2013. "NSA Whistleblower Edward Snowden: 'I Don't Want to Live in a Society That Does These Sort of Things.'" *Guardian*. Last modified June 9, 2013. http://www.theguardian.com.

Roberts, Dan. 2013. "FBI Admits to Using Surveillance Drones over US Soil." *Guardian*. Last modified June 19, 2013. http://www.theguardian.com.

Scriberia, Scott Cawley, Jemima Kiss, Paul Boyd, and James Ball. 2013. "The NSA and Surveillance . . . Made Simple—Video Animation." *Guardian*. Last modified November 26, 2013. http://www.theguardian.com.

CHAPTER REFERENCES

Baruh, Lemi, and Mihaela Popescu. 2017. "Big Data Analytics and the Limits of Privacy Self-Management." *New Media & Society* 19 (4): 579–96.

Bauman, Zygmunt, Didier Bigo, Paulo Esteves, Elspeth Guild, Vivienne Jabri, David Lyon, and R. B. J. Walker. 2014. "After Snowden: Rethinking the Impact of Surveillance." *International Political Sociology* 8 (2): 121–44.

Bulger, Monica, Patrick Burton, Brian O'Neill, and Elisabeth Staksrud. 2017. "Where Policy and Practice Collide: Comparing United States, South African and European

Union Approaches to Protecting Children Online." *New Media & Society* 19 (5): 750–64.

Choudhury, Tufyal, and Helen Fenwick. 2011. "The Impact of Counter-Terrorism Measures on Muslim Communities." *International Review of Law, Computers & Technology* 25 (3): 151–81.

Cunningham, David. 2004. *There's Something Happening Here: The New Left, the Klan, and FBI Counterintelligence*. Los Angeles: University of California Press.

Earl, Jennifer. 2009. "Information Access and Protest Policing Post-9/11: Studying the Policing of the 2004 Republican National Convention." *American Behavioral Scientist* 53 (1): 44–60.

Fuchs, Christian, Kees Boersma, Anders Albrechtslund, and Marisol Sandoval. 2013. *Internet and Surveillance: The Challenges of Web 2.0 and Social Media*. New York: Routledge.

Gangadharan, Seeta Peña. 2017. "The Downside of Digital Inclusion: Expectations and Experiences of Privacy and Surveillance among Marginal Internet Users." *New Media & Society* 19 (4): 597–615.

Koskela, Hille, and Liisa A. Mäkinen. 2016. "Ludic Encounters—Understanding Surveillance through Game Metaphors." *Information, Communication & Society* 19 (11): 1523–38.

Lupton, Deborah, and Ben Williamson. 2017. "The Datafied Child: The Dataveillance of Children and Implications for Their Rights." *New Media & Society* 19 (5): 1–15. https://doi.org/10.1177/1461444816686328.

Lyon, David. 2015. *Surveillance after Snowden*. Malden, MA: Polity Press.

MacKinnon, Rebecca. 2013. *Consent of the Networked: The Worldwide Struggle for Internet Freedom*. New York: Basic Books.

Marwick, Alice, and Danah Boyd. 2014. "Networked Privacy: How Teenagers Negotiate Context in Social Media." *New Media & Society* 16 (7): 1051–67.

Schildkraut, Deborah. 2002. "The More Things Change . . . American Identity and Mass and Elite Responses to 9/11." *Political Psychology* 23 (3): 511–55.

———. 2009. "The Dynamics of Public Opinion on Ethnic Profiling after 9/11: Results from a Survey Experiment." *American Behavioral Scientist* 53 (1): 61–79.

Spalek, Basia, and Bob Lambert. 2007. "Muslim Communities under Surveillance." *Criminal Justice Matters* 68 (1): 12–13.

Staples, William. 2013. *Everyday Surveillance: Vigilance and Visibility in Postmodern Life*. 2nd ed. Lanham, MD: Rowman & Littlefield.

Tsay-Vogel, Mina, James Shanahan, and Nancy Signorielli. 2016. "Social Media Cultivating Perceptions of Privacy: A 5-Year Analysis of Privacy Attitudes and Self-Disclosure Behaviors among Facebook Users." *New Media & Society* 20 (1): 141–61. https://doi.org/10.1177/1461444816660731.

Wood, David, ed. 2003. "Foucault and Panopticism Revisited." *Surveillance & Society* 1 (3): 234–430.

5

The Changing World of Work

KEY CONCEPTS

Alienation refers to the idea that individuals can feel estranged
from their work because they have no control over it. Karl
Marx argued that work, and our ability to control it, is central
to our sense of self. He argued that capitalism exploited workers and led to alienation.

Autonomy is the opposite of alienation. Karl Marx argued that the
only way individuals could be truly autonomous was to have
control over what they made, how they made it, and how they
sold it.

Taylorism describes a theory of management developed by Frederick Winslow Taylor in the 1880s and 1890s. Taylor analyzed
how workers did their jobs in order to make them more efficient and productive. Unlike Marx, Taylor was not concerned
with workers' experiences.

McDonaldization refers to sociologist George Ritzer's theory
about how Taylorism looks in modern society. His theory
stresses how modern-day employers increasingly rely on
technology to make workers more efficient and productive
and consumer experiences predictable.

You probably have spent a lot of time thinking about the kind of
job you want after college. In fact, you may have spent a fair amount
of time online trying to figure out what life looks like once you flip the
tassel on your mortarboard and enter the workforce. You probably have
spent far less time thinking about the role media plays in your hunt for
a job. Just thirty years ago, job seekers were reliant on newspapers and
career centers to learn about new jobs. Job seekers would buy the newspaper, go to the classified section, see if they were qualified for any of the

positions listed, and then mail a prospective employee their cover letter. Finding and applying for jobs is much easier in the digital age. There are dozens of websites that can assist with your job search. CareerBuilder, Job.com, and Monster all list thousands of jobs that you can easily search to find a potential job. CareerBuilder, for instance, allows you to create a profile, resume, cover letter, and apply for jobs through its website. If you don't want to do all this work, you can simply search for jobs by job title, skills, or company or search for jobs in a specific city or state. If you enter New York City, NY, for instance, a list of more than 2,500 jobs appears.

According to a November 2015 Pew Research Center survey, new media play a critical role in both finding and applying for jobs. As you can see in the chart below (figure 5.1), 79 percent of those surveyed said that they used the internet when looking for a new job. If you compare this to the other categories, you will see that more job seekers relied on the internet than they did their close personal connections (66 percent), professional contacts (63 percent), employment agencies (32 percent), print advertisements (32 percent), or job fairs and other events (28 percent). In fact, 34 percent of respondents said that the internet was the most important resource in their job search. The same survey also found that job seekers increasingly use smartphones to find and apply for jobs. Job seekers between eighteen and twenty-nine years old are the most likely to use their smartphones to browse job listings, send a potential employer an email, fill out an online application, and create a resume.

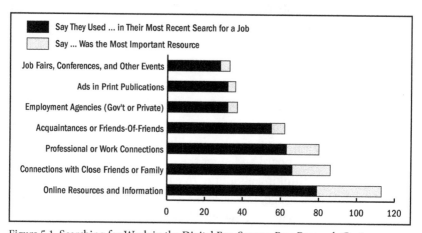

Figure 5.1. Searching for Work in the Digital Era. Source: Pew Research Center.

New media have changed a lot more than the job search. They also change the hiring process. Before the advent of the internet, employers knew very little about applicants beyond what they included in their resume. Sure, many employers conducted background checks on potential employees to verify information provided in a resume, but most of the records employers had access to are already public. For example, background checks typically include your driving record, credit record, criminal record, education record, military record, and drug test record. While these records can provide employers some useful information about potential employees, such as whether they are good drivers or have been convicted of a crime, they don't give employers a sense of the kind of person potential employees are. Employers increasingly check out potential employees on social media sites. According to a CareerBuilder news release about a survey conducted with 2,138 hiring managers and human resource professionals in 2014, 43 percent of employers research job candidates on social media and 45 percent use search engines such as Google to learn more about potential employees. As you can see below in table 5.1, employers passed on candidates for a number of reasons including the following: the job candidate posted inappropriate photos (46 percent);

TABLE 5.1. CareerBuilder Survey with Hiring Managers and Human Resource Professionals

Reasons for Eliminating a Job Candidate	Reasons for Hiring a Job Candidate
Job Candidate	Employer
Posted inappropriate photographs (46%)	Got a good feel for the candidate's personality, could see a good fit with the company (46%)
Posted information about drinking or drugs (41%)	Candidate's background information supported their professional qualifications for the job (45%)
Negative comments about their previous company or fellow employee (36%)	Candidate's site was professional (43%)
Had poor communication skills (32%)	Candidate was well-rounded / showed a wide range of interests (40%)
Made discriminatory comments (28%)	Candidate had great communication skills (40%)
Lied about his qualifications (25%)	Candidate was creative (36%)
Shared confidential information from previous employers (24%)	Candidate received awards and accolades (31%)
Was linked to criminal behavior (22%)	Other people posted great references about the job candidate (30%)
Had an unprofessional screen name (21%)	Candidate interacted with company's social media accounts (24%)
Lied about an absence (13%)	Candidate had a large number of followers/subscribers (14%)

shared information about drinking and drug use (41 percent); bad-mouthed a previous employer or fellow employee (36 percent); made discriminatory comments related to race, gender, religion, or sexuality (28 percent); and had an unprofessional screen name (21 percent). Of course, employers also opted to offer job seekers a position based on their internet presence. Employers offered candidates' jobs when they got a good feel for a candidate's personality and thought he or she would be a good fit with the company (46 percent), the candidate's site conveyed a professional image (43 percent), the job candidate seemed well rounded (40 percent), the candidate had awards and accolades (31 percent), and the candidate had interacted with the company's social media accounts (24 percent).

Not surprisingly, not all job seekers are happy with potential employers investigating them online. They consider it an invasion of their privacy. In fact, many workers and job seekers try to protect their privacy by only sharing posts with friends and family (47 percent of those surveyed by CareerBuilder), keeping their profile private (41 percent of those surveyed), and maintaining separate professional and personal profiles (18 percent of those surveyed). State legislatures are weighing in on whether employers can access prospective and current employee social media pages. Since 2012, twenty-five states, which are listed below in table 5.2, have passed laws preventing employers from "media snooping," or requiring potential or current employees to provide passwords to their personal internet accounts to get or keep a job.

Finally, new media have dramatically changed our experiences at work. This may not have occurred to you, but new media such as email

TABLE 5.2. List of States That Don't Allow Media Snooping

Arkansas	Michigan	Rhode Island
California	Montana	Tennessee
Colorado	Nebraska	Utah
Connecticut	Nevada	Vermont
Delaware	New Hampshire	Virginia
Illinois	New Jersey	Washington
Louisiana	New Mexico	West Virginia
Maine	Oklahoma	Wisconsin
Maryland	Oregon	

have changed what the traditional workday looks like. Think about it. Before email and telecommuting, employees either stayed late at the office or went home when the day ended. Either way, once they left the office, work basically was done for the day. This is far less true today. A 2008 Pew Internet & American Life Project report found that 50 percent of employees who use email as part of their job check their work email on the weekends—and 34 percent check their email while on vacation. In fact, some companies require employees to check and respond to email outside of their shifts. T-Mobile, for example, requires employees to check and respond to work-related emails while off the clock. Employees, who have to deal with customers early in the morning or late at night, sometimes argue that they should be paid overtime for this work. Companies that make use of this practice disagree. They see these after-hour calls as part of their employees' jobs. These disagreements can lead to lawsuits. In July 2009, several ex-employees of T-Mobile sued the corporation for overtime. They claimed that T-Mobile forced them to reply to work-related emails after hours on company-provided phones. T-Mobile ex-employees were not the only ones to sue. Since the height of the great recession in 2008, American workers increasingly have sued employers under federal and state wage-and-hour laws. In fact, between 2008 and 2011 employee lawsuits increased to 32 percent—a 378 percent increase from 2000. Clearly, new media have disrupted the American notion of the eight-hour workday and we are seeing how disputes over workplace practices are playing out.

This chapter examines how new media change the way we feel about the work we do as well as our experiences in the workplace. We begin by discussing two concepts critical to understanding work as a social institution: alienation and autonomy. We experience alienation when we have no control over our work or how it is done. In contrast, we experience autonomy when we have control over our work and how it is sold in the marketplace. Then we discuss alienation and autonomy in our digital economy. We will see that individuals' feelings about the effects of new media on their work vary dramatically. Individuals' feelings of alienation and autonomy vary not only by the kind of work they do but also according to their employment status. We conclude the chapter with a discussion of how new media affect the workplace itself. Digital technology give corporations and managers a great deal of control over how employees do their work. This helps companies increase their profits and makes it easy for them to train new employees and replace those who quit.

ALIENATION VS. AUTONOMY

Much of the sociological thinking about *alienation*, which generally refers to when we feel isolated or estranged from our work, and *autonomy*, which refers to when we have control over our workplaces and the products we make, go back to the well-known social scientist, Karl Marx. His theories regarding capitalism are complicated and changed over the course of his life. Here, we just want a sense of what alienation and autonomy mean for workers in capitalist economies, or economies where a country's trade and industry are controlled by private owners rather than the government. In capitalist economies, individuals are relatively free to use and sell their labor and property without government interference. As you may know, Marx was very interested in how the conflicting interests of the ruling classes (those with money and power, such as corporate owners) and the oppressed classes (those with limited money and power, such as workers) shaped the economy and society. While Marx is popularly known for advocating that workers rise up, overthrow capitalism, and replace it with communism, or an economy where the government controls most of the trade and industry and distributes money and resources, his understanding of why socialism was better for workers is very interesting. In a nutshell, he believed that changing the economy would free us, or make us more autonomous.

Here's Marx's general argument about alienation and autonomy: Marx, who started writing all about the capitalism in the 1840s, observed that the world was organized into two groups or social classes: workers who worked in factories, in offices, and on farms (which he called the proletariat) and the owners who owned the factories, buildings, and land that the workers used (which he called the bourgeoisie). Marx considered the bourgeoisie the ruling class because they owned all the tools workers needed to do their jobs (which Marx labeled the means of production). Because the bourgeoisie owned the means of production, they did not have to work themselves. They lived off of the work of their employees. If they wanted to increase their profits, the bourgeoisie would simply exploit the proletariat by using their knowledge and their labor to make their businesses more profitable. You probably guessed by now that Marx was a conflict theorist. He understood capitalism as a battle over resources and outlined how the bourgeoisie maintained its power over the proletariat.

What does this have to do with alienation? A lot. Marx believed that when the proletariat lost control of their work, they lost control of their lives. The result was alienation or the estrangement from work and self. Let's break this down with an example from my life. One of the part-time jobs I had in college was at a fast food place, which I will not name. I hated this job for a lot of reasons. First, I had no control over when I worked. One day, I would be scheduled for three hours during the peak lunch period, and the next day, I would have to work a nine-hour shift that had me closing the restaurant at 2 a.m. Second, I had no control over what I did when I was at work. Some days, I worked the drive thru, and other days, I scrubbed food-encrusted pots and pans for hours on end. Third, the fast food restaurant had crazy procedures that felt like they were designed to make me feel bad about myself. For example, the restaurant policy stated I had to enter a customer's coupon before I could enter their order. If the coupon wasn't entered first, then a manager would have to cancel the order and I (the employee) would be written up for violating company policy. After three violations, the offending employee (in this case, me) would be fired. As you can imagine, even if I asked first, customers sometimes forgot they had a coupon. After I was written up the first time for this violation (the customer produced a coupon after he had paid), I understood that employees weren't just avoiding the company's stupid catchphrase we were forced to say when greeting customers. Employees avoided drive-thru and walk-up costumers because they knew it was only a matter of time before they got fired for unintentionally violating the coupon rule three times.

Finally, I had no way to enforce my rights to things like a break or payment for working overtime. When this particular fast food restaurant was busy, the manager refused to let me take a bathroom break or grab something to eat. If I insisted that I really needed a break, the manager threatened to fire me. When the restaurant was slow, the manager would force me to clock out and sit in the break room. She wouldn't let me go home because she was worried business might pick up and she would need me to work. She made it very clear that if I wanted to keep my job, I couldn't leave. You can imagine my frustration. Sometimes I would have to sit there for two or three hours at a time. Since we were not allowed to bring personal items to work, I couldn't even study or do homework during this time. I literally had to sit there and wait for the manager to either summon me back to work or send me home. In short, I did not have control over what I made (cheap, unhealthy food), the conditions where I worked (I couldn't choose my hours or breaks), or how I sold the food (there were rules about what I said and how I entered their orders). In Marx's words, I was experiencing alienation.

Since Marx believed that work was central to our human nature, he argued that we create ourselves through our labor. Capitalism reduces work to wages rather than as a way to express creativity and build our intellects. Consequently, alienation in the workplace also affects how we feel about ourselves. The opposite of alienation is autonomy. Marx argued that the only way individuals could be autonomous was to have control over what they made, how they made it, and how they sold it. If you think about my experience in the food industry, I would have been autonomous if I had been able to choose what food I made, how I made it, when I made it, and who I sold it too.

Before we start talking about alienation in the digital economy, it is important to note that sociologists do not think, like Marx, that there are only two classes. In fact, sociologists often identify five social classes where people have similar levels of wealth, power, and prestige in society:

1. Upper class and elites, which consist of occupations that have very high salaries and a lot of power such as CEOs and CFOs and other top positions. These are the individuals that own the means of production.
2. Upper middle class, which consist of occupations that have high salaries and prestige such as computer engineers, academics, accountants, lawyers, and directors of organizations.

3. Lower middle class, which consists of occupations that are designed to support the upper middle class such as clerical and administrative positions, data entry and record keeping jobs, and paralegal positions. These jobs have moderate salaries and prestige.

4. Working class, which consists of occupations that require a high school diploma and are often "hands on," such as factory and restaurant workers, laborers, bank tellers, customer service representatives, and telemarketers. These jobs have moderate salaries and low prestige.

5. Poor, which consist of occupations that require limited education and are minimum wage, such as fast food workers and big-box-store clerks. Individuals with such jobs may work full time but still require social services (EBT and Medicaid) to make ends meet. These jobs have low pay and low prestige.

These distinctions matter because, as we already discussed, they reflect unequal access to resources, which affects things like the quality of education kids get and, later, the kinds of jobs they are competitive for.

These distinctions also are important for our understanding of alienation in the digital economy. New media can be empowering for some and increase the alienation of others. You can imagine, for example, that a telemarketer has a very different experience with alienation than an academic. Read the excerpt below titled "I Work as a Telemarketer and I Hate My Life," which was posted on the now defunct Experience Project website in June 2012. Notice that that poster notes how little control he has over his work. He cannot control who he calls, what he says, what his boss considers rude, how much time elapses between the calls, when he goes to the bathroom or has a break, or whether he is sent home for the day. Also notice that he talks about how work affects his personal life. Since he doesn't have sick days, when he or his child gets sick, he has to use a vacation day or make up the hours. This, as you can tell, is a source of great annoyance, since he is very eager to use his vacation days to get away from the telemarketing job he hates. The telemarketer, in short, is alienated from his work, and new media plays an important role in this alienation. How (and how quickly) he does his work is almost completely determined by a computer.

I Work as a Telemarketer and I Hate My Life

ANONYMOUS POST

JUNE 2012

I hate my job. I hate it with everything in me. I work at a telemarketing place that does fundraising calls for charitable organizations. I hate it with everything in me. I cannot say that enough. It barely pays the bills and it feels more like prison or some sweat shop in some 3rd world country. Let me tell you of my typical day at this job. I get there at 8am then calls begin. We have NO control over who we are calling or what part of the country we are calling. We read from a script. We have to do a 2nd request no matter what the person says to us. If the person says they have been without a job for such and such period of time we still go for that 2nd request. If they tell us, "wife is dying" we still go for that 2nd request. It does not matter if they say "NO" we still go for that 2nd request as if NO was never said. At times we even ask for money. If the caller is disabled and old as can be we still do our 2nd request and a money ask. If we do not we are either: written up or sent home without pay or both. So we have no choice. Plus if we are cussed out or insulted we have to be nice and kind and not say anything the boss says is rude. Rude can be anything from, changing your tone of voice or even talking nicer. Seriously they consider that rude. So we have to put with being insulted and cussed out and top it off we have very little time between calls. Remember, we are not the ones dialing. The computer dials for us. We have no control over how fast the calls are coming or who we call. So when one call ends another one comes in within 1 second or 2. You have no time to get a drink of water or anything. Forbid if you have a runny nose or must cough. That is why some of us who work for this company calls it a prison or some sweat shop. We must have permission to go to the bath room. They time us when we go so we don't stay gone for long. Long being a few minutes. They expect us to go down the hall and use the bath room and wash our hands and come back in the maximum of 4 or 5 minutes tops. After that you risk getting in trouble or being put off on an unpaid break of 30 minutes. They also listen to your calls and will harass you if you are kind and give sick people a break or very old people a break. Forbid you get some compassion for someone whose crying due to a loved one is dying of cancer and cannot help you at this time.

Also forbid if you get sick. The company I work for does not give sick pay ONLY vacation pay. And forbid if you or a child of yours gets sick and need to take time off. You must work your hours or risk being fired. The company I work for does not accept doctor's excuses. So you risk your job if you get sick or if you need to stay home to take care of a sick child. Yes you can use your vacation pay but then you will not get off for an actual vacation or even a holiday if you want to. Yes we must use vacation pay for everything that or make the time back up. Which means being at that prison (sweat shop) for a longer period of time.

There is a high turnover with this particular company due to how difficult and crappy a place it is. They change rules like some people go through toilet paper. One week it's this rule and then another week it's another rule. You have to get used to your supervisors lying and telling you "it's always been a rule we are just now applying it."

I must mention how if your performance is down and you do not get enough volunteers you will be sent home without pay. Also if they run out of work you will be sent home without pay. I hate this job. I hate the supervisors. I hate the boredom. I hate the calling and harassing others. I hate how I am basically tied to that computer reading from a script. Don't ever work for any telemarketing call center. Keep looking for another job. They will lie to you and tell you it's a great job. It's not. It's called prison and a sweat shop by those working and doing the actual work for a reason. I cannot wait till I find another job.

Here is a list of some of the technology that is required to make a telemarketing business work:

- data network/internet
- automatic call distributor system
- interactive voice response system
- predictive dialer
- web applications (such as email, online chat, and online collaboration)
- customer relationship management tools, such as a billing system, scripting, and customer analytics
- computer—telephony integration software and hardware
- agent performance dashboard

- workforce management software
- call-recording equipment
- voice over internet protocol (VoIP) communications technology

It is easy to see why telemarketers have very little control over their work lives. Their entire experience is mediated and evaluated by computer software and equipment. Telemarketing is not less alienating when you work from home. Telemarketers who work from home still report their hours and work experiences are completely out of their hands.

Compare this experience with new media in the digital economy to that of an academic whose job it is to teach graduate and undergraduate students as well as to conduct research. New media can give academics more control over their work lives and time. I will use my work experience as an example again. New media makes teaching courses easier and more fun. I can put content on my course website, share interesting information and links I find online quickly via email, hold virtual office hours, and discuss course content with students one-on-one through Twitter and Facebook. New media also makes my research easier and more exciting. For example, I study, among other things, how citizens use media in their political participation. Because new media makes it easier for individuals to tell politicians what they think about an issue (see chapter 6), I can collect the emails sent to political leaders and analyze how citizens argue for (or against) important political issues. Getting real insight into how individuals make their political arguments was impossible before the advent of the internet and email because scholars had to rely on what individuals told them—and we know that sometimes what people say they did and what they actually did do not line up. New media (and laws that make politicians' emails available to the public) gives me access to new kinds of data, which generate new understanding about how the political world works. For me, this is liberating and exciting. Unlike the telemarketer, new media increases my ability to do the work I want, how I want.

FLEXICURITY: WHAT DOES THIS MEAN FOR ALIENATION AND AUTONOMY?

<u>Flexicurity</u>, which is short for flexible security, refers to a social model from the Nordic countries. The term, which was first coined by the Prime Minister of Denmark Poul Nyrup Rasmussen in the 1990s, refers to a model of governing that tries to protect the health and well-being of its citizens by balancing employers' need for a flexible workforce with workers' need for job security. In other words, employers want workers who can perform a variety of different jobs for a company and who they can allocate as needed to different positions, and employees want to know that they won't be unemployed for long periods of time. Flexicurity, in short, is intended to help companies maximize their profits while giving employees job security. In the United States, companies often make the workforce flexible by employing freelancers, independent professionals, temporary contract workers, and independent contractors or consultants on an as-needed basis. These <u>contingent workers</u> are great for employers because they can hire these temporary workers when the demand for their product is high, when they are starting a new project, or when they need more employees to help, and fire these workers when the demand for their product returns to normal or the project is complete. For example, there are a lot of contingent workers hired around Christmas and Hanukkah to handle the influx of shoppers at retail stores and the increase in mail. In 2016, Federal Express hired an additional fifty thousand workers to deliver mail and presents during the holiday season. The United States Postal Service also increases its workforce at the holidays, hiring additional workers to sort packages that come into the processing and distribution centers and bulk mail centers during the month of December.

Since the Department of Labor's Bureau of Labor Statistics has not collected data on the contingent workforce since 2005, it is not clear how large the contingent labor force is in the United States. In 2015, the Bureau of Labor Statistics used national survey data and estimated that approximately 7.9 percent of the employed labor force was made up of contingent workers. This figure, however, does not include agency temp workers or day laborers. When these workers are included in the definition of contingent workers, the figure jumps to 40.5 percent—a huge increase. The Bureau of Labor Statistics also found that contingent workers experience job instability at higher rates than permanent workers, have lower pay than permanent workers, and get few (if any) benefits. On its website, the Department of Labor notes that many companies are turning to a contingent workforce not just for flexibility and efficiency but also as a way to increase their profit margins. Employers do not have to make contributions to Social Security, unemployment insurance, workers' compensation, and health insurance for contingent workers. This not only saves the company money on employee benefits but also saves them money in administrative expenses and potential costs related to employee injuries and lawsuits. Contingent workers have far less protection under labor and employment laws because they are, by definition, temporary or part-time workers.

Why are there so many contingent workers? This is, in part, a response to the Great Recession of 2008. The Great Recession, which officially lasted from December 2007 to June 2009, began with the bursting of an eight-trillion-dollar housing bubble. Basically, housing prices increased dramatically throughout the 1990s and early 2000s in response to an increase in demand for homes and an increase in speculation in the real estate market. As you may know from shows like A&E's *Flip This House* and HGTV's *Flip or Flop*, many Americans tried to make money off of buying and flipping homes. Since interest rates were low, some Americans bought multiple properties and others, who previously could not qualify for a loan for one reason or another (such as a bad credit rating or unemployment), suddenly found themselves qualifying for loans for hundreds of thousands of dollars. However, housing prices peaked in 2006 and began to decline. All of a sudden, many Americans found themselves with negative equity—meaning their mortgage debts were higher than the value of their homes. People who had speculated on real estate let the banks foreclose on their properties and others cut back their spending on other things in an effort to hold onto their homes.

As you can imagine, this had a rippling effect. The sharp cutbacks in consumer spending affected business investment and caused massive job loss. In 2008 and 2009, the US labor market lost 8.4 million jobs, which was the most dramatic employment contraction of any recession since the Great Depression. By comparison, in the deep recession that began in 1981, job loss was 3.1 percent, or only about half as severe as the Great Recession. Just to give you a bit of context, in 2001, before the Great Recession, there was one person looking for work for every job opening. This increased dramatically during the Great Recession. In 2010, there were seven people looking for work for every one job opening. The employment situation has improved. In 2015, there were two people looking for work for every job opening.

Given this economic context, the idea of flexicurity is widely criticized. Like the Department of Labor noted, many companies and states use contingent workers so that they can increase their profit at the expense of worker security. This leads to alienation, rather than autonomy, for workers. Let's consider two examples. First, consider the temporary worker at the United States Post Office. It is not unusual for a call for temporary workers to post on the Federal Jobs blog. Here is an example of a job advertisement posted online in 2014:

It's beginning to look a lot like Christmas at the post office! It's that time of year again. Time to start thinking of hiring temporary employees to help with the Christmas rush. The United States Postal Service will hire temporary clerks and mail handlers for a 21-day period to get them through the holiday season. These positions pay on average eleven dollars per hour, no benefits; but can lead to a 360-day appointment. . . .

The job of a casual clerk and mail handler in the processing and distribution centers can be physically demanding. They will load and unload postal trucks and move mail around a mail-processing center with forklifts, small electric tractors and hand-pushed carts. These workers are usually on their feet, reaching for sacks and trays of mail or placing packages and bundles of mail into sacks and trays. The clerk and mail handler positions can be a very tedious, tiring and stressful job. The mail sacks can be very heavy, so you must be able to lift 70 pounds. You will have time restraints in getting the job done and you will be working in a fast pace environment.

Notice in the call that temporary workers can earn eleven dollars per hour but receive no benefits for a "physically demanding," "tedious," "tiring," and "stressful" job. If their supervisors like them, these "casual" workers can get a 360-day contract. They still will not have benefits and are unlikely to be offered a permanent position.

A big complaint of postal employees in these positions is that they are evaluated on the aspects of their jobs that they cannot control. For example, in order for the mail to go out on time, the sorting machines must be running on schedule. Once the mail is sorted, clerks organize them by route for delivery. When the sorting machines are behind so are the clerks. The problem, of course, is that postal workers can lose their jobs for being behind schedule. One "casual" employee who managed to land a longer-term contract blogged about his constant worry of getting fired for reasons he couldn't control on the website, Federal Soup. He wrote,

> This is no way to come to work, worried every day if this day is going to be your last! I mean jeez, today for example, today was the first day in WEEKS that every machine got its mail out on time. Usually at least 2 or 3 machines are late by 20, 30, sometimes even 45 minutes or more. It's not that we're inept or inefficient, it's just that that's the way it is when dealing with machines . . . [that are] prone to jams and breakdowns, multiplied by the number of machines we have running.

This description is not so different from that of the telemarketer's complaints discussed above. Like the telemarketer, the postal employee has very little control over his work.

Temporary workers for the postal service are not the only ones who experience alienation in the wake of the Great Recession. All kinds of employers, including colleges and universities, are increasingly reliant on contingent workers, which they typically call adjunct professors or teaching faculty. In fact, the percentage of temporary or part-time faculty increased from 30 percent in 1975 to 51 percent in 2011. Rita Kirshstein, who studies how colleges and universities spend money, compiled data on the percentage of part-time faculty at US educational institutions. Some of her data are featured in table 5.3. Notice that even private institutions rely heavily on contingent workers. At the University of California, Berkeley, a public school where an education will cost you around $12,864, only 29 percent of the faculty are part time.

TABLE 5.3. Table of the Tuition and Fees, Percentage of Part-Time Faculty, and Percentage of Graduate Students at Selected US Colleges

School	Tuition and Fees ($)	Percent Part-Time Faculty	Percent Part-Time Faculty and Graduate Assistants
PUBLIC			
University of Illinois, Urbana-Champaign	14,750	13	58
University of North Carolina, Chapel Hill	8,340	18	50
University of California, Berkeley	12,864	29	68
University of Delaware	12,112	4	34
Virginia Commonwealth University	12,002	32	46
PRIVATE			
Boston University	44,880	32	50
Northwestern University	45,527	13	32
Syracuse University	40,458	35	57
George Washington University	47,343	54	61
Emory University	44,008	25	30

Note: In-state tuition and fees are reported for public universities. Source: Rita Kirshstein.

Compare this to George Washington University. The tuition and fees ($47,343) as well as the percentage of part-time faculty (54 percent) are considerably higher. In other words, the chance that a part-time professor is teaching your class is just as likely at a private school as it is at a public one.

Like other contingent workers, adjunct professors are paid less (on average $2,700 for each class) and have no benefits. As a result, most adjuncts teach at two or more colleges and universities at the same time and only earn between twenty thousand dollars and twenty-five thousand dollars per year even though many have doctoral degrees. Not surprisingly, like the telemarketer and the postal worker, adjunct faculty describe their temporary positions as "alienating" and "exploitative." Adjuncts point out that they are only paid for their time in the classroom and earn nothing for preparing classes and meeting with students; a practice they refer to as wage theft. In a report conducted by the Service Employees International Union in the Boston area in 2013, one adjunct described herself as "Kleenex," since she was disposable. She noted,

> As an adjunct there is no job security. I am scheduled to teach a class at [a Boston university] in the fall. That class can be canceled up to the morning it is supposed to start—and that is it. No pay. So all of us are hustling for work. If I am offered another class and there is a conflict, I have to pick one or the other—but if the one I picked is canceled, then I lose my compensation because the other one will no longer be available. They treat us like we are Kleenex.

Her story is not unusual. There are similar accounts on Adjunctnation .com in which faculty talk about the difficulties of doing their work when their time is so taken up by trying to make a living. One author, Jodi Campbell, documents her struggle as an advanced graduate student to find stable work that pays enough for her to move out of her parents' house. Campbell notes that she will take any job, but no one wants to hire her either because she is overqualified for the position or because of her spotty work record. She notes,

> I live in a perpetual cycle of fear and self-criticism. I constantly doubt myself because I can't get a job, even as a receptionist at the local gym or a waitress at a pizza place. I worry that I am either not good enough a scholar or have made all the wrong choices because, otherwise, I wouldn't be struggling to find a job, any job. I worry that I will never be able to finish writing my dissertation because all I can think about is how I can't pay my bills. I worry that once I do finish my dissertation, I will have spent five years of my life with nothing to show for it, other than a dissertation no one will read.

Of course, not everyone experiences alienation in the digital economy. According to Gallup polls, 37 percent of American workers reported that they had telecommuted, or used the internet, email, and mobile phones to work from home, an average of six days per month in 2015. As you can see in the chart below (figure 5.2), most telecommuters

	Yes (%)
College graduate	55
Noncollege graduate	26
Annual household income $75,000 or more	52
Annual household income less than $75,000	26
White-collar profession	44
Blue-collar profession	16

Aug. 5–9, 2015
Note: White-collar professions are those categorized as being executive/managerial, professional specialty, technical, sales, or administrative.

Figure 5.2. Ever Telecommuted—by Education, Income, and Job Type. Based on Employed Adults. Source: Gallup.

are college graduates (55 percent) in professional positions (44 percent) with annual incomes of seventy-five thousand dollars or more per year (52 percent). Importantly, Gallup found that professionals are increasingly telecommuting during the regular workday instead of going to the office (46 percent of telecommuters) or simply putting in additional hours after the regular workday ends. This is a change from 2006 in which most workers reported they telecommuted to in order to supplement their regular workday. Social scientists find that telecommuting increases employee job satisfaction, productivity, and commitment. More important for thinking about autonomy, telecommuting reduces employee stress and work-family conflicts because it gives workers more control over their jobs and their time.

Let's look at the example of Handy, a worldwide platform that connects individuals looking for household services such as cleaners and handymen with prescreened independent contractors through a smartphone app. If there is a job around the house that you don't want to do, Handy can help you find a nearby professional to get the job done. Handy guarantees its customers that workers are competent and honest and guarantees workers a steady flow of work and prompt payment. More important for our discussion about autonomy, the majority of employees like working for the company. Glassdoor, which has a database of more than eight million company reviews, CEO approval ratings, salary reports, and benefits reviews, reports that individuals generally are happy working for Handy. In fact, independent contractors rate Handy 3.5 or more stars (out of five stars) on their work/life balance, compensation and benefits, and career opportunities. The majority also would recommend that a friend work for Handy and agree that the company has a positive business outlook. Glassdoor, which also provides an overall trend in employee satisfaction, reports that individuals were the unhappiest working at Handy in 2015. This decline in worker happiness trends with the company's growth. Handy, which was founded in 2012, experienced tremendous growth in 2014 and had difficulty scaling up its business effectively. This led to lots of hiring and firing, not to mention dissatisfaction with Handy as a company to work for. This trend reversed in 2016. Once again, independent contractors appear mostly happy with the work they get through Handy.

In the comment section on Glassdoor, independent contractors frequently note that they like working for Handy because they can make their own schedules, which allows them to spend more time with their friends and family. A cleaner in New York gave Handy five stars and reported, "Probably the best thing about working at Handy is that I am able to make my own schedule, which enables me to better balance my work and free time, and spend more time with my family and friends. The salary is quite satisfactory and the work is not really that hard. I got to meet a lot of interesting people and make some significant acquaintances. Also, the management here is great, we are like one big family!" Another poster from Los Angeles, California, agreed, noting that she likes that she doesn't have to sit down at a "boring old job all day" and is her "own boss." She added, "There are a couple of things that I really like about working for this company. Most of the customers have been awesome to deal with, and I am my own boss, which means I make my own schedule. The management has been good, and I am the only person held responsible for the work done. I have been pretty happy since starting with them about 1 yr. ago now." These posts, in other words, show workers expressing more autonomy than the telemarketer, postal worker, and adjunct faculty above.

Freelance writers report similar levels of autonomy. Miranda Miller blogged about her job and how she feels about being a freelance business and marketing writer in June 2014. She admits that it is a lot of work essentially running her own business but appreciates the flexibility it gives her so that she can try to be "super mom." Her schedule is flexible enough that she can take her sons to school in the morning, pick them up in the afternoon, and spend time with them in the afternoon doing homework and activities. Miller specifically credits new media for her ability to be a successful freelancer. She uses new media, and social media in particular, to make business connections and find new clients to write for. She notes that this is easier in the digital age because "social media have massively leveled the playing field, removing geographical and other barriers." New media enable Miller to do the work she wants, when she wants it. Freelancers point out that there are other benefits as well. They have more opportunities to take on new or challenging jobs at their convenience and, as contingent workers, they can demand higher pay for their work, since their employer is not paying them benefits such as health care or giving them office space. In fact, according to *Time* magazine, as of 2015, contingent workers earn 17 percent more per hour than full-time workers. Some freelancers argue that the biggest hurdle is knowing that they can ask for more.

In sum, it is difficult to determine whether new media make work more alienating or more autonomous. New media, we see, have diversified the experiences of workers. Some contingent workers, for example, are very alienated by the integration of new media into the workplace. Telemarketers report that every aspect of their workday is controlled by computer software and managers monitoring everything from how many calls they place per hour to the number of minutes they spend on each call. Research professors such as myself have a different experience with new media. I find that it makes some aspects of my job easier. I can search books and access articles almost instantly, which helps me complete my own research and writing projects. We see, however, that the difference between the working experiences of the telemarketer and myself cannot be explained by education alone. There are growing numbers of adjunct professors who cannot get permanent work despite their advanced degrees. Additionally, we see that employment status, or whether a worker is a contingent or permanent employee, does not explain the differences in how individuals feel about their work. There are a lot of contingent workers who like the freedom they have as temporary employees because it gives them more say in whom they work for and how this work is done.

REPRODUCING INEQUALITY
The Case of Uber

If you haven't heard of Uber, it is a digital taxi service. Uber provides an app for smartphones that connects drivers, who are independent contractors, with riders. Basically, you use the app to request a ride with a registered driver. Once a driver accepts the request, the app gives you an estimated time of arrival and information about your driver as well as his or her vehicle. Your account is automatically billed when you arrive at your destination, and you are asked to rate your driver with one through five stars. Uber takes a roughly 25 percent commission from each fare.

Here are some basic demographics on Uber drivers from the magazine *Entrepreneur* (January 22, 2015). Notice that for many Uber drivers, this is a second job and that the drivers are largely men:

- Eighty-six percent of Uber drivers are men.
- Thirty-seven percent of drivers are white, 18 percent are African American, 16 percent Hispanic, and 15 percent are Asian or Pacific Islander.
- Fifty-six percent of drivers are between the ages of thirty and forty-nine.
- Forty-eight percent of drivers have a college or advanced degree.
- Fifty percent of drivers are married and 46 percent have children.
- Twenty-five percent of drivers are financially supporting parents or other relatives.
- More than 60 percent of drivers report that they have full- or part-time jobs that they work in addition to driving for Uber.

With more than 160,000 drivers, Uber attracts a lot of attention. Recently, a lot of that attention has been negative. For example, in June 2017, nearly two dozen employees were fired after Susan Fowler alleged that Uber's human resource team ignored her reports of sexual harassment during the year she worked for the company. Fowler's allegations, which are outlined in a blog post on her "strange year at Uber," triggered an internal investigation and the mass firings. In her post, Fowler discusses several incidents at Uber. The first involved a male manager who basically asked Fowler to have sex with him. The second incident involved a male manager who altered her performance evaluation so that Fowler could not transfer to another team. One of the last incidents involved leather jackets. A male manager sent the six remaining female engineers an email stating that they would only purchase jackets for the 120 male employees because Uber could get a bulk discount on male jackets. Leather jackets would not be ordered for the women because there were not enough women in the organization to justify placing an order. When Fowler questioned this logic, her manager replied, "If we women really wanted equality, then we should realize we were getting equality by not getting the leather jackets. He said that because there were so many men in the org, they had gotten a significant discount on the men's jackets but not on the women's jackets, and it wouldn't be equal or fair, he argued, to give the women leather jackets that cost a little more than the men's jackets." Fowler accepted another position and left Uber a week later. More recently, a group of lawmakers demanded that Uber explain how the company dealt with allegations of sexual violence against its drivers. Between 2014 and 2018, 103 Uber drivers have been accused of and sued over sexual assault and abuse.

Uber has also been accused of psychologically manipulating its drivers in an effort to get them to work longer hours. It turns out that Uber employs hundreds of social scientists and data scientists in order to find ways to make drivers work longer and harder. It specifically models its approach off of video games. Of course, instead of gaming longer, drivers will drive longer. Uber is particularly interested in creating an internalized motivation system so that drivers will keep picking up fares long after they want to. How does Uber do it? Consider the following:

- Uber exploits drivers' tendency to set specific earning goals and desire to reach a goal that is just out of reach. It alerts drivers that they are close to their target when they try to log off. For example, a driver will get a message on the app that notes he is $10 away from netting $330 and asks him if he is sure if he wants to go offline. This is often accompanied by a graphic of an engine gauge with a needle that is close to, but short of, a dollar sign.
- Uber uses algorithms (similar to Netflix), which loads the next fare opportunity before the current fare has left the car. This is designed to keep more drivers on the road and defuse fare surges.
- Uber drivers can earn badges for achievements such as providing excellent service and being entertaining. This is can be a point of pride among drivers. One Florida driver noted that he earned

twelve excellent service badges and nine great conversation badges. He also earned less than twenty thousand dollars before expenses (e.g., gas and car maintenance).

- Uber texts, emails, and uses pop-ups in an effort to get drivers on the road and to the locations they want them. Some local managers, who were male, even adopted a female persona when dealing with drivers because they found that this induced more drivers to take to the road; remember, most of the drivers are male.
- Uber ranks drivers according to the number of trips they've taken in the current week, how much money they've made, their overall passenger rating, and how many hours they've been logged on. These metrics are designed to induce competition among drivers.

In short, while Uber promises drivers autonomy, it uses new technology and psychological techniques to shape drivers' behaviors in ways that serve the company's, rather than drivers', interests.

EFFICIENCY AND PRODUCTIVITY

In order to understand the workplace adequately, we also have to think about how the workplace is structured and affects the ways in which work is done. As seen above, my experience as a faculty member at a research institution is very different than that of a telemarketer or even an adjunct faculty member. As long as I find ways to be an effective researcher, teacher, and community member, I can structure my time how I see fit. This is not true of a telemarketer who has to clock in and is expected to make call after call throughout her shift. The telemarketer's experience at work is designed to maximize her efficiency as an employee. Much of the telemarketer's experience is shaped by *Taylorism*, a theory of management that analyzes how people work in an effort to make workers more efficient and productive when doing their jobs. Taylorism is named after Frederick Winslow Taylor who, in the 1880s and 1890s, observed manual laborers as they worked doing things such as shoveling ore out of railroad cars, lifting and moving ore at the steel mill, and inspecting the products made, such as ball bearings.

Taylor drew several conclusions from his analyses of workers. First, he concluded that every job could be broken down into isolated, simple tasks that a single worker could perform. For example, instead of making a complete horse-drawn wagon one at a time, building the wagon would be broken down into parts. One worker would make benches for wagons, another would attach the benches to the wagon, and a third would put the wheels on one wagon. The worker performs one task all day, which makes him more efficient and productive. Second, and related, breaking down a job into individual tasks would standardize the product. In this case, the horse-drawn wagons would look very similar because they had been put together the same way. Finally, Taylor concluded that most workers were motivated by money and, since they were paid by the hour, generally slow to complete their jobs. His solution for this was to link worker pay to worker output in order to encourage them to work harder and faster.

Read the excerpt below from Taylor's 1911 book *The Principles of Scientific Management*. Here, he describes his success at Bethlehem Steel Company, with workers who were charged with carrying pieces of iron (called pig iron) from one place to another. Taylor chose a man he calls Schmidt to show how money can be used to make men work harder and faster. Notice in the excerpt below that Taylor assumes that Schmidt's desire to build a home can be used as leverage to get him to carry more pig iron. Also notice that Taylor is pretty demeaning throughout their conversation. He assumes that Schmidt is stupid (he calls him "mentally sluggish") and that Schmidt needs to learn that his job is to follow orders, or carry pig iron when he is told to and rest when he is told to. The result, Taylor notes, was positive. Schmidt increased the amount of pig iron carried per day and his wages. This, of course, only considers efficiency and productivity—worker satisfaction is not considered at all.

Excerpt from Chapter 2, The Principles of Scientific Management

WRITTEN BY FREDERICK WINSLOW TAYLOR (1911)
HARPER & BROTHERS PUBLISHERS

He was a little Pennsylvania Dutchman who had been observed to trot back home for a mile or so after his work in the evening about as fresh as he was when he came trotting down to work in the morning. We found that upon wages of $1.15 a day he had succeeded in buying a small plot of ground, and that he was engaged in putting up the walls of a little house for himself in the morning before starting to work and at night after leaving. He also had the reputation of being exceedingly "close," that is, of placing a very high value on a dollar. As one man whom we talked to about him said, "A penny looks about the size of a cartwheel to him." This man we will call Schmidt.

The task before us, then, narrowed itself down to getting Schmidt to handle 47 tons of pig iron per day and making him glad to do it. This was done as follows. Schmidt was called out from among the gang of pig-iron handlers and talked to somewhat in this way:

"Schmidt, are you a high-priced man?"

"Vell, I don't know vat you mean."

"Oh yes, you do. What I want to know is whether you are a high-priced man or not."

"Vell, I don't know vat you mean."

"Oh, come now, you answer my questions. What I want to find out is whether you are a high-priced man or one of these cheap fellows here. What I want to find out is whether you want to earn $1.85 a day or whether you are satisfied with $1.15, just the same as all those cheap fellows are getting."

"Did I vant $1.85 a day? Vas dot a high-priced man? Vell, yes, I vas a high-priced man."

"Oh, you're aggravating me. Of course you want $1.85 a day—everyone wants it! You know perfectly well that that has very little to do with your being a high-priced man. For goodness' sake answer my questions, and don't waste any more of my time. Now come over here. You see that pile of pig iron?"

"Yes."

"You see that car?"

"Yes."

"Well, if you are a high-priced man, you will load that pig iron on that car tomorrow for $1.85. Now do wake up and answer my question. Tell me whether you are a high-priced man or not."

"Vell—did I got $1.85 for loading dot pig iron on dot car to-morrow?"

"Yes, of course you do, and you get $1.85 for loading a pile like that every day right through the year. That is what a high-priced man does, and you know it just as well as I do."

"Vell, dot's all right. I could load dot pig iron on the car to-morrow for $1.85, and I get it every day, don't I?"

"Certainly you do—certainly you do."

"Vell, den, I vas a high-priced man."

"Now, hold on, hold on. You know just as well as I do that a high-priced man has to do exactly as he's told from morning till night. You have seen this man here before, haven't you?"

"No, I never saw him."

"Well, if you are a high-priced man, you will do exactly as this man tells you to-morrow, from morning till night. When he tells you to pick up a pig and walk, you pick it up and you walk, and when he tells you to sit down and rest, you sit down. You do that right straight through the day. And what's more, no back talk. Now a high-priced man does just what he's told to do, and no back talk. Do you understand that? When this man tells you to walk, you walk; when he tells you to sit down, you sit down, and you don't talk back at him. Now you come on to work here to-morrow morning and I'll know before night whether you are really a high-priced man or not."

This seems to be rather rough talk. And indeed it would be if applied to an educated mechanic, or even an intelligent laborer. With a man of the mentally sluggish type of Schmidt it is appropriate and not unkind, since it is effective in fixing his attention on the high wages which he wants and away from what, if it were called to his attention, he probably would consider impossibly hard work. . . .

Schmidt started to work, and all day long, and at regular intervals, was told by the man who stood over him with a watch, "Now pick up a pig and walk. Now sit down and rest. Now walk—now rest," etc. He worked when he was told to work, and rested when he was told to rest, and at half-past five in the afternoon had his 47½ tons loaded on the car. And he practically never failed to work at this pace and do the task that was set him during the three years that the writer was at Bethlehem. And throughout this time he averaged a little more than $1.85 per day, whereas before he had never received over $1.15 per day, which was the ruling rate of wages at that time in Bethlehem. That is, he received 60 percent higher wages than were paid to other men who were not working on task work.

Some sociologists argue that Taylor's ideas have been implemented to an extreme. Basically, tasks have been broken down into the smallest possible level so that companies can find the most efficient way to complete a job. All employees are taught each of the tasks, which are to be completed the same way and in the same order every time the job is performed. Sociologist George Ritzer calls this modern-day Taylorism, *McDonaldization*. Ritzer references the famous fast food chain for several reasons. First, McDonald's is a useful example for understanding how simple jobs are broken down to the smallest, most efficient steps. At McDonald's, employees are instructed to get several beef patties, put them on the grill, and push a button over the grill so that it gets cooked the proper amount. While the burgers are cooking, employees are instructed to get buns, toast them (also done with timers), and start putting the ingredients (sauce, onion, lettuce, pickles, and cheese) on the buns. Once the timer sounds, the employee gets the patties and puts them on the prepared buns.

Second, Ritzer uses McDonald's as a reference point because the fast food giant's procedures clearly illustrate how all aspects of a process can be easily controlled by employers so that the outcome is calculable and predictable. Calculability refers to the ability of the employer and the consumer to quantify the product. McDonald's knows how many Big Macs were made and, consequently, the amount of ingredients used on any given day and the cost associated with the ingredients, and customers know just how big the Big Mac (not to mention the large fries and supersized soda) will be. In this way, McDonald's is predictable. We know what to expect when we go to McDonald's, and the food will be pretty much the same no matter which McDonald's we visit. Third, Ritzer points out how McDonaldization deskills the workforce so that workers can be quickly and cheaply trained and easily replaced if they quit or are fired. If you have ever worked in a fast food restaurant like I have, training literally consists of a few videos. Generally, the videos cover safety guidelines and teach you the steps of your first job at the restaurant, which often is on the fryer, making French fries.

Finally, McDonaldization draws attention to the ways in which customers get tricked into performing jobs that used to be done by the company. At McDonald's and most fast food restaurants, we are expected to clean up our tables and put our trash in the bin marked "Thank You."

Bussing tables used to be the job of the restaurant. Now it is done by us. Of course, McDonaldization is not specific to McDonald's. We get tricked into doing work the company used to do every time we go to an all-you-can-eat buffet where we serve ourselves, use an automated telephone menu to make an appointment or reservation, or get money out of an ATM. More important, the McDonaldization of work is visible in all kinds of jobs that involve new media. Factories that produce cell phones, customer service centers, and even primary schools all adopt procedures designed to make products, service customers, and teach students in efficient, calculable, and predictable ways. Remember the telemarketer? He described in great detail how his work experience was controlled and evaluated via computer programs.

In sum, while the debate over alienation and autonomy focus on workers' experiences and their satisfaction with their jobs, discussions of efficiency and productivity focus on how the workplace can be controlled to ensure that employees are working quickly, customers getting a product that meets their expectations, and making sure the company

---

CASE STUDY

Marina Shifrin's YouTube Resignation

In September 2013, Marina Shifrin went to work at 4:30 am and made a resignation video. The video, which features Kanye West's "Gone," uses pointed remarks and interpretive dance to tell her supervisors at Next Media Animation that she too is gone.

The video, which shows Shifrin dancing everywhere from a deserted office to a bathroom, notes that "for almost two years I've sacrificed my relationships, time and energy for this job. And my boss only cares about quantity and how many views each video gets. So I figured I'd make ONE video of my own." As she dances, "I Quit" appears across the bottom of the screen.

Watch the video in its entirety (there is a link to the YouTube video at the end of the chapter) and discuss how Shifrin's workplace is an example of McDonaldization. Specifically, think about how Shifrin's work is evaluated and the extent to which these evaluation criteria are calculable and predictable.

---

makes a profit. We can see that new media play an important role in efficiency and productivity. Specifically, new media make it easier for employers to control how workers' do their jobs—everything from when they flip burgers to how many calls they make to customers per hour.

CONCLUSION

In this chapter, we explored the effects of new media on work. We began with a discussion of Karl Marx and an explanation of two concepts that help us understand our relationship to work: alienation and autonomy. We learned that we experience alienation when we feel estranged from our work. We experience autonomy when we feel connected to our work. Specifically, we have control over what we do and how we do it. We explored alienation and autonomy in the digital era and found that new media have mixed effects on our experience with work. Some individuals find that new media contributes to their alienation because it allows companies and managers to control every aspect of their work. Other individuals find that new media gives them autonomy, allowing them to structure when and how they work better. We learned that neither education nor employment status (whether they are contingent workers) can completely explain the different experiences of workers.

Then we discussed efficiency and productivity in the digital age. We learned that new media give companies a great deal of control over their employees and that this control is intended to make the companies more profitable. This theory of management called Taylorism, which has been around for more than one hundred years, cares very little about workers' experiences. The emphasis is only on making workers more efficient and productive in their positions. Employers increasingly rely on new media to make workers more efficient and productive as well as to make consumer experiences predictable. Sociologist George Ritzer refers to this as McDonaldization. He argues that companies model themselves after the fast food giant in an effort to control how employees work and how customers experience their products. McDonaldization shifts some of the work onto customers and increases the profits of the company as well as their control over their workers.

CHAPTER LINKS

"Number of Employers Passing on Applicants Due to Social Media Posts Continues to Rise, According to New CareerBuilder Survey." 2014. CareerBuilder. Last modified June 26, 2014. http://www.careerbuilder.com.

"State Social Media Privacy Laws." 2017. National Conference of State Legislatures. Last modified May 5, 2017. http://www.ncsl.org.

"I Hate Myself and I Want to Die." 2012. Experience Project. Last modified June 27, 2012. http://www.experienceproject.com.

"Chart Book: The Legacy of the Great Recession." 2017. Center on Budget and Policy Priorities. Last modified November 7, 2017. http://www.cbpp.org.

Adjunct Action. 2013. "The High Cost of Adjunct Living: Boston." Service Employees International Union. Last modified November 2013. http://www.campaign-media .seiumedia.net.

"Handy's Rating Trends." 2017. Glassdoor. Last modified October 31, 2017. http://www .glassdoor.com.

Clifford, Catherine. 2015. "Who Exactly Are Uber's Drivers?" *Entrepreneur*. Last modified January 22, 2015. http://www.entrepreneur.com.

Fowler, Susan. 2017. "Reflecting on One Very Strange Year at Uber." Susan Fowler. Last modified February 2, 2017. http://www.susanjfowler.com.

Scheiber, Noam. 2017. "How Uber Uses Psychological Tricks to Push Its Drivers' Buttons." *New York Times*. Last modified April 2, 2017. http://www.nytimes.com.

Moon, Mariella. 2018. "US Lawmakers Demand Answers from Uber about Sexual Assaults." Engadget. Last modified May 22, 2018, https://www.engadget.com.

Shifrin, Marina. 2013. "Quit Your Job by Dancing to Kanye, like Marina Shifrin." YouTube. Last modified October 1, 2013. http://www.youtube.com.

CHAPTER REVIEW QUESTIONS

1. How have new media, such as email, changed the way we work as Americans?
2. How, in Karl Marx's view, did the battle over resources play out in capitalism?
3. What is the difference between alienation and autonomy?
4. How does the digital economy shape our work experiences with alienation and autonomy? Are workers' experiences the same? Why or why not?
5. How are Taylorism and McDonaldization similar and different from one another?

LEARN MORE

Alton, Larry. 2016. "Can't Wait to Freelance in the Gig Economy? Read This First." *Huffington Post*. Last modified June 9, 2016. http://www.huffingtonpost.com.

Cole, Nicki Lisa. 2017. "What Is Social Class, and Why Does It Matter?" ThoughtCo. Last modified March 2, 2017. http://www.thoughtco.com.

"Contingent Workforce: Size, Characteristics, Earnings, and Benefits." 2015. US Government Accountability Office. Last modified April 20, 2015. http://www.gao.gov.

"Digital Taylorism." 2015. *Economist*. Last modified September 10, 2015. http://www.economist.com.

Ehrenreich, Barbara. 2001. "Excerpt of Nickel and Dimed: On (Not) Getting by in America." *New York Times*. http://www.nytimes.com.

Friedman, Thomas L. 2013. "How to Monetize Your Closet." *New York Times*. Last modified December 21, 2013. http://www.nytimes.com.

Fruscione, Joseph. 2014. "When a College Contracts 'Adjunctivitis,' It's the Students Who Lose." *PBS*. Last modified July 25, 2014. http://www.pbs.org.

"The Future of Work: There's an App for That." 2014. *Economist*. Last modified December 30, 2014. http://www.economist.com.

Griswold, Alison. 2015. "Dirty Work." *Slate*. Last modified July 24, 2015. http://www.slate.com.

Kessler, Sarah. 2014. "Pixel & Dimed On (Not) Getting by in the Gig Economy." *Fast Company*. Last modified March 18, 2014. http://www.fastcompany.com.

Kirshstein, Rita. 2015. "Percentage of Part-Time Faculty at U.S. Universities." Google Sheets. Last modified October 5, 2015. http://docs.google.com.

McGee, Suzanne. 2016. "How the Gig Economy Is Helping Make the Case for Universal Basic Income." *Guardian*. Last modified June 9, 2016. http://www.theguardian.com.

NPR Money. 2014. "Episode 509: Will A Computer Decide Whether You Get Your Next Job?" *NPR*. Last modified January 15, 2014. http://www.npr.org.

O'Leary, Michael Boyer. 2013. "Telecommuting Can Boost Productivity and Job Performance." *U.S. News and World Report*. Last modified March 15, 2013. http://www.usnews.com.

Weissmann, Jordan. 2013. "The Ever-Shrinking Role of Tenured College Professors (in 1 Chart)." *Atlantic*. Last modified April 10, 2013. http://www.theatlantic.com.

White, Gillian B. 2015. "Working from Home: Awesome or Awful?" *Atlantic*. Last modified October 22, 2015. http://www.theatlantic.com.

Williams, Joseph. 2014. "My Life as a Retail Worker: Nasty, Brutish, and Poor." *Atlantic*. Last modified March 11, 2014. http://www.theatlantic.com.

Wladawsky-Berger, Irving. 2015. "Flexible Security: A Sensible Social Policy for Our Digital Age." *Wall Street Journal*. Last modified July 10, 2015. http://blogs.wsj.com.

VIDEOS AND MOVIES

BBC Radio 4. 2015. "Karl Marx on Alienation." YouTube. Last modified January 4, 2015. http://www.youtube.com.

Botsman, Rachel. 2012. "The Currency of the New Economy Is Trust." *TED*. Last modified June 2012. http://www.ted.com.

Business Insider. 2012. "Nine Ways Your Employer May Be Legally Spying on You." *Financial Post*. Last modified December 15, 2012. http://www.business.financialpost.com.

FOX 47 News. 2012. "Employers Turning to Social Media in Hiring Process." YouTube. Last modified March 22, 2012. http://www.youtube.com.

Helmrich, Brittney. 2015. "Seven Ways Your Work Technology Is Betraying Your Privacy." *News*. Last modified April 24, 2015. http://www.news.com.au.

Jacobs, Deborah L. 2013. "The Six Best Ways to Find Your Next Job." *Forbes*. Last modified March 22, 2013. http://www.forbes.com.

Judge, Mike. 1999. *Office Space*. Twentieth Century Fox Film Corporation. DVD.

Kashdan, Jason. 2015. "New Ways Your Boss Could Be Keeping Tabs on You." *CBS*. Last modified August 21, 2015. http://www.cbsnews.com.

Kirby, John. 2005. *The American Ruling Class*. Alive Mind. DVD.

"McDonaldization." 2015. *Sociology Live!* Last modified September 28, 2015. http://www.youtube.com.

"Taylorism on ABC World Report." 2011. YouTube. Last modified October 28, 2011. http://www.youtube.com.

WISN 12 News. 2014. "Using Improper Social Media Etiquette Can Affect Your Jobs." YouTube. Last modified March 18, 2014. http://www.youtube.com.

CHAPTER REFERENCES

Bucher, Eliane, and Christian Fieseler. 2016. "The Flow of Digital Labor." *New Media & Society* 19 (11): 1868–86. https://doi.org/10.1177/1461444816644566.

Comor, Edward. 2010. "Digital Prosumption and Alienation." *Ephemera: Theory & Politics in Organization* 10 (3/4): 439–54.

Fish, Adam, and Ramesh Srinivasan. 2012. "Digital Labor Is the New Killer App." *New Media & Society* 14 (1): 137–52.

Fuchs, Christian, and Sebastian Sevignani. 2013. "What Is Digital Labour? What Is Digital Work? What's Their Difference? And Why Do These Questions Matter for Understanding Social Media?" *TripleC: Communication, Capitalism & Critique. Open Access Journal for a Global Sustainable Information Society* 11 (2): 237–93.

Gajendran, Ravi, David Harrison, and Kelly Delaney-Klinger. 2015. "Are Telecommuters Remotely Good Citizens? Unpacking Telecommuting's Effects on Performance via I-Deals and Job Resources." *Personnel Psychology* 68 (2): 353–93.

Golden, Timothy, and John Veiga. 2008. "The Impact of Superior–Subordinate Relationships on the Commitment, Job Satisfaction, and Performance of Virtual Workers." *Leadership Quarterly* 19 (1): 77–88.

Grint, Keith, and Darren Nixon. 2015. *The Sociology of Work*. 4th ed. Cambridge, UK: Polity Press.

Grint, Keith, and Steve Woolgar, eds. 1997. *The Machine at Work: Technology, Work and Organization*. Cambridge, UK: Polity Press.

Huws, Ursula. 2015. "iCapitalism and the Cybertariat: Contradictions of the Digital Economy." *Monthly Review* 66 (8): 42–57.

Jacobs, Jerry A., and Kathleen Gerson. 2004. *The Time Divide: Work, Family, and Gender Inequality*. Cambridge, MA: Harvard University Press.

Keune, Maarten, and Amparo Serrano, eds. 2014. *Deconstructing Flexicurity and Developing Alternative Approaches: Toward New Concepts and Approaches for Employment and Social Policy*. New York: Routledge.

Marx, Karl. 1978. *The Marx-Engels Reader*. Edited by Robert Tucker. New York: W. W. Norton.

Ritzer, George. 2014. *The McDonaldization of Society*. 8th ed. Thousand Oaks, CA: Sage.

Scholz, Trebor, ed. 2012. *Digital Labor: The Internet as Playground and Factory*. New York: Routledge.

Taylor, Frederick Winslow. 1911. *The Principles of Scientific Management*. New York: Harper & Brothers.

Thompson, Terrie Lynn. 2016. "The Making of Mobilities in Online Work-Learning Practices." *New Media & Society* 20 (3): 1031–46. https://doi.org/10.1177/1461444816678946.

Tomaskovic-Devey, Donald, and Barbara J. Risman. 1993. "Telecommuting Innovation and Organization: A Contingency Theory of Labor Process Change." *Social Science Quarterly* 74 (2): 367–85.

Wellman, Barry, Janet Salaff, Dimitrina Dimitrova, Laura Garton, Melina Gulia, and Caroline Haythornthwaite. 1996. "Computer Networks as Social Networks: Collaborative Work, Telework, and Virtual Community." *Annual Review of Sociology* 22:213–38.

6

Is This What Democracy Looks Like?

Try to imagine America in 1963; a country where segregation was common and African Americans were prevented from voting, particularly in
the South. For years, activists had pushed for equal rights under the law
for black Americans. Yet what made 1963 significant was the civil rights
movement's use of mass media (television, newspapers, and magazines)

to make the horrors of racial discrimination visible to the general public. The Southern Christian Leadership Conference's (SCLC's) Children's March in Birmingham, Alabama, is a well-known example. Birmingham was one of America's most racially divided cities. Civil rights activists, including Fred Shuttlesworth, had boycotted Birmingham businesses unsuccessfully and asked the SCLC for assistance. The SCLC, led by Dr. Martin Luther King Jr., organized a series of sit-ins and marches designed to provoke mass arrests and fill the Birmingham jails. When the movement ran low on adult volunteers, the SCLC asked students to get involved in the demonstrations. The commissioner of public safety, Eugene "Bull" Connor, was determined to keep segregation in place and civil rights activists in check. When the students marched down the streets of Birmingham, Connor responded with violence. He ordered his men to spray the children with high-pressure water hoses and released attack dogs on the demonstrators. The hose pressure was

Figure 6.1. Student Protestors, Birmingham, Alabama. Photo by Charles Moore. Originally Published in *Life Magazine*.

set high enough to peel bark off a tree. It knocked the children to the ground and tore the clothes from their bodies.

The violence against young, unarmed demonstrators was documented by Charles Moore, a photographer for *Life* magazine. Moore knew that pictures like the one above would obliterate assumptions about "good Southerners" and change America. He was right. *Life* magazine published Moore's photographs and public support for civil rights swelled in the United States. In fact, figure 6.2 shows that when Gallup asked "what do you think is the most important problem facing the country today?" 52 percent of the people surveyed thought race relations and racism were the most important problems in 1963. If you compare this percentage over time (1948–2014), in which there are many years where the people surveyed did not think race relations and racism were problems at all, you can see just how important images of violence against African Americans really were.

The outrage over what was happening in the South sent a clear signal to the White House. The citizenry expected President John F. Kennedy, a Democrat, to act. This is not something Kennedy was eager to do. Most Southern Democrats supported segregation, and Kennedy worried that a showdown over civil rights would tear the Democratic Party apart. Mass media—in this case, radio, television, and newspapers—brought what was happening in the American South into living rooms around the world. The Democratic Party had no choice but to take a stronger

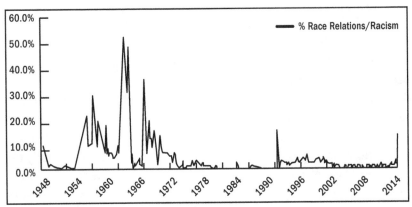

Figure 6.2. Trends for "Race Relations/Racism" as Most Important Problem in the United States. Source: Gallup.

position on civil rights. The following month, Kennedy addressed the nation and announced that major civil rights legislation would be introduced to Congress in order to ensure equal access to public facilities, end segregation in education, and combat discriminatory hiring practices.

Fast forward to the summer of 2015. On the campaign trail, presidential hopefuls are confronted by Black Lives Matter activists, who want to know how the Democratic Party is going to deal with racial profiling, police brutality, and racism in the criminal justice system. Black Lives Matter began as a hashtag on social media in the summer of 2013 and was a direct response to the acquittal of George Zimmerman, who shot and killed Trayvon Martin, an unarmed teenager, in Sanford, Florida. Three community organizers—Alicia Garza, Patrisse Cullors-Brignac, and Opal Tometi—transformed the hashtag and public outrage over Martin's death into an online movement. Within the year, Black Lives Matter used social media to organize massive protests in Ferguson, Missouri, and New York City after police officers killed two unarmed men, Michael Brown and Eric Garner, and a twelve-year-old boy, Tamir Rice. By summer 2015, Black Lives Matter activists began to challenge Democratic presidential candidates Hillary Clinton and Bernie Sanders to address racism in America. The organizers credit social media for their success. Patrisse Cullors-Brignac explained, "Because of social media we reach people in the smallest corners of America. We are plucking at a cord that has not been plucked forever."

Hillary Clinton initially avoided talking to Black Lives Matter activists publicly. In August 2015, activists were denied entry into a campaign event in New Hampshire. Instead, she met with the activists backstage and a heated discussion on race in America ensued. Activists wanted Clinton to accept responsibility for her past policy positions on stronger prison sentences, and Clinton asked the activists for a list of policy solutions. The conversation was documented, uploaded to YouTube by *Good* magazine, viewed hundreds of thousands of times online, and covered by the national news. Bernie Sanders found himself in a similar situation in Seattle, Washington. Black Lives Matter activists took over a rally on Social Security in an effort to question Sanders on how he would address racial inequality in America. Sanders refused to engage the protestors and, instead, stood offstage with his aides and wife. After a moment of silence for Michael Brown, the rally was ended. The video went viral and the event received global media coverage. Conversations about racism and Black Lives Matter erupted online and offline, and some citizens tweeted the candidates directly about their positions on the issue.

As the movement picked up steam throughout the summer, Americans increasingly identified race relations and racism as an important problem in the country. You can see the increase in concern over racism in America in figure 6.3. Again, respondents were asked, "What do you think is the most important problem facing the country today?" Notice that only 1 to 3 percent of the respondents think racism is an important issue between June 2014 and November 2014. This percentage increases dramatically in December after Black Lives Matter activists protested the killing of twelve-year-old Tamir Rice, who was playing with an airsoft pistol that was missing the orange safety feature, in a Cleveland, Ohio, park. Video showed the police officer, Timothy Loehmann, firing two shots, one of which hit Rice in the torso, before the squad car had come to a stop. Black Lives Matter activists used social media and protest to let the public know that this was the fourth death of a black man at the hands of police officers in less than six months.

Again, because of mass media and growing public discontent, politicians responded to the civil rights crisis. By fall 2015, both Clinton and Sanders had addressed some of the movement's claims on their campaign websites. "Criminal justice reform" appeared as an issue on Clinton's website with the promise to "come to terms with some hard truths about race and justice in America." On her website, Clinton promised to

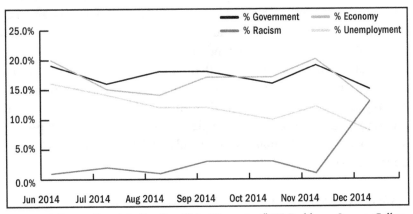

Figure 6.3. Recent Trends in Top Four "Most Important" US Problems. Source: Gallup

- end the era of mass incarceration, reform mandatory minimum sentences, and end private prisons;
- encourage the use of smart strategies—like police body cameras—and end racial profiling to rebuild trust between law enforcement and communities; and
- help formerly incarcerated individuals successfully reenter society.

The site also notes that "although the United States has less than 5 percent of the world's population, we have almost 25 percent of the total prison population. A significant percentage of the more than 2 million American incarcerated today are nonviolent offenders. African American men are far more likely to be stopped and searched by police, charged with crimes, and sentenced to longer prison terms than white men found guilty of the same offenses."

The webpage even included a quote from Clinton with the famous "black lives matter" phrase and a call for action. Her July 20, 2015, quote reads, "Black lives matter. Everyone in this country should stand firmly behind that. . . . Since this campaign started I've been talking about the work we must do to address the systemic inequalities that persist in education, in economic opportunity, in our justice system. But we have to do more than talk—we have to take action." To be clear, her webpage was not short on substance. Clinton outlined a detailed six-point plan to strengthen trust between police and community members, reduce mandatory minimum sentences on nonviolent drug offenders, focus federal enforcement resources on violent crime rather than marijuana possession, make rehabilitation a priority for nonviolent drug offenders, end the privatization of prisons, and promote the economic and social success of formerly incarcerated individuals.

Sanders also took up the call on his website. In fact, Sanders listed "racial justice" as one of his campaign issues; outlined five types of violence—physical, political, legal, economic, and environmental—waged against people of color in America; and promised a societal transformation that would make clear that black lives matter. He bluntly noted,

We must pursue policies to transform this country into a nation that affirms the value of its people of color. That starts with address the five central types of violence waged against black, brown and indigenous Americans: physical, political, legal, economic and environmental. We are far from eradicating racism in this country. Today in America, if you are black, you can be killed for getting a pack of Skittles during a basketball game. Or murdered in your church while you were praying. This violence fills us with outrage, disgust and a deep, deep sadness. These hateful acts of violence amount to acts of terror. They are perpetuated by extremists who want to intimidate and terrorized black, brown and indigenous people in this country.

Sanders addressed physical violence head on, noting,

It is an outrage that in these early years of the 21st century we are seeing intolerable actions of violence being perpetuated by police and racist acts of terrorism by white supremacists. A growing number of communities do not trust the police. Law enforcement officers have become disconnected from the communities they are sworn to protect. Violence and brutality of any kind, particularly at the hands of the policy meant to protect and serve our communities, is unacceptable and must not be tolerated. We need a societal transformation to make it clear that black lives matter and racism will not be accepted in a civilized country.

Some of Sanders's solutions for dealing with physical violence perpetrated by the state and extremists included demilitarizing America's police forces, investing in community policing, making sure the police force reflects the diversity of the community, and cracking down on the illegal activities of hate groups.

Both examples—the Children's March in Birmingham and the disruption of campaign events by Black Lives Matter activists—illustrate the importance of mass media to *social inclusion*, or the ability of individuals and groups to fully participate in society and control their life chances. A key reason citizens get politically involved is so that they have a voice in *political institutions*, or the organizations that create laws, mediate conflict, and represent the citizenry. Individuals hope that by making their voices heard, elected officials will act in ways that improve their social inclusion in political institutions. In 1963, SCLC successfully pushed Kennedy into announcing legislation that would protect the civil rights of African Americans and, in 2015, Black Lives Matter pressured Democratic presidential candidates to offer plans to address racism in the criminal justice system.

Of course, elected officials generally have very limited interactions with the citizens they represent once they take office. As the examples above illustrate, mass media are a key way for politicians to get a sense of what issues their constituents care about as well as their thoughts on these issues. The process through which an issue is identified as a problem that should be solved by government involvement is called *agenda setting*, and this process has changed with our technology. In 1963, the ways in which citizens advocated for social inclusion were pretty direct. Let's use figure 6.4 and the example of the 1963 Children's March described above to follow how the agenda-setting process worked. The SCLC (which was composed of citizens) engaged in actions, including the Children's March in Birmingham, Alabama, to attract the attention of traditional media such as newspapers, magazines, radio reports, and television news. This attention alerted the broader public to the civil rights problems in the South, polls such as those conducted by Gallup measured whether Americans regarded race relations and racism as a serious political problem, and elected officials such as President Kennedy acted on the information. Kennedy used traditional media outlets to announce that major civil rights legislation was forthcoming. As you can see in figure 6.4, this was a fairly straightforward process. Citizens organized in ways that attracted the attention of traditional news outlets. Companies like Gallup polled citizens to get the pulse of the people

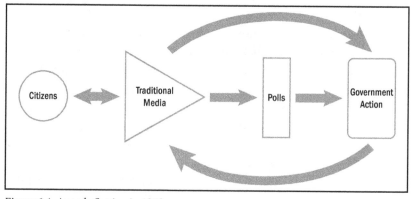

Figure 6.4. Agenda Setting in 1963.

on an issue and politicians paid attention to the media coverage and the polling numbers before deciding whether to act. If they decided to act, politicians outlined their plans in traditional media.

Agenda setting is more complicated in the digital age because there are more mediums available to carry citizens' concerns and more opportunities for politicians to hear (and respond to) their constituents' complaints. Citizens do not have to do something that attracts the attention of traditional news media. They can organize campaigns that get thousands of concerned voters to email, tweet, and petition politicians directly. Likewise, politicians do not have to wait for a poll to get the pulse of the people on an issue. They can follow hashtags to see what citizens are saying, look for groups on Facebook that are talking about the issue, and use online surveys to quickly get a sense of what their constituents care most about.

Let's explore the contemporary agenda-setting process in more detail using figure 6.5 and the Black Lives Matter example. Notice that there are a lot more lines in this chart. This is because there are more ways for citizens to indirectly influence the agenda-setting process. In the case of Black Lives Matter, citizens used Twitter (social media) to bypass traditional media outlets and put their concerns regarding the criminal justice system on politician's radar. Citizens used Twitter to build support for their ideas and organize protests in Ferguson, Missouri, and

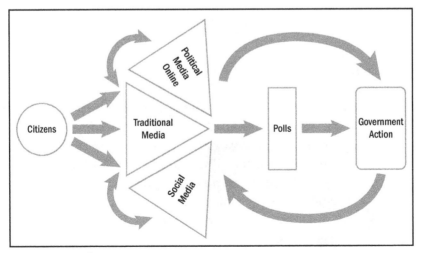

Figure 6.5. Agenda Setting in 2018.

New York City. The hashtag BlackLivesMatter trended and reached a broader public long before it received coverage from political media online, such as the *Huffington Post* and *Slate*, or coverage in traditional news media outlets, such as the nightly broadcast news. In fact, traditional media initially did a poor job covering the movement because journalists were not sure who was leading the movement or clear on the movement's long-term goals. Polling companies like Gallup assessed the shift in citizen's concerns over racism in America and politicians talked more about it on their websites and in their speeches.

While social scientists are still trying to assess precisely how new media affect agenda-setting processes, it is clear from figure 6.5 and the example that traditional media outlets no longer dominate the process. This means that the role of media in social inclusion in political institutions have changed as well. Older mediums such as radio, print, and television allowed citizens and elected officials to interact indirectly: citizens could make their concerns visible to politicians, and politicians would use media to update constituents on their political positions. New media make communication between citizens and elected officials as well as political participation easier and more direct. As we see in the example of Black Lives Matter, new media make it relatively easy for citizens—in this case, citizens concerned about racism in the criminal justice system—to organize and pressure politicians to address their concerns publicly.

Social scientists study the effects of new media on our political institutions more than any other topic we have discussed in the book so far. Since we cannot cover everything, this chapter takes a closer look at social inclusion in political institutions. We start by looking at individual political participation, or what individuals can do to get political institutions to better represent their interests. In this section, we discuss the obstacles to acting alone and outline how new media help overcome some of these challenges. Then we turn our attention to *political organizations*, or groups that represent individuals who share a common political interest or goal. These groups play a critical role in social inclusion because they amplify the voices of average citizens and have the ability to use traditional, social, and political media to influence the policy agenda-setting process outlined above.

INDIVIDUAL POLITICAL PARTICIPATION AND
SOCIAL INCLUSION

Pick a political issue you care about—the environment, animal rights, human rights—and imagine that you wanted to spearhead a letter writing campaign urging politicians to take action on the issue. This would be relatively easy. You would write a clear letter that tells politicians why you are angry and outline the reasonable action you want them to take. New media make it easy for you to alert others of your campaign via email, social media, and discussion boards and easy for them to sign and send the letter to politicians. This was not always the case. Before hashtags, petition websites, and social media, making people aware of your issue and campaign was much more difficult—particularly if you wanted citizens beyond your immediate geographic area to participate. Think of it! After putting together a convincing, well-researched letter, you then had to find people to sign it and send it to their representative. Sure, you could start by asking your family and friends to sign and send letters, but beyond these immediate networks, sharing your ideas and getting support for them was not an easy task. Even if you stood outside of pedestrian hotspots, such as the grocery store or the post office, people who did not know you may be reluctant to get involved. After all, how are they to know if you are an upstanding citizen or if the information you provided in your letter is correct?

The point is that political participation was a lot of work. If you were spearheading a letter writing campaign, you had to be willing to give time, energy, and money to a cause. If you were participating in a letter writing campaign, you wanted to be somewhat knowledgeable about the issue (or willing to research the issue in the library—remember, no internet!) and able to assess whether the ideas and course of action presented in the letter were reasonable. This took time and energy—and you still would have needed to find the address of the appropriate politicians to whom you could mail the letter. Even if you did all this work, there was still no guarantee that politicians would read and act on your letter.

New media help reduce the costs associated with participation and make getting politically involved easier. This is in part because new media change our <u>social networks</u> or personal connections. Before new media, social networks were based primarily on geography, meaning we interacted with those who lived or worked relatively nearby. As we already discussed, new media have substantially broadened with whom we can connect. Now we can chat with individuals whom we never met in person and who live on the other side of the world. New media make it much easier for us to find communities of people who share our political and other interests. In this section of the chapter, we will consider three reasons individuals might not get involved in politics and discuss how new media make individual action easier. Again, participation matters because if individuals do not make an effort to get their voices heard, they are very unlikely to see their interests reflected in political institutions.

First, political participation often is more difficult as you age and the demands on your time shift. Generally speaking, you have more free time for political participation (and other activities) during college than you do after you graduate. After graduation, you hopefully find meaningful work that supports you financially. Work, of course, reduces the amount of free time you have available for yourself and political activities. If you find a partner, start a family, or have health issues, you have even more demands on your time, and the energy you are willing to spend on researching political issues and getting involved in campaigns may be very limited. New media make finding—and checking—political information fast and easy.

For example, when you hear a politician make an outrageous comment, and virtually all of them do, you can quickly go to websites such as PolitiFact to check the truthfulness of the statement. PolitiFact is an excellent resource because it not only evaluates each of the outrageous statements made by a given politician but also provides a "scorecard" that allows you to see his or her pattern of honesty or dishonesty in his or her public behavior. The scorecard on Donald Trump (table 6.1) shows that the majority of his statements—a total of 475 statements as of November 30, 2017—fall into the "mostly false," "false," and "pants on fire" (meaning there is no truth to the statement at all) categories. For instance, Trump's statements regarding America's tax situation ("We're the highest developed nation taxed in the world"), the Republican tax plan (it is "the biggest tax cut in U.S. history"), and whether Trump would personally benefit from the tax plan (Trump said, "No,

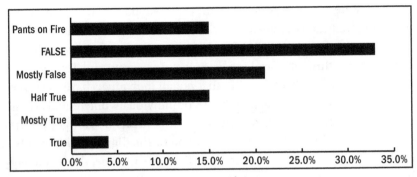

Figure 6.6. Donald Trump Scorecard. Source: PolitiFact.

I don't benefit, I don't benefit," talking about his tax proposal) were all false.

Political inexperience is the second reason individuals avoid getting politically involved. While basic political skills such as voting are taught in most elementary schools, spearheading a letter writing campaign, organizing a rally or protest, and canvassing a neighborhood before a presidential election are skills that are learned primarily through participation in civic, political, and church groups. Absent these informative experiences, individuals are unlikely to know how to undertake these more complicated political projects. Again, new media make political participation easier because they lower the costs associated with it. Individuals can easily go to a petition website such as Change.org or find a *political organization*, a group that engages in actions intended to forward a specific political goal, online that is organizing around the issues they care about.

Political organizations give individuals not only opportunities to get involved but also a chance to learn new political skills. Let's use the National Rifle Association's Institute for Legislative Action webpage, where individuals interested in gun rights have a number of ways that they can get involved, as an example. Visitors can request speakers, tweet their legislators, order a yard sign, sign up for alerts, volunteer, and get involved with the upcoming election locally. If you explore the site more, you will see that individuals can contact their legislators with a personalized message by simply filling in the empty fields, using drop-down menus to identify their local, state, and federal representatives, and, when they are ready, click "send." Gun rights supporters who want to be more involved can volunteer their time and learn how to do everything from canvassing their neighborhoods door-to-door to facilitate political conversations through social media such as Instagram and Twitter.

It is important to keep in mind that not all individuals have the same access to new media. The digital divide, or individuals' differential access to the internet, is the last reason some individuals do not get politically involved. In the United States, some of the digital divide can be explained by income. The lower an individual's income, the less likely he is to have access to broadband at home and to go online. You can see this relationship in figure 6.7, which is based on data from the Pew Research Center. Notice that only 31 percent of individuals who make less than twenty thousand dollars have broadband at home and only 52 percent go online. Compare this to individuals making one hundred thousand dollars or more. Eighty-eight percent of individuals in this category have home broadband and 97 percent of these individuals go online. This means that individuals with the highest incomes are about 50 percent more likely to have broadband and go online than those with the lowest incomes. Income affects individual involvement as well. A 2009 study by Aaron Smith and his colleagues found that individuals with higher incomes and higher levels of education are more involved in politics. As you can see in figure 6.8, individuals with an income of one hundred thousand dollars or more are far more likely to contact a government official, send a letter to the editor, or make a political contribution compared to those individuals with an income of twenty thousand dollars or less.

We do have to be careful about how we interpret these findings. It is not correct to assume that individuals with lower incomes are disengaged completely. In fact, if you look at table 6.1, you will see that most of the differences by income disappear when we consider a broader range of political activities such as writing or posting about a political or social issue on a blog or social media site, searching for candidate information online, and joining a political group or cause. Notice that individuals in the lowest income bracket who are internet users or have internet access at home are just as likely to post political content online and use social networking sites for political purposes as those individuals with incomes of one hundred thousand dollars or more.

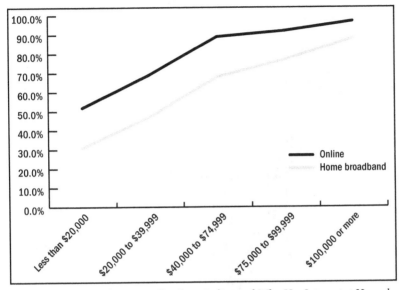

Figure 6.7. Differences between Who Goes Online and Who Has Internet at Home by Income. Source: Pew Research Center.

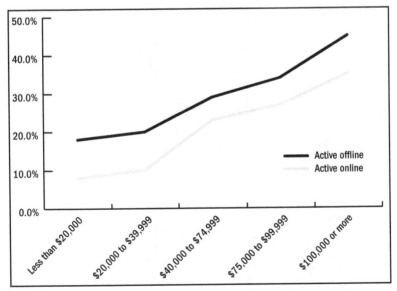

Figure 6.8. The Proportion of Adults within Each Income Category Who Have Participated in Two or More Online/Offline Political Activities within the Last Twelve Months. Source: Pew Research Center.

TABLE 6.1. The Proportion within Each Income Group That Take Part in the Following Activities

	Less than $20,000 (%)	$20,000–$39,999 (%)	$40,000–$74,999 (%)	$75,000–$99,999 (%)	$100,000 or More	Difference between Less-than-$20,000 and $100,000-or-More Groups (%)
Two or more offline political activities	18	20	29	34	45	+27
Among all adults						
Two or more offline political activities	8	10	23	27	35	+27
Make political use of social network sites	6	6	11	9	9	+3
Post political content online	9	9	14	14	14	+5
Among internet users						
Two or more offline political activities	15	14	26	30	37	+22
Make political use of social network sites	11	9	12	10	9	−2
Post political content online	17	13	16	16	15	−2
Among home broadband users						
Two or more offline political activities	21	15	28	32	40	+19
Make political use of social network sites	15	11	15	12	10	−5
Post political content online	22	16	19	18	16	−6

What does all this mean for social inclusion in political institutions? The effects of new media on individual political engagement are mixed. On the one hand, new media reduce the costs of participation by making it easier for individuals to find political information, get involved in a range of political activities, and learn new political skills. On the other hand, how individuals get politically involved varies by factors such as income and access to the internet, which potentially gives wealthy individuals more visibility in political processes than those with lower incomes. Individuals with the highest incomes are the most likely to engage in political activities that attract politicians' attention, such as writing a letter to the editor. These kinds of activities are easier for politicians to track than the number of constituents posting a comment on Facebook and, consequently, may have more influence on whose interests they consider when making political decisions.

POLITICAL ORGANIZATIONS AND SOCIAL INCLUSION

Political organizations can exert more pressure on the political system than individuals alone because they allow those who share an interest or point of view to act as a collective. As a result, individuals who get involved in political organizations often are better represented in political institutions. Of course, not all political organizations are the same, they can be formal or informal. For instance, the US Chamber of Commerce, which represents millions of companies and advocates for "probusiness" policies such as minimizing taxes on corporations in Washington, DC, is a formal political organization, or a group that is clearly structured, bureaucratic, and has a paid, professional staff. The US Chamber of Commerce has a president and CEO, policy experts who craft sample legislation for politicians to consider, public relations experts who promote the organization's ideas to the broader public, and a team of lobbyists who periodically check in with politicians when they are in DC or in their hometown. All of these activities are funded by members who agree with the organization's goals and want to see political change in state legislatures and on Capitol Hill. The same is true of groups such as the National Rifle Association (discussed above), the Sierra Club, and the Humane Society. It is easy to see how membership in formal political organizations translates into social inclusion

CASE STUDY

Vote Swapping and Presidential Elections

The 2000 presidential race between Al Gore and George W. Bush was one for the history books. Not only was it the first time the Supreme Court weighed in on a presidential election, but it also was the first election where citizens used "vote swapping" websites to try to change the electoral outcome. Vote-swapping websites are exactly what you think they are. Individuals go to a website and trade their vote with someone else. For example, a Republican living in a blue state swaps his vote with a like-minded Libertarian, who intends on voting third party, living in a swing state. Both individuals win because their votes were not wasted. The Republican had his vote cast in a battleground state, and the Libertarian had her vote cast for a third-party candidate.

In 2000, progressives rallied around Green Party candidate Ralph Nader, a well-known consumer rights activist. There was a lot of speculation whether Nader would get 5 percent of the vote, which had huge benefits. Third-party candidates that meet this benchmark qualify their next presidential candidate for federal funding. In an effort to defeat George W. Bush and qualify the Green Party for federal funds in the 2004 presidential election, progressives went online and set up a number of vote swapping websites, including Vote Exchange, Nader Trader, Voteswap 2000, WinWin Campaign, and nadergore.org.

While vote swapping was unsuccessful in 2000, vote swapping websites and discussions about vote swapping pop up every presidential election cycle. In fact, you may have heard about the #NeverTrump vote swapping app. It was created by Amit Kumar to encourage anti-Trump Republicans to swap their vote. Kumar explained to *Business Insider* that "this is really about those people who just don't like Clinton, but also know that Trump would be the worst case scenario. So we're saying, that's fine, let's figure out a way to have someone else vote for Clinton instead of you."

The app improved on vote swapping websites. First, the app goes through your existing contacts in order to see if you have any friends in a swing state so that you can swap votes with someone you know. Second, the app connects you with strangers who are interested in vote swapping. Not unlike a dating app, #NeverTrump gives you the names of five voters with similar political interests. You can look at their profiles, find a voter you like, and then start a conversation.

Get into small groups and brainstorm a list of problems with vote swapping websites. After you have a list of three to seven problems, brainstorm a list of potential solutions. Be sure to pay attention to whether current technology can be used to solve each of the problems. Look back at your list and discuss the benefits and shortcomings of new media and social inclusion.

---

in political institutions on at least one issue. Formal political organizations have full-time employees advocating on their behalf, giving them a much better chance of affecting political change than individuals alone.

There also are thousands of informal political organizations in the United States. Unlike formal political organizations, informal political organizations are not always clearly structured and are often run by unpaid volunteers. Typically, informal political organizations are grassroots groups that want to change a local condition such as city policies toward homeless individuals or the placement of landfills and nuclear power plants within counties. The Occupy movement, which started in New York in 2011 and quickly spread to cities across the country, is a great example of an informal political organization. While nationally groups rallied around the concerns of the "99 percent" over social and economic inequality, corruption, and corporate influence on politics, Occupy groups primarily focused on local concerns. For instance, in Denver, Colorado, the Occupy Denver group protested the eviction of families from foreclosed homes after the "Great Recession" in 2008, and in Oakland, California, Occupy Oakland challenged the effects of pollution and environmental degradation on low-income communities. The differences between formal and informal political organizations are summarized in table 6.2.

NEW MEDIA, NEW ORGANIZATIONS

New media have changed dramatically how political organizations are structured. Political organizations no longer have to have a brick-and-mortar location in the real world; they can exist completely online. Above, we distinguished formal organizations from informal political

TABLE 6.2. Summary of Differences between Formal and Informal Political Organizations

	Formal Political Organizations	Informal Political Organizations
Funding	Membership dues	Donations, which may be time, money, or space, from supporters
Structure	Clear roles such as president, policy expert, and public relations	May (or may not) have clear roles
Staff	Paid, professional staff	Unpaid volunteers

organizations. While these distinctions are still relevant, new media have made communication even more central to organizational structure because political organizations can use websites, discussion boards, and social media to affect how individuals interact with one another. Political organizations, of course, do not structure communication the same way. Some groups structure communication hierarchically, while others structure communication horizontally. Political organizations that structure communication more hierarchically limit how supporters can interact via new media and, like formal political organizations, typically have clear leaders, who are the decision-makers and spokespeople for the group. In contrast, political organizations that structure communication more horizontally have far fewer limits on how supporters can interact and, like informal political organization, often are grassroots groups that depend on volunteers and donations to keep the group going.

MoveOn, which was founded in 1998 to get progressives and moderate independents more involved in the political process, structures communication hierarchically. MoveOn limits interaction to topics associated with its agenda and limits the forums in which supporters can interact with one another. For example, citizens can tweet (and tweet about) MoveOn, but the organization primarily uses Twitter to advertise its positions, issues, and campaigns. The same is true of Instagram and Tumblr. The main forum where supporters can interact directly is MoveOn's Facebook page. MoveOn posts content related to its issues and campaigns and allows supporters to comment. For example, in December 2017, MoveOn supporters encouraged one another to call their legislators and urge them to vote against a tax reform bill (figures 6.9–6.10). Opponents of the bill charged that the reform largely reduced the tax burden of wealthy Americans as well as corporations while increasing

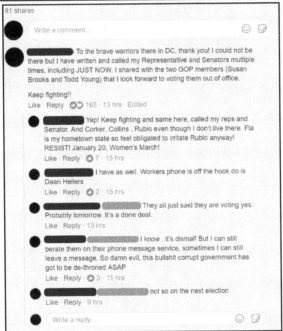

Figures 6.9–10. MoveOn Supporters Encourage One Another to Call Their Legislators.
Source: Facebook.

the taxes for middle- and lower-income families. As you can see in figures 6.9–10, groups such as MoveOn labeled this a "GOP Tax Scam" and supporters used social media to encourage one another to "keep fighting." Before Facebook, MoveOn supporters could not interact with one another online outside of the occasional online event.

A key benefit of a hierarchical communication structure is that it makes it much easier for individuals to get involved with a political organization. MoveOn has an executive director and a handful of paid activists (like a formal political organization), who create campaigns around political issues such as the environment, gun control, voting rights, immigrant rights, and health care. Once MoveOn leaders have created a campaign, they email supporters and ask them to sign a petition, donate money, host a film screening or letter-writing event at their homes, spearhead a rally or vigil, or canvas their neighborhood ahead of an election. While activities such as signing a petition and donating money do not require much time or energy, organizing a rally or letter writing campaign do, especially if you have never done it before. MoveOn makes organizing easy by providing individuals to-do lists leading up to the event, emails prepopulated with attendee email addresses so that organizers can send information and reminders, and event materials. For a letter writing event, MoveOn provides organizers a film for attendees to watch together, discussion question prompts about the film, sample letters, a list of politicians to whom letters should be sent, and envelops and stamps so that the letters can be mailed at the end of the meeting. Because MoveOn makes it easy to get involved in its activities, the political organization has more than seven million members.

Not all political organizations that use new media structure their communication hierarchically. Black Lives Matter, for instance, structures communication more horizontally than MoveOn. Black Lives Matter uses new media to create forums where supporters can share information with one another, discuss goals, and hash out ways to affect political change. A key reason the organization tries to maximize interaction is because Black Lives Matter founders want supporters to start groups in their own communities and share their experiences with one another. This is similar to informal political organizations that focus on shared leadership and open communication. Black Lives Matter also use new media to communicate its ideas directly to politicians. For example, during the Democratic Party's presidential debate in January 2016, the organization commented on candidate responses, advising Clinton and Sanders to acknowledge the killing of transgender, black women and offer a solution for state violence (e.g., gerrymandering and poverty).

While structuring communication horizontally can help political organizations strengthen grassroots participation, there are drawbacks. Open forums, for instance, can attract opponents and trolls, who intentionally post inflammatory statements and arguments in order to upset those who support a cause or community. In the example (figures 6.11–13), you can see that a few individuals post racist comments in order to denigrate the Black Lives Matter movement and those who support it. Here, a conversation about a fan throwing beer on an ejected Seahawks football player is periodically disrupted by individuals calling the player, and African Americans more generally, monkeys. Comparing people of color to animals has been used throughout American history to dehumanize African Americans and justify their subordination in society. As you can see here, these kinds of posts can completely disrupt the conversation—in this case, a conversation about race and sports etiquette. Another drawback of horizontal communication is that leaders have very little control over how their ideas and slogans are used by individuals. Political activities that draw public criticism can hurt a political organization's ability to influence the agenda-setting process. Black Lives Matter, for example, has taken a lot of heat for disrupting Democratic presidential candidate rallies and Martin Luther King Jr. events as well as for staging blockades on highways, bridges, and airports. Blockades in particular raise the broader public's hackles because it disrupts everyday movements, such as going to work, and can cause long delays, which citizens find inconvenient regardless of the cause.

Another example involves the Tea Party movement, which is, in part, a grassroots movement that emerged in response to the passage of the Troubled Asset Relief Program (a bill signed into law by President George W. Bush in October 2008), which "bailed out" banks from the economic crisis. Many local Tea Party groups tried to broaden the appeal of their claims by avoiding party politics and urging citizens to vote out political insiders. This, however, was not universally true. Some local Tea Party organizations attacked President Obama, likening his leadership during the Great Recession of 2008 to that of Adolf Hitler and Vladimir

Black Lives Matter shared a link.
12 December at 05:37 · 🌐

Seahawks Game Turns Ugly As Fans Throw Food At Ejected Player

"I'm a human just like anybody else. I'm a man just like the other man in the stands. I'm not going to let somebody disrespect me, throw a beer on me."

HUFFINGTONPOST.COM

👍 Like   💬 Comment   ➤ Share

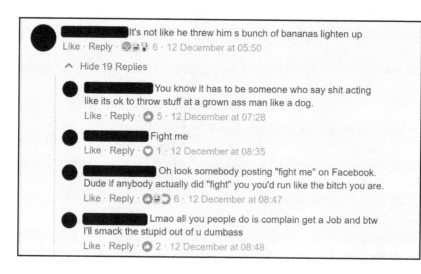

██████████ It's not like he threw him s bunch of bananas lighten up
Like · Reply · 😊👍😮 6 · 12 December at 05:50

∧ Hide 19 Replies

██████████ You know it has to be someone who say shit acting like its ok to throw stuff at a grown ass man like a dog.
Like · Reply · 👍 5 · 12 December at 07:28

██████████ Fight me
Like · Reply · 👍 1 · 12 December at 08:35

██████████ Oh look somebody posting "fight me" on Facebook. Dude if anybody actually did "fight" you you'd run like the bitch you are.
Like · Reply · 👍😆 6 · 12 December at 08:47

██████████ Lmao all you people do is complain get a Job and btw I'll smack the stupid out of u dumbass
Like · Reply · 👍 2 · 12 December at 08:48

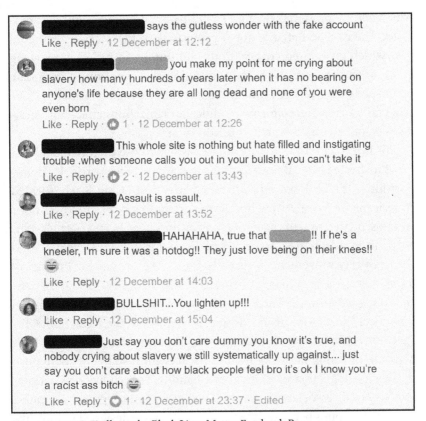

Figures 6.11–13. Trolls on the Black Lives Matter Facebook Page.

Lenin. A North Iowa Tea Party group even sponsored a billboard to make its more partisan positions on Obama known. In the billboard, it labeled Obama a "radical leader" and argued that like Hitler and Lenin, Obama was "preying" on "the fearful & naïve." These kinds of comparisons drew flak and international scrutiny given the controversial ideas and actions of the historical figures mentioned. In short, these types of actions rarely get support from the public and make it harder for political organizations to influence the agenda-setting process. Their ideas are seen as too extreme to be taken seriously.

These new organizational forms have a drawback for citizens as well. It sometimes can be difficult to tell whether political organizations represent the concerns of corporations or those of citizens. This is particularly true given the 2010 *Citizens United v. FEC* Supreme Court decision, which allows unlimited election spending by individuals and corporations. The decision struck down provisions in the McCain-Feingold Act, which prohibited corporations and unions from "electioneering communication," which is communication that mentions a candidate within sixty days of a general election or thirty days of a primary. Consequently, ads by newly formed political organizations attacking candidates before an election are not uncommon.

Nor is it uncommon for corporate owners to use their personal fortunes to create political organizations that advocate for particular policy positions. The billionaire brothers, Charles and David Koch, formed Americans for Prosperity, a libertarian group that works to lower taxes and lessen government regulation on corporations. In an effort to influence the agenda-setting process, Americans for Prosperity helped fund the Tea Party movement in its early stages. Americans for Prosperity bussed citizens to rallies and funded town hall meetings across the country, giving the Tea Party movement national visibility and political influence. While Americans for Prosperity helped the ideas of the Tea Party movement gain influence, some local groups denounced the organization for trying to co-opt their grassroots effort so that it could push its own agenda. Organizations created and/or funded by corporations, industry trade associations, or public relations firms typically are called *"astroturf"* groups because, like fake grass, they are designed to look like real grassroots, citizen groups but are not. Regardless, astroturf organizations are politically influential because they capitalize on popular discontent and channel frustrations expressed by citizens into actions and policies that forward their goals.

POLITICAL ORGANIZATIONS AND THE AGENDA-SETTING PROCESS

Like citizens, political organizations want to affect the agenda-setting process. As discussed above, political organizations have an advantage because they often represent thousands of citizens. Political organizations have two other advantages as well. First, they can use their resources to frame how we—including politicians—understand political issues and their solutions. If these frames become part of the policy agenda-setting process, political organizations can shape legislation.

A political *frame* is not unlike a camera frame insofar as we have to decide what is included and excluded from the picture. With a camera, we choose what part of the landscape on which to focus. If we focus our camera on the mountain peaks disappearing into the dark clouds, we miss the ducks playing in the lake at its base. If we make the ducks the center of our picture, we cannot capture the dramatic image of the mountains puncturing the clouds. How we frame our picture, in other words, has consequences. This same is true of a political frame. Political organizations selectively choose how to interpret a problem and, in doing so, narrow the range of relevant solutions discussed by the public and politicians.

Let's use the example of legal abortion to think about how frames work. Organizations that support safe and legal abortion in America often frame the issue in terms of women's health. They argue that legal abortion is a safe way for a woman to end an unwanted pregnancy and often remind us that women went to great lengths to end their unwanted pregnancies when abortion was illegal; sometimes dying as a result. Political organizations advocating for safe and legal abortion use symbols such as the coat hanger, which was used by women to induce an abortion prior to its legality, to dramatically argue that politicians should not consider policies that restrict abortion rights, since they would put women's lives at risk. Organizations that oppose legal abortion, in contrast, frame the issue in terms of the "rights" of "unborn babies." They argue that the public needs to prioritize the rights of "unborn children" over those of the mother and make abortion illegal in most circumstances. One of the symbols organizations on this side of the debate use to dramatically argue that fetuses are children and that politicians should protect their rights by making abortion illegal is tiny feet. In short, political organizations advocating for and against legal abortion frame the issue in ways that are consistent with their goals. These frames are very successful. Politicians frequently cite these frames when considering new abortion policies.

The second, and related, advantage political organizations have over individuals is that they can effectively disseminate their frames via mass media. Political organizations often have employees or members that have media expertise and know how to promote their frames. Again, this matters because politicians pay attention to media in order to understand what issues their constituents care about. Politicians also are exposed to frames, which affects how political institutions address these issues. Let's look at how political organizations use traditional and new media in more detail.

POLITICAL ORGANIZATIONS AND TRADITIONAL NEWS OUTLETS

While it is tempting to focus our attention on how political organizations use new media to disseminate their frames, traditional outlets such as newspapers and TV news still play a role in the agenda-setting process. According to Pew's 2016 State of the News Media report, Americans continue to tune into traditional news outlets, which means they still matter to the agenda-setting process. Consequently, political organizations target traditional mass media so that citizens and politicians are exposed to—and accept—their political frames.

Getting political frames into traditional outlets is not easy to do. This is particularly true because media professionals, editors, and owners are gatekeepers of information and decide what stories will be brought to the larger public as well as how they will be presented. Not surprisingly, news stories rarely convey the ideas of political organizations perfectly, and, more often than not, their frames are excluded from coverage altogether. Sometimes the distortion or omission of political organizations is a function of outlet bias, which is when an outlet is prejudiced in favor of or against an idea, person, or group compared with another. For example, sometimes conservative magazines like *Human Events* distort the ideas of progressive political organizations and sometimes progressive outlets like *Mother Jones* distort the ideas of conservative political organizations in an effort to appeal to their target audiences. Other times, this is a function of journalistic practices. News outlets that appeal to general audiences such as broadcast news, for instance, try to be objective, or neutral, in their presentation of political issues. In practice, this means that journalists summarize the opposing perspectives in their news stories. This is why when you see or read stories on topics such as abortion rights and gun rights both points of view—the perspective of groups opposing and perspectives of groups supporting these rights—are included in the coverage. As a result, political organizations do not have much of an opportunity to convey their ideas in their own words. If they are lucky, political organizations are mentioned or quoted in these stories.

Some political groups will try to get traditional media attention by using new or interesting tactics that catch the eye of journalists. Let's look at the example of Operation Rescue, which used direct action to attract the attention of traditional media outlets. The organization became the topic of news when its members began blocking the entrances to—and shutting down—abortion clinics. Journalists flocked to the clinics and documented the protestors getting arrested as they talked about the importance of ending abortion. This tactic got Operation Rescue news coverage across the country. Journalists in mainstream, general-interest outlets often provided balanced coverage of the organization, meaning they include different points of view. For example, in a story about some of Operation Rescue's first demonstrations at clinics, which took place in Atlanta, Georgia, around the 1988 Democratic National Convention, journalists included Operation Rescue's frame—abortion kills an unborn baby—in the story. It, however, was not the only frame included. Clinic personnel, who opposed the protests, were also included in the coverage in an effort to make the story more objective. Political organizations rarely if ever have their issues and frames presented in coverage without a contrasting point of view.

Political organizations also try to get their frames in guest op-eds, commentary, and letters to the editor. Like news coverage, opportunities for political organizations to write op-eds, write commentaries, and publish letters to the editor are pretty rare. Letters to the editor typically feature the perspectives of average citizens and op-eds often shed light on one or more of an outlet's journalistic staff. In the op-ed titled "Lose Friends and Influence People," which appeared in the *Providence Journal*, unnamed editors criticize Operation Rescue's demonstrations outside of clinics for using "guerilla tactics" that "endanger civil order." The editors wrote,

> But just as abortion opponents may exercise those rights, they must also consider the rights of fellow citizens. So it was not only ill-advised to descend en masse for a surprise demonstration, causing public disturbances and distracting the police, it was also simply wrong. Indeed, the

demonstration was so explosive, and so clearly unexpected, that police were unable to perform their vital duties in other sections of the city. If anti-abortion demonstrators seek to influence opinion, they would be well advised to avoid guerrilla tactics that endanger civil order. In Providence, as in other cities, the authorities did what they clearly had to do (November 1, 1988; *Providence Journal*).

Notice that while the editors are critical of Operation Rescue, they do not mention its frame (abortion kills an unborn baby), nor does the op-ed discuss the ideas of organizations that support legal abortion. In short, political organizations may put a lot of time and effort into trying to get media attention in traditional outlets and find that they are criticized for their tactics and goals.

Paid advertising may seem like an obvious solution to this problem. After all, political organizations can just buy space and create ads that convey the frames they want. Advertising, however, is very expensive. Political organizations have to pay marketing experts to create and test their political messages and then purchase the advertising space in the cities and states where their frames will have the most impact on politicians. Corporations pass the costs of advertising to consumers by increasing the price of the product. Political organizations, however, are not selling products and have no one to pass these costs to. Some political organizations, particularly informal groups, do not have enough money to buy advertising space. Even political organizations that do have the funds have to be careful how they use them. Supporters of political organizations expect their donations to be spent on pushing forward group goals rather than advertising campaigns. Even if a political organization does put together an advertisement, there is no guarantee that a media outlet will carry it.

There are lots of examples where newspapers, radio stations, and networks have refused to carry the advertisements of political organizations because they are worried about offending some portion of their audience. For example, the National Right to Life Committee, a group opposing legal abortion, could not get local papers to carry an advertisement that visually depicted the so-called partial birth abortion procedure, a rare procedure that doctors used to terminate a pregnancy.

Newspapers were concerned that the advertisement, which showed the procedure in a comic strip format, would offend its readership. Similarly, the political organization, People for the Ethical Treatment of Animals found that it could not get networks to carry its ad. The advertisement, which spoofed the popular "Girls Gone Wild" series by showing women ripping open their tops to bare their cow utters (rather than their breasts), was deemed too controversial to air during the Super Bowl. People for the Ethical Treatment of Animals has had similar difficulty getting newspapers and magazines to carry its ads of scantily clad celebrities advocating animal rights. One ad featuring bikini-clad Pamela Anderson with her body parts (e.g., leg, breast, shoulder, ribs, rump, round, and feet) labeled read, "All animals have the same parts." Another ad featuring a nude Joanna Krupa wearing angel wings and holding a strategically placed crucifix urged viewers, "Be an angel for animals. Always adopt. Never buy." Political organizations, in short, cannot always get their ideas in traditional media outlets even when they want to pay for it.

These examples highlight the fact that communication through traditional media outlets is one-way and that there are a number of gatekeepers (in this case, journalists, editors, and owners) who decide what issues, ideas, and political organizations are included in television broadcasts, in newspapers, and on the radio. As a consequence, it is not only difficult for political organizations to get their ideas in traditional outlets but also hard to determine whether their efforts are effective. Let's use the example of advertising. Political organizations often try to use paid advertising when they need to rally the public around their issues. We see television ads from the National Rifle Association when gun control is the topic of conversation and billboards paid for by People for the Ethical Treatment of Animals when they want to expose how factory farms treat the animals that we eat. It is very difficult to figure out whether a given ad is a good use of money because most of the viewing public will not offer an organization feedback on their positions. Sure, individuals that vehemently agree and disagree might email the organization and, perhaps if they support what it is doing, give the group money. Most individuals, however, do not respond, making it very difficult to determine whether an ad was worth the expense.

REPRODUCING INEQUALITY
The "Alt Right" Online

During the 2016 presidential election, we heard a lot about the "Alt Right," which refers to individuals who believe that "white civilization" is under attack by advocates of multiculturalism. Basically, the Alt Right sees the changing demographics of the United States and calls for equality as a threat to white, heterosexual, male dominance. Alt Right supporters see "political correctness" and "social justice" as the main tools of their opponents and combat their efforts online, where they can be anonymous. Specifically, Alt Right advocates use the following:

- Memes that denigrate mainstream conservatives, Jews, and people of color. Alt Righters, for example, refer to conservatives as "cuckservatives," which combines the words "conservative" and "cuckold" and is used to describe Republicans who are seen as emasculated or "selling out." This meme often explicitly refers to sex acts—a husband allowing strangers to have sex with his wife—to highlight the weakness and effeminateness of politicians. Alt Righters also use the 1980s McDonald's character, Moon Man, as a "front man" for rap parodies and explicit descriptions of gruesome scenes murdering people of color.
- Reddit, which is very popular among the Alt Right in large part because it allows posters to remain anonymous when they post content. The Alt Right forums on Reddit as well as Donald Trump's willingness to retweet material posted on them are central to debates over politics online. For instance, Trump shared a GIF of him beating up a CNN reporter via Twitter. The video was created by "HansAssholeSolo," who is one of 448,000 members of the subreddit The_Donald. While "HansAssholeSolo" argued that the video was satire, several investigations of the subreddit argue that The_Donald is filled with openly Islamophobic, misogynistic, and racist hate speech.
- Political channels on YouTube, which are dominated by the Alt Right. Zack Exley, a Joan Shorenstein Fellow at Harvard University, conducted research on YouTube and found that political YouTube channels receive millions of views, and the vast majority of them espouse white nationalism with a modern twist. Exley specifically examines the videos of Black Pigeon Speaks, who has 180,000

subscribers as of April 2017 and whose videos typically have more than 100,000 views. Using the producer's own words, Exley unpacks Alt Right positions and attitudes toward women, progressives, Islam, immigration, and Jews. Exley notes that the Alt Right is cornering the market on political rants and that this is problematic insofar as this way of communicating has gained traction among the YouTube viewing population.

Given Americans' tendency to only view content in which they politically agree, it is easy to imagine how the Alt Right undermine social inclusion. By arguing that women, people of color, progressives, Jews, Muslims, immigrants, and lesbian, gay, and transgender individuals are, at best, inferior to white, heterosexual men and, at worst, legitimate targets of violence, Alt Right supporters clearly define who should—and shouldn't—be included in our political system.

POLITICAL ORGANIZATIONS AND NEW MEDIA

New media provide alternative ways for political organizations to affect the agenda-setting process. Political organizations can use new media to connect constituents directly to the politicians representing them. Let's consider the example of MomsRising, a political organization that takes on pressing issues for mothers and families such as affordable medical care. MomsRising used their website and social media to collect stories about how Medicaid helps American families. Once it collected stories, MomsRising forwarded some of these stories to politicians who wanted to cut funds from Medicaid via social media. MomsRising, for instance, tweeted Senator Mitch McConnell (a Republican from Kentucky) to educate him about how Medicaid helped the citizens of his state. MomsRising encouraged McConnell to learn more about fellow Kentuckian Rolanda, a mother of two who would not have access to medical care without the program. MomsRising compiled all the stories into a collection titled "Moms Speak Up for Medicaid," which it hand delivered to members of Congress and President Obama.

Political organizations also can disseminate their advertisements and videos without worrying about whether gatekeepers like their ideas. This is important for political organizations because it allows them to circumvent traditional media outlets and get their frames to a broader public. For example, Dan Savage and Terry Miller, Savage's husband, sidestepped traditional outlets altogether and started the "It Gets Better" project on YouTube. Savage and Miller were responding to an increase in suicides by teens who were bullied because of their sexual orientation. The first video, which was posted on September 21, 2010, has been viewed more than two million times and thousands of celebrities and citizens from around the world have shared their messages of hope on the site. Likewise, Sustainable Table, a political organization that advocates for sustainable farming made a video called "The Meatrix" (a spoof on the blockbuster film *The Matrix*) to show how industrial agriculture causes environmental damage and health problems. More recently, the World Wildlife Fund used Snapchat to try to raise awareness regarding animal populations at risk of extinction. The organization snapped pictures of a gorilla, tiger, and panda, noting that, just like the selfies on Snapchat, which disappear every ten seconds, so do endangered animals.

New media, in sum, make it easier for political organizations to frame issues to a broader audience and pressure politicians to take up their causes. This is important for social inclusion because organizations that represent significant groups of the citizenry will have more sway with politicians and in agenda-setting processes. This is particularly true if political organizations can find ways to use new media to leverage the personal experiences of their supporters against the politicians representing them. Politicians may find it more difficult to downplay or ignore issues after political organizations advertise the stories of constituents affected by them.

CONCLUSION

In this chapter, we learned that new media have changed our interactions with political institutions. Specifically, new media offer individuals and political organizations more ways to influence the agenda-setting process. At the individual level, new media help reduce the costs associated with participation and make it easier for individuals to get politically involved. New media, for instance, make it easier for individuals to learn political skills. Individuals can go to websites associated with the National Rifle Association and quickly learn how to do everything from canvassing their neighborhoods to facilitating political conversations on

CASE STUDY

People for the Ethical Treatment of Animals

People for the Ethical Treatment of Animals (PETA) is well known for its creative, effective, and sometimes offensive use of new media. The political organization has the following:

- Different websites for different target audiences. In addition to its general website (PETA.org), the group maintains PETA Kids for elementary and middle school kids, PETA2 for high school and college students, and PETA Prime for the fifty and older crowd.
- Different websites for different campaigns. PETA campaigns often attack corporations for their use of fur or their treatment of animals. Check out their campaigns against the Olsen twins (*Dress Up the Trollsens*) and KFC (*Kentucky Fried Cruelty*).
- A number of satirical games designed to educate the public about animal rights. Two examples are *Revenge of the PETA Tomatoes* (based on Frogger) in which users throw tomatoes at fur wearers and *New Super Chick Sisters*, where users try to save celebrity Pamela Anderson from becoming the secret ingredient in Ronald McDonald's food.

Go online and check out the following PETA websites and games (the links are at the end of the chapter):

- PETA kids
- PETA2
- *Super Chick Sisters*
- *Super Tofu Boy*

    Discuss the following questions:
- Do you think PETA effectively uses new media to educate a broader public?
- Do you think this helps with social inclusion? Why or why not?

social media. These activities are consequential because they potentially give individuals more influence in agenda setting, which could translate into legislative change and more social inclusion.

Political organizations also benefit from new media. Political organizations can use new media to organize themselves in different ways. Groups no longer have to have a brick-and-mortar location in the real world; they can exist completely online. We learned that new media make communication even more important to political organizations and that groups can use new technology to either limit or facilitate interactions among supporters. MoveOn.org, for example, structures its communications hierarchically and limits how supporters can interact with one another via new media. Black Lives Matter, in contrast, structures its communications horizontally and allows its supporters to interact more freely. We discussed the advantages and disadvantages of each. Groups with a hierarchical communication structure make it easier for individuals to get involved with the political organization but make it very hard for supporters to regularly connect in the "real" world. Political organizations with a horizontal structure cultivate a grassroots base but cannot control how their ideas are used by others.

A key advantage political organizations have over individuals is their ability to effectively influence the agenda-setting process. We learned that political organizations use traditional media and new media to disseminate their frames to the public and politicians alike. Because political organizations have more resources than individuals, they have a relatively easier time disseminating their ideas and affecting agenda-setting processes. New media allow political organizations to target politicians with their frames more effectively. As we saw with Moms-Rising, political organizations can creatively connect constituents and politicians in ways that publicly pressure politicians to take up their issues—or, at least, make them difficult to ignore.

That said, new media do not necessarily lead to more social inclusion. It is important to remember that some individuals have more and better access to new media and that this shapes the ability of citizens to engage politically and advocate on behalf of their own interests. Likewise, it is important to remember that some political organizations are more representative of a community and more powerful in the political process. Grassroots political organizations are far more representative of a community than "astroturf" political organizations, which simply capitalize on popular ideas for their own purposes. Despite this fact, astroturf political organizations can use their wealth to disproportionately affect politics and social inclusion.

CHAPTER LINKS

"Home Page." n.d. National Rifle Association Institute for Legislative Action. http:// www.nraila.org.

Marikar, Sheila. 2016. "An App for Political Organizing." *New Yorker*. Last modified October 17, 2016. http://www.newyorker.com.

Janjigian, Lori. 2016. "#NeverTrump App Helps Facilitate Vote Swapping to Safely Vote for a Third-Party." *Business Insider*. Last modified October 6, 2016. http://www .businessinsider.com.

Atkinson, Robert. 2010. "Voices: Reactions to the North Iowa Tea Party Billboard Comparing President Barack Obama to Adolf Hitler and Vladimir Lenin." *Kalama-zoo Gazette*. Last modified July 20, 2010. http://www.mlive.com.

"Last Selfie." n.d. World Wildlife Fund. http://www.justforthis.com.

Caffier, Justin. 2017. "Get to Know the Memes of the Alt-Right and Never Miss a Dog-Whistle Again." *Vice*. Last modified January 25, 2017. http://www.vice.com.

Ellis, Emma Grey. 2017. "The Alt-Right's Newest Ploy? Trolling with False Symbols." *Wired*. Last modified May 10, 2017. http://www.wired.com.

Exley, Zack. 2017. "Black Pigeon Speaks: The Anatomy of the Worldview of an Alt-Right YouTuber." Shorenstein Center on Media, Politics and Public Policy. Last modified June 2017. http://www.shorensteincenter.org.

"Home Page." n.d. PETA Kids. http://www.petakids.com.

"Home Page." n.d. PETA 2. http://www.peta2.com.

"Super Chick Sisters." n.d. PETA. http://www.mccruelty.com.

"Super Tofu Boy." n.d. PETA. http://www.peta.org.

CHAPTER REVIEW QUESTIONS

1. How has the agenda setting changed with new technology?
2. What is the relationship between agenda setting and social inclusion?
3. How do new media help individuals overcome the obstacles associated with political participation?
4. How is the digital divide an obstacle to social inclusion?
5. What are the drawbacks for political organizations that structure communication hierarchically? How about horizontally?
6. Why do political organizations create frames?

LEARN MORE

Capecchi, Christina. 2015. "'Black Lives Matter' Protesters Gather; Mall Is Shut in Response." *New York Times*. Last modified December 23, 2015. http://www.nytimes .com.

"Civil Rights Movement." n.d. John F. Kennedy Presidential Library and Museum. Retrieved June 2016. http://www.jfklibrary.org.

Cornish, Audie. 2013. "How the Civil Rights Movement Was Covered in Birmingham." *NPR*. Last modified June 18, 2013. http://www.npr.org.

Farley, Robert. 2011. "Americans for Prosperity." FactCheck.org. Last modified October 10, 2011. http://www.factcheck.org.

Freelon, Deen, Charlton D. McIlwain, and Meredith D. Clark. 2016. "Beyond the Hashtags: #Ferguson, #BlackLivesMatter, and the Online Struggle for Offline Justice." Center for Media & Social Impact. Last modified February 29, 2016. http://www.cmsimpact.org.

Garza, Alicia. 2014. "A Herstory of the #BlackLivesMatter Movement." The Feminist Wire. Last modified October 7, 2014. http://www.thefeministwire.com.

"How the Media Covered the Civil Rights Movement: The Children's March." 2015. *Alabama Public Radio*. Last modified April 25, 2013. http://www.apr.org.

Kanter, Beth. 2011. "Likes on Facebook Are Not a Victory: Results Are!" Beth's Blog. Last modified August 9, 2011. http://www.bethkanter.org.

"Mapping the Digital Divide." 2015. Council of Economic Advisers Issue Brief. Last modified July 2015. http://www.obamawhitehouse.archives.gov.

McClain, Dani. 2016. "The Black Lives Matter Movement Is Most Visible on Twitter. Its True Home Is Elsewhere." *Nation*. Last modified April 19, 2016. http://www.thenation.com.

Mohdin, Aamna. 2015. "From #PrayForParis to #BlackLivesMatter, Twitter Looks Back at This Year's Biggest Moments." *Quartz*. Last modified December 7, 2015. http://www.qz.com.

Savage, Dan, and Terry Miller. 2010. "It Gets Better: Dan & Terry." It Gets Better Project. Last modified October 13, 2010. http://www.youtube.com.

"Selma, Alabama: The Role of News Media in the Civil Rights Movement." n.d. *PBS LearningMedia*. Retrieved June 2016. http://www.pbslearningmedia.org.

Sidner, Sara, and Mallory Simon. 2015. "This Is How and Why the Black Lives Matter Movement Continues to Grow." *Las Vegas Review-Journal*. Last modified December 28, 2015. http://www.reviewjournal.com.

Smith, Aaron, Kay Lehman Schlozman, Sidney Verba, and Henry Brady. 2009. "The Demographics of Online and Offline Political Participation." Pew Research Center. Last modified September 1, 2009. http://www.pewinternet.org.

———. 2009. "Will Political Engagement on Blogs and Social Networking Sites Change Everything?" Pew Research Center. Last modified September 1, 2009. http://www.pewinternet.org.

Spillius, Alex. 2010. "Barack Obama Compared to Hitler and Lenin in Tea Party Billboard." *Telegraph*. Last modified July 13, 2010. http://www.telegraph.co.uk.

"The State of Broadband: Broadband Catalyzing Sustainable Development." 2016. Broadband Commission. Last modified September 2016. http://www.broadbandcommission.org.

"State of the News Media 2016." 2016. Pew Research Center. Last modified June 15, 2016. http://www.pewresearch.org.

VIDEOS AND MOVIES

ABC News. 2010. "Social Networking Is Revolutionizing Politics." YouTube. Last modified July 22, 2010. http://www.youtube.com.

Anschuetz, Nika. 2015. "Is Hashtag-Based Activism All Talk, No Action?" *USA Today College*. Last modified October 26, 2015. http://www.college.usatoday.com.

Attkisson, Sharyl. 2015. "Astroturf and Manipulation of Media Messages." *TEDxUniversityofNevada*. Last modified February 6, 2015. http://www.youtube.com.

Auerbach, David. 2016. "The Bernie Bubble." *Slate*. Last modified February 17, 2016. http://www.slate.com.

BBC News. 2014. "Social Media & Twitter Abuse in Politics." YouTube. Last modified September 13, 2014. http://www.youtube.com.

Cleary, Ronica. 2016. "Impacts of Social Media on Politics, Presidential Race." *FOX 5*. Last modified March 2, 2016. http://www.fox5dc.com.

Daniels, Eugene. 2016. "House Democrats Use Social Media to Show House Floor Takeover." *Newsy*. Last modified June 22, 2016. http://www.newsy.com.

"Is Social Media Ruining Politics in the United States?" 2015. *MSNBC*. Last modified September 4, 2015. http://www.msnbc.com.

Keen, Andrew. 2009. "Social Media and the Internet Do Not Spread Democracy." *Telegraph*. Last modified August 18, 2009. http://www.telegraph.co.uk.

Maddow, Rachel. 2015. "Full Video: Hillary Clinton Meets Black Lives Matter." *MSNBC*. Last modified August 20, 2015. http://www.msnbc.com.

Patterson, Dan. 2016. "Election Tech: Let's Get Vertical—How Presidential Campaigns Use Data and Social Media to Microtarget Voters." TechRepublic. Last modified February 12, 2016. http://www.techrepublic.com.

Perry, Melissa Harris. 2016. "Engaging in Politics through Social Media." *MSNBC*. Last modified February 7, 2016. http://www.msnbc.com.

PETA. 2012. "Milk Gone Wild." YouTube. Last modified January 23, 2012. http://www.youtube.com.

"Political Change: What Social Media Can—and Can't Do." 2011. *NATO Review*. http://www.nato.int.

"Political Talk on Facebook Mirrors Political Talk Offline." 2015. Phys.org. Last modified May 12, 2015. http://www.phys.org.

"Politics and Religion Don't Mix, Neither Do Politics and Social Media." 2012. *CBS DFW*. Last modified October 15, 2012. http://www.dfw.cbslocal.com.

Retherford, John. 2015. "Black Lives Matters Demonstration at Bernie Sanders Westlake Event Seattle (Unedited)." YouTube. Last modified August 10, 2015. http://www.youtube.com.

Ridgwell, Henry. 2013. "Global Politics Shaken by Social Media." *VOA*. Last modified March 13, 2013. http://www.voanews.com.

"Role of Social Media in 2016 Presidential Campaign Coverage." 2016. *C-SPAN*. Last modified July 24, 2016. http://www.c-span.org.

"The Role of Tech in Women's Political Participation—Video." 2013. *Guardian.* Last modified December 10, 2013. http://www.theguardian.com.

Shirky, Clay. 2009. "How Social Media Can Make History." *TED.* Last modified June 2009. http://www.ted.com.

"The Sustainable Table." n.d. *Meatrix.* Last modified July 2016. http://www.themeatrix .com.

CHAPTER REFERENCES

Andrews, Kenneth, and Neal Caren. 2010. "Making the News: Movement Organizations, Media Attention, and the Public Agenda." *American Sociological Review* 75 (6): 841–66.

Bennett, Lance, and Alexandra Segerberg. 2012. "The Logic of Connective Action." *Information, Communication & Society* 15 (5): 739–68.

Bimber, Bruce, Andrew Flanagin, and Cynthia Stohl. 2012. *Collective Action in Organizations: Interaction and Engagement in an Era of Technological Change.* New York: Cambridge University Press.

Castells, Manuel. 2012. *Networks of Outrage and Hope: Social Movements in the Internet Age.* Malden, MA: Polity Press.

Earl, Jennifer, and Katrina Kimport. 2011. *Digitally Enabled Social Change: Activism in the Internet Age.* New York: MIT Press.

Faris, Rob, Hal Roberts, Bruce Etling, Nikki Bourassa, and Ethan Zucherman. 2017. "Partisanship, Propaganda, and Disinformation: Online Media and the 2016 U.S. Presidential Election." Bekman Klein Center for Internet & Society. Last modified August 2018. https://cyber.harvard.edu/publications/2017/08/mediacloud.

Freelon, Deen, Charlton McIlwain, and Meredith Clark. 2016. "Quantifying the Power and Consequences of Social Media Protest." *New Media & Society* 20 (3): 990–1011. https://doi.org/10.1177/1461444816676646.

Gamson, William, and David Meyer. 1996. "Framing Political Opportunity." In *Comparative Perspectives on Social Movements: Political Opportunities, Mobilizing Structures, and Cultural Framings,* edited by D. McAdam, J. McCarthy, and M. Zald, 275–90. Cambridge: Cambridge University Press.

Gamson, William, and Gadi Wolfsfeld. 1993. "Movement and Media as Interacting Systems." *Annals of the American Academy of Political and Social Science* 578:104–25.

Haines, Herbert. 1988. *Black Radicals and the Civil Rights Mainstream, 1954–1970.* Knoxville: University of Tennessee Press.

Heatherly, Kyle A., Yanqin Lu, and Jae Kook Lee. 2016. "Filtering Out the Other Side? Cross-Cutting and Like-Minded Discussions on Social Networking Sites." *New Media & Society* 19 (8): 1271–89. https://doi.org/10.1177/1461444816634677.

Hilgartner, Stephen, and Charles Bosk. 1988. "The Rise and Fall of Social Problems: A Public Arenas Model." *American Journal of Sociology* 94:53–78.

LeFebvre, Rebecca Kay, and Crystal Armstrong. 2016. "Grievance-Based Social Movement Mobilization in the #Ferguson Twitter Storm." *New Media & Society* 20 (1): 8. https://doi.org/10.1177/1461444816644697.

McCombs, Maxwell, and Donald Shaw. 1972. "The Agenda-Setting Function of Mass Media." *The Public Opinion Quarterly* 36 (2): 176–87.

Phillips, Whitney. 2018. "The Oxygen of Amplification: Better Practices for Reporting on Extremists, Antagonists, and Manipulators Online." Data & Society. Last modified May 2018. https://datasociety.net/wp-content/uploads/2018/05/FULLREPORT _Oxygen_of_Amplification_DS.pdf.

Rohlinger, Deana. 2015. *Abortion Politics, Mass Media, and Social Movements in America*. New York: Cambridge University Press.

Rohlinger, Deana, and Leslie Bunnage. 2015. "Connecting People to Politics over Time? Internet Communication Technology and Retention in Moveon.org and the Florida Tea Party Movement." *Information, Communication & Society* 18 (5): 539–52.

Rojecki, Andrew, and Sharon Meraz. 2016. "Rumors and Factitious Informational Blends: The Role of the Web in Speculative Politics." *New Media & Society* 18 (1): 25–43.

Ryan, Charlotte. 1991. *Prime Time Activism: Media Strategies for Grassroots Organizing*. Boston: South End Press.

Shin, Jieun, Lian Jian, Kevin Driscoll, and François Bar. 2017. "Political Rumoring on Twitter During the 2012 US Presidential Election: Rumor Diffusion and Correction." *New Media & Society* 19 (8):1214–35.

Snow, David, and Robert Benford. 1992. "Master Frames and Cycles of Protest." In *Frontiers in Social Movement Theory*, edited by A. Morris and C. M. Mueller, 133–55. New Haven: Yale University Press.

Sobieraj, Sarah. 2011. *Soundbitten: The Perils of Media-Centered Political Activism*. New York: New York University Press.

Wiewiura, Joachim S., and Vincent F. Hendricks. 2017. "Informational Pathologies and Interest Bubbles: Exploring the Structural Mobilization of Knowledge, Ignorance, and Slack." *New Media & Society* 20 (3): 1123–38. https://doi.org/10.1177/ 1461444816686095.

Conclusion

At the outset of the book, I compared us to fish. Like fish, we have a difficult time understanding the water in which we swim. Only for us, new media are the water. While you may have some sense of how reliant you are on digital technology, you probably have not tracked the amount of time you spend on your devices online much less thought about how new technologies have changed the way we interact and the social institutions on which we rely. In the concluding chapter of the book, we revisit the two questions posed in the introduction:

1. How do new media shape our interactions and experiences with one another?
2. How do new media change the social institutions, or the systems of established social rules that create stable expectations for behavior, governing our lives?

We will discuss the each of the questions in turn.

EXERCISE

Do you really know how much time you spend engaged with mass media? Find out! Keep a journal that records your use of different devices for a week. The best way to do this is to create an Excel sheet that notes (1) the medium/device, (2) the number of minutes spent per medium/device, and (3) what the medium/device was used to do (e.g., 10 minutes talking to parents, 90 minutes playing music while studying, 120 minutes of recreational TV, etc.). Mediums and devices you should include in your Excel sheet are as follows:
- computer
- TV
- tablet
- newspapers/magazines
- radio
- stereo/CD

- books
- telephone
- other

It is really important that you are specific about how you are using a medium/device so that you can see how often you use mass media for work and pleasure. For example, you may spend five hours total on your smartphone, but most of this time may be spent texting friends.

At the end of the week, assess how much time you spend on each medium/device on average and determine how much time you engage in various activities such as using a computer for work. Did anything surprise you about the results? Compare your results to one or more of your classmates. How similar/different is your media use?

NEW MEDIA AND US

The first question asked how new media affect our interactions and experiences with one another. As we saw in chapter 1, the answer to this question is complicated. In fact, we find that new media potentially have positive and negative influences on our relationships. Here's what we know.

New media make it much easier for us to connect with one another and provide us additional ways to connect with one another around a broad range of interests. If we want to chat with other folks about the latest episode of *Westworld*, the teams in contention for the World Series, or even a difficult passage from the Torah (or the teachings from the Hebrew Bible), it is easy to find an online community ready and willing to discuss each of these topics in great detail. It also is easy to find collective entertainment in the digital age. We can get on our mobile devices and play everything from *Words with Friends* to *Fortnite Battle Royale*. More important, we know that these online social networks matter. Remember the Pew Research survey on teens, technology, and friendship from chapter 1? Pew found that the majority of teens met someone that they would not have otherwise via social media or online gaming and that 20 percent of teens met these digital friends in the "real" world. We also learned that communicating online helps teens transition to adulthood. Teens in particular can go online and experiment with different aspects of their personalities and develop virtual friendships, which can make going to college easier. New media, in short, provide forums where we can form meaningful and positive relationships.

New media, however, do not necessarily help us foster happy and healthy relationships. In chapter 1, we learned about the importance of ontological security, which comes from our relationships with friends and family, for dealing with events beyond our control. We also learned that new media put a strain on these relationships. Teens, for instance, report that they wish their parents would put down their devices and engage them in conversation. Teens resent their parents for ignoring them when they are in the same room while, at the same time, trying to track their friends and activities through social media. New media put a strain on friendships as well. We saw that teens and adults alike sometimes are much more concerned with how they appear online than the quality of their friendships. Consequently, we often engage our friends carefully online and post content that we hope will make us look good—and will be "liked" by others. This ongoing curation of our lives for friends and family ultimately creates distance between us, which affects our ability to deal with interpersonal conflict and embarrassing interactions in face-to-face interactions.

We are not necessarily nicer to one another in the digital age. New media create a distance in interactions, and this distance makes it easy for some individuals to do and say things that they might not otherwise. Teens and adults alike sometimes engage in rude behavior online. The strange focus on Serena Williams's nipples during Wimbledon is just one example of average people using new media to post unseemly comments about another human being. The trolls that went after feminist Lindy West were worse. One troll even impersonated her dead father and, using this persona, threatened West with rape. Finally, we do not appear to challenge racial or ethnic discrimination online. Virtual forums such as *Second Life* are dominated by white avatars, making them less diverse than our lived realities. While some of this is a function of the forum (remember, *Second Life* offered users light-skinned avatars, since they more closely mirror a presumed white ideal), racial and ethnic minorities are often called names and harassed online.

REPRODUCING INEQUALITY
Net Neutrality

We often think about the internet as a space where information flows quickly and freely. Anything that we want to know or any product we want to buy, we are just one click away. This notion that we can go online, communicate freely, and access information about the world is central to the principle of net neutrality. We believe that we—not companies—should be in charge of our internet experience.

Internet service providers such as AT&T, Comcast, and Verizon disagree. They argue that since they have provided some of the physical infrastructure necessary for the internet as we know it, they should have more control over how we receive our content and how they profit from it. This is contentious because internet service providers can affect the flow of information and influence what kinds of content to which we have access. Absent net neutrality, internet service providers could block our access to content they do not like, silence individuals and groups with whom they do not agree, and make "fast lanes" so that we can only quickly access the content and services of companies that pay them a premium. We might also find that internet services are more expensive. Internet service providers could bundle content like they do on cable. For example, Comcast could decide that access to "popular" websites such as Google, CNN, and the *New York Times* costs customers sixty dollars per month.

What does this have to do with inequality? A lot. First, having "fast" and "slow" lanes favors large corporations. Smaller businesses and startups will have a much harder time coming up with the funds to get their content on the "fast lane," which will make it more difficult for them to survive. Second, allowing internet service providers to censure content makes it more difficult for people of color, the LGBTQ community, indigenous peoples, and religious minorities to organize and fight back against discrimination. Finally, it will deepen the digital divide in America. As the cost of access to the internet increase, the number of Americans able to pay for it shrinks.

NEW MEDIA AND SOCIAL INSTITUTIONS

The second question asked how new media change the social institutions, or the systems of established social rules that create stable expectations for behavior, governing our lives. To better understand the interactions between individuals, institutions, and new media, we used the social exchange model. This model highlights the importance of relational dynamics, or how the behavior of one actor is shaped by the behaviors of other actors and by changes in the institutional context. In other words, the social exchange model doesn't argue that new media are good or bad for American society. It simply draws our attention to the fact that the interactions between mass media, social institutions, and individuals change our behavior and society as well as recognizes that the consequences associated with change are likely positive *and* negative Throughout the book, we explored how these interactions are changing education, religion, legal institutions, the workplace, and political institutions. Here, we will briefly summarize some of the consequences associated with new media in the various social institutions. You can find an overview in table C.1.

Let's start with education. In chapter 2, we learned that new media are used to increase connections among students, teachers, professionals, and experts as well as to expand the educational opportunities available to students. For instance, students in poor communities can learn basic and specialized skills through free platforms such as Khan Academy or learn advanced material from experts in the field through massive open online courses (MOOCs). Additionally, new media diversifies how teachers can deliver lessons, allowing them to accommodate a range of learning styles. Fast learners can read a lesson and jump to the required quiz, while slow learners can take advantage of different formats featuring the material they need to learn. Slow learners can read a lesson (or have it read to them), watch a short video on the material, and play a game that tests their knowledge before they take the required quiz. New media also make it easier for shy students and slow learners to participate in classroom discussions—not to mention digital classrooms downplay the importance of teachers' subjective evaluations of students and their likelihood of success.

TABLE C.1. The Consequences of New Media on American Institutions

Social Institution	New Media Usage	Positive Consequences	Negative Consequences
Education	Increase connections among students	Connect students, experts, and professionals globally.	Enables cyber bullying.
	Reduce inequality	Creates opportunities for learning such as Khan Academy and MOOCs.	Focuses on providing internet services in schools that can't afford teachers let alone tech support.
	Enhance learning	Provides more opportunities for slow learners and buffers teacher evaluations of individual students.	Emphasizes "fun" education and downplays teacher expertise in student learning.
Religion	Make religious teaching more accessible	Allows individuals to keep up their faith regardless of constraints on their time or mobility.	Undermines some religious practices, including the creation of a sacred space.
	Make religious leaders more accessible	Provides religious leaders a platform through which they can translate doctrine and share their personal stories.	Allows extremist religious leaders to share propaganda and find new recruits.
	Build religious community	Enables individuals to find others and practice religions such as Buddhism and Wicca and deepen their faith.	Supports extremist religious communities, such as Christian Identity, and communities that engage in religious persecution, such as Jihad Watch.
Legal institutions	Improve national security	Allows legal actors to better identify threats and thwart some terrorist attacks.	Enables legal actors to monitor virtually every digital transaction, including emails and texts.
	Improve community safety	Facilitates predictive policing so that departments can target policy resources where they are needed most.	Uses incomplete and flawed data to unfairly target poor communities and communities of color.

2

Social Institution	New Media Usage	Positive Consequences	Negative Consequences
Work	Help employers make better choices about their employees	Helps employers better ensure that an employee fits with a given workplace and saves both parties time and money.	Violates the privacy of potential employees by requiring them to provide social media passwords.
	Make work more efficient and standardize production	Makes a range of work-related tasks easier through programs and automation.	Alienates employees from their work as they have no control over what they do and when they do it.
	Increase company profitability	Can give some employees a more flexible schedule and allows telecommuting, which helps with work-family balance.	Ensures that some workers are consistently underemployed, lengthens the workday, and allows work to encroach on vacations.
Politics	Increase citizen participation	Eases the costs associated with participation and makes it easier for individuals to learn new political skills.	Access to the internet varies, which means some kinds of participation vary by income and education level.
	Increased the voice of citizens who share a common political interest	Provides a forum in which average citizens can effect grassroots change.	Enables extremist groups to organize and mobilize and is vulnerable to astroturfing.

Access to high-speed internet, however, will not solve all of America's educational woes. Resource-strapped schools can't afford teachers, let alone technicians to install and fix the technological problems that inevitably arise. Moreover, not all educational settings prioritize education. For-profit companies such as the University of Phoenix and Everest Institute—the now-defunct college owned by Corinthian Colleges—worry about getting paid first and student education second. There are problems with new media in the classroom as well. New media often gamifies education and reinforces students' expectations that learning should be enjoyable, if not downright fun. New media also provide students news ways to connect with—and sometimes bully—one another during and after school hours. Finally, downplaying the expertise of teachers has consequences. Teachers are trained to identify the strengths and weakness of individual students. Treating them like online facilitators means that students probably are not being properly developed and challenged in the classroom.

We see similar mixed results for religious institutions. New media hold a lot of positives for religious practice and for religious leaders. Digital technology makes it possible for individuals to celebrate their faith regardless of constraints on their time or mobility. It doesn't matter if you are a workaholic or disabled, new media allow you to download your favorite Godcast or watch a recorded sermon online. Additionally, new media make religious leaders more accessible to their congregation. Religious leaders such as priests and rabbis can use social media to make their lives—and their teachings—more accessible through personal stories. New media potentially expand who we consider religious leaders and look to for inspiration in our lives. For some, Sam and Nia may epitomize Christian living, and they watch them faithfully on YouTube. Others, however, may find Christian blogger and writer Priscilla Shirer more relatable and appreciate how she finds religious experience in mundane activities such as washing dishes. Finally, new media provide ways for individuals to practice less popular religions such as Buddhism and Wicca and create communities of faith online. As we saw with the Ship of Fools example, individuals can create religious communities that extend across time and social media platforms.

Of course, new media has its fair share of negative consequences on religious institutions. Arguably, new media undermine religious practices, particularly as it relates to the creation of a sacred space. While new media makes religious practice convenient, some believe that it is impossible to truly practice your faith if you are listening to a sermon on the treadmill or while you take care of your grocery shopping. More troublesome, new media make it easier for religious extremists to share propaganda, find new recruits, and build communities based on lies and hate. We learned about several instances in which religious extremists used social media to share information on how to build and plant bombs (e.g., the attack on the Boston Marathon) or tried to recruit new members to their cause. BuzzFeed reporter Sheera Frenkel recounts how ISIS used chat rooms and dating websites to target women. We also learned more about communities, including Christian Identity and Jihad Watch, which use distorted religious doctrine to persecute ethnic and racial minorities as well as Muslims.

The implications of new media are particularly interesting when we consider legal institutions. New media are supposed to improve the safety of our communities and our nation. Certainly, the NSA has used programs such as PRISM and XKeyScore to filter through Americans' communications and stop terrorist attacks. According to an unnamed official, who appeared before a House committee on the issue in 2013, NSA programs disrupted more than fifty terrorist plots around the world. Police departments claim similar success with predictive policing programs. The research on the effectiveness of predictive policing, however, is mixed. John Hollywood, an analyst for the RAND Corporation in Arlington, Virginia, who coauthored a report on the issue, found that the advantage of predictive policing over traditional policing is "incremental at best." Moreover, we find that these community and national programs do not always have good data and may ultimately perpetuate racial, ethnic, and religious prejudices. It is difficult to forget what we learned about the "Mapping Muslims" project, where the NYPD monitored more than 250 mosques and student groups in an effort to root out would-be terrorists.

As you enter the workforce, you should think about how new media change your job search, the work you do, and the way you do it. New media certainly make searching and applying for jobs easier, especially if you are applying to jobs on the other side of the country. You can quickly upload a cover letter and resume for several jobs at a time. New media also make it much easier for us to research prospective employers. We can go online and see if a company has a good reputation and whether it has decent benefits. The same is true for employers. They can go online and see what you post publicly and determine whether you are someone they want to interview. This, however, can feel like a violation of your privacy when prospective employers require you to provide login information for your social media accounts before they grant you an interview.

Much of the new technology is designed to make the workplace more efficient and profitable. On the one hand, this can involve the standardization of production, which can make work easier to do and provide a consistent product to customers. Remember the McDonald's worker? A series of timers tell him or her when to turn the hamburger patties, take the bread out of the toaster, and assemble the Big Macs. Similarly, telemarketers report that employers provide them with scripts that tell them exactly what to say to customers and that a computer automatically dials the next phone number once a call has ended. In these instances, digital technologies break down work to its specific tasks and allow companies to standardize how work is done, what their product looks like, and how it is delivered. Consistency helps profitability. On the other hand, new media can alienate workers because they have little to no say in how their time is spent during the workday. While it is easy to write off this complaint with a simple "boo hoo for you," it is worth remembering the work experiences of telemarketers and temporary post office employees. They have no say over the pace of their work or even when they can go to the bathroom. Likewise, it is important to think about whether work already encroaches on your free time. If so, imagine how this will feel when you are having dinner with a loved one or on vacation in Hawaii. Having some control over what you do and how you do it generates satisfaction, which is important to well-being.

In the last chapter, we discussed the effects of new media on political institutions. Here, we saw that new media can aid in social inclusion because digital technologies can ease the costs of participation. It doesn't matter if we work full time, are caregivers, or are managing a family, new media make it easy for us to learn about political issues. More important, new media make it easier for us to get involved. We can share information about an issue, contribute money to an organization, or volunteer to help out at an event supporting a cause. We can even learn new political skills online. Groups such as the National Rifle Association and People for the Ethical Treatment of Animals provide instructions on how to do everything from penning an email to your legislators to launching a grassroots campaign. We also learned that political organizations play an important role in increasing citizens' voices in the political system. While organizations such as PETA and the Humane Society advocate for animal rights nationally, there are lots of grassroots groups that use new media to organize and mobilize citizens in local communities.

Of course, new media do not completely solve the social inclusion problem. We learned that there is a digital divide in America and that this influences who gets politically involved online as well as the kinds of activities in which they engage. Individuals with higher household incomes and higher levels of education use new media to engage in a broad range of political activities, including writing legislators and letters to the editor, contributing money to candidates and causes, joining organizations online, and sharing political content through social media. Individuals with lower household incomes and lower levels of education primarily engage in the latter—joining organizations and sharing content. Education and income are obstacles to social inclusion. We also learned that new media enable groups with extremist views (such as the Alt Right) to flourish and allow astroturfing. Organizations funded by corporations, industry trade associations, or public relations firms try to capitalize on citizen discontent to push for legislation that helps their bottom lines.

NOW WHAT?

The purpose of this book is to provide you with a sociological framework for understanding the role of new media in American society. You should not only be able to think about new media a bit differently but also be able to use sociological tools to undertake your own research project. For example, you could analyze a specific company. It would be interesting to visit a few Starbucks or Dunkin' Donuts in town to see how new media and McDonaldization shape the ways in which your morning coffee and bagel are prepared. Pay attention to how employees move, the buttons they push, and how they use their registers.

If you are more interested in religion, you can analyze the religious community of a denomination with which you are unfamiliar. While it may feel a bit uncomfortable, it is really helpful to choose a religion with which you are unfamiliar because it makes observing religious community much easier. Start by going to a virtual forum like *Second Life* and learn more about the religion. Chat with greeters, attend a service, and take notes on the experience. Then attend service in the real world. Do the same thing. Chat with fellow attendees, stay for a service, and write down what happened. Reflect on the two experiences. Did you see religious community? How? Consider how they were similar and different and whether online and offline practices might work together to create a more satisfying religious experience.

Are you interested in online education? Sign up for two MOOC classes and take notes on how the course is structured as well as how the professors engage their students. Also pay attention to whether (and how) students engage one another. Compare your observations across the courses. Do you see dramatic differences? What do your observations say about the benefits and drawbacks of education online? Of course, you can always apply these sociological tools to other interests not covered in the book. If you are interested in the American health care system, you could explore how new media facilitate the spread of information outside of academic journal such as the *Journal of Pediatrics*, which nonmedical professionals seldom read. For instance, you could analyze how physicians and pharmacists use websites, blogs, and wikis to discuss diagnoses and medications with individuals looking for medical information online. Wikis such as RxWiki can only be edited by pharmacists but provides visitors with information about medications, including their side effects and drug interactions, as well as medical conditions.

If you are more interested in how hospitals work, you could observe how new media and McDonaldization affect efficiency and patient care. For those of you who've been in the hospital lately, you may have noticed that everyone seems to have a tablet and is very good about taking patient vitals and entering the information into a program that ensures patient information is readily available—and that the patient's vitals are checked again at the appropriate time. In this regard, new media has increased hospital efficiency. However, digital technology doesn't necessarily translate into better care. A doctor, for example, may opt not to give a patient a needed surgery because he is on a ventilator, not realizing that a portable ventilator, which would make the surgery possible, is on site.

In 1959, sociologist C. Wright Mills asked readers to think about how our lives are linked to the forces of history and the society in which we live. Mills challenged us to think outside of ourselves and consider how the realities and problems we face are shared by many others and are directly related to the structure of society and changes happening within it. He called our ability to make these connections between ourselves, history, and society the "sociological imagination." With it, we can better understand how rapidly changing technology affects our relationships with one another and alters the social institutions upon which we depend. The sociological imagination helps us explain the water in which we swim.

ACKNOWLEDGMENTS

This book began as a disjointed series of posts and tweets that I had collected and shared with my students over the years. Thanks to the urging and support of Ilene Kalish, I turned these "teachable moments" into the book I wanted to use in my class. This book would not have been possible without the tireless assistance of editorial assistant extraordinaire Maryam Arain and three wonderful graduate students at Florida State University: Tara Stamm, Shawn Gaulden, and Cynthia Williams. Each played a critical role in helping me bring the book over the proverbial finish line. I am grateful to the Department of Sociology, the Pepper Institute on Aging and Public Policy, and the College of Social Science and Public Policy at Florida State University for providing me such wonderful students at critical times during the project. I also thank my mom, Dee Styborski, who read each of the chapters and gave me lively feedback. If you can't rely on your mom to tell you that your examples are boring, then who can you count on? I am indebted to my husband and sons for their love and unending support. I couldn't do my work without them.

GLOSSARY

Agency refers to individuals' decisions to conform to or challenge the rules or practices of a social institution (introduction, page 1).

Agenda-setting process denotes how an issue is identified as a problem that should be solved by political institutions. Policy agenda setting affects the social inclusion of individuals and groups (chapter 6, page 183).

Alienation refers to the idea that individuals can feel estranged from their work because they have no control over it. Karl Marx argued that work, and our ability to control it, is central to our sense of self. He argued that capitalism exploited workers and led to alienation (chapter 5, page 149).

Astroturf groups are organizations created and/or funded by corporations, industry trade associations, or public relations firms (chapter 6, page 208).

Authority refers to the power of an institution to give orders, make decisions, and force citizens to comply (chapter 4, page 110).

Autonomy is the opposite of alienation. Karl Marx argued that the only way individuals could be truly autonomous was to have control over what they made, how they made it, and how they sold it (chapter 5, page 149).

Bourgeoisie is what Karl Marx called the capitalist class who owned the means of production. The bourgeoisie were the owners of the factories, buildings, and land that the workers used (chapter 5, page 154).

Bureaucratization is the adoption of a clear organizational structure, protocols, and procedures. Weber observed that bureaucratization was a key feature of modern institutions and played an important role in maintaining power over the citizenry (chapter 4, page 110).

Capitalist economy describes an economy where a country's trade and industry are controlled by private owners rather than the government (chapter 5, page 154).

Communication structured hierarchically limits how supporters can interact with political organizations, which typically have clear leaders who are decision-makers and spokespeople for the group (chapter 6, page 204).

Communication structured horizontally has fewer limits on how supporters can interact with political organizations, which are often grassroots groups that depend on volunteers and donations to keep the group going (chapter 6, page 204).

Communism describes an economy where the government controls most of the trade and industry and distributes money and resources (chapter 5, page 154).

Conflict theory describes sociological theories that focus on contention, power, and inequality in America. As the name suggests, these perspectives highlight how competition for scarce resources brings different groups into conflict with one another in ways that may not be immediately visible. The education system, for example, perpetuates income inequality in the United States by training students in poor schools to accept their position as lower-income-earning members of American society (chapter 2, page 50).

Contingent workers are temporary workers, such as freelancers, independent professionals, temporary contract workers, independent contractors, or consultants, who are hired by employers when they need them and fired when they don't (chapter 5, page 161).

Corporate legitimacy is a result of how people evaluate a company, its goals, and its appropriateness. Some of a corporation's legitimacy results from its compliance with the rules and regulations of a country. However, we also evaluate the legitimacy of a corporation based on the social values it represents (chapter 4, page 110).

Data mining refers to the practice of searching large stores of data in order to find trends and patterns in it. Companies engage in data mining so that they can forecast their sales, create profiles of the people who buy and use their products, and discover the best ways to market their products to consumers—among many other things (chapter 4, page 133).

Digital divide refers to the gap between those who have access to the internet and those who do not (chapter 6, page 196).

Ethnic profiling describes the practice by which law enforcement use racial or ethnic characteristics to determine who is likely to commit a crime and prevent these crimes from occurring (chapter 4, page 120).

Family consists of people who consider themselves related by blood, marriage, or adoption. Family is a universal social institution, meaning that while its form may vary, no matter where you go in the world or how remote the culture, you will find family (chapter 1, page 21).

Flexicurity is short for "flexible security" and refers to a social model of governing that tries to protect the health and well-being of its citizens by balancing employee's need for a flexible workforce with workers' need for job security (chapter 5, page 161).

Frame outlines a problem and its solution. Political organizations frame issues in ways designed to influence the agenda-setting process (chapter 6, page 183).

Formal political organizations are groups that are clearly structured and bureaucratic and have a paid, professional staff (chapter 6, page 199).

Functionalism (or *functionalist perspective*) refers to sociological theories that emphasize how social institutions help create consensus and cooperation in a society. Education, for instance, passes basic knowledge and skills to the next generation, teaches young people what is (and is not) acceptable behavior in society, and prepares them for the workforce (chapter 2, page 50).

Gamification of education describes the use of game thinking and game mechanics to stimulate learning (chapter 2, page 53).

Globalism refers to the networks of connections that bridge space and time (chapter 1, page 21).

Godcasts are religious podcasts that can be downloaded to mobile devices. Religious leaders create Godcasts to spread their messages of faith (chapter 3, page 83).

Identity refers to the behaviors we perform in a setting that are related to the self. We perform many identities including student, sibling, child, friend, worker, partner, and so on—all of which constitute the self (chapter 1, page 21).

Imperialism describes a country's practice of extending its power through policy and military force (chapter 4, page 113).

Individuality is the characteristics that distinguish us from one another (chapter 1, page 21).

Informal political organizations are groups without a clear structure and are often run by unpaid volunteers (chapter 6, page 201).

Latent functions refer to the unintended consequences of a social institution (chapter 2, page 54).

Legal actors are the individuals who work for and represent legal institutions, including police officers, FBI agents, NSA analysts, lawyers, and judges (chapter 4, page 110).

Legal institutions refer to those organizations charged with enforcing laws and protecting the populace. The Federal Bureau of Investigation (FBI), Central Intelligence Agency (CIA), National Security Agency (NSA), and law enforcement are examples of legal institutions (chapter 4, page 110).

Manifest functions refer to the intended consequences of a social institution (chapter 2, page 54).

McDonaldization refers to sociologist George Ritzer's theory about how Taylorism looks in modern society. His theory stresses how modern-day employers increasingly rely on technology to make workers more efficient and productive and consumer experiences more predictable (chapter 5, page 149).

Means of production are the tools the workers need to do their jobs such as farm equipment or computers. The means of production, according to Karl Marx, are owned by the bourgeoisie (chapter 5, page 154).

Media logic refers to how the structure of the medium and the format of the content affect communication. Medium structure outlines how different medium structures shape the information we receive. Format refers to how information is presented (chapter 3, page 79).

National security refers to the idea that the government should protect itself and its citizens from threats (chapter 4, page 111).

New media are the mass communications that rely on digital technologies such as social media, online games and applications, multimedia, productivity applications, cloud computing, interoperable systems, and mobile devices. New media are part of mass media (introduction, page 1).

Objectivity describes a journalistic practice by which reporters try to be neutral in their presentation of political issues (chapter 6, page 210).

Ontological security refers to our existential sense of self. According to Anthony Giddens, ontological security comes from our relationships with family members and friends and is achieved when we experience the positive and stable emotions that help us deal with events beyond our control (chapter 1, page 21).

Outlet bias refers to when an outlet is prejudiced in favor of or against an idea, person, or group compared with another (chapter 6, page 210).

Panopticon is a model of an ideal prison created by philosopher and social theorist Jeremy Bentham in the eighteenth century where all the cells are open to a central tower with a guard. The prisoners cannot interact with one another, nor can they tell when they are being watched by the guard in the tower (chapter 4, page 121).

Political institutions are the organizations that create laws, mediate political conflict, and represent the citizenry. Individuals hope that by making their voices heard elected officials will act in ways that improve their social inclusion (chapter 6, page 183).

Political organizations are groups that engage in actions intended to forward a specific political goal such as the National Rifle Association or People for the Ethical Treatment of Animals.

Political organizations, which represent thousands of individuals who care about the same cause, can give citizens a louder voice in the agenda-setting process and increase their social inclusion (chapter 6, page 183).

Proletariat refers to the workers who worked in factories, in offices, and on farms. Karl Marx noted that the proletariat did not own the means of production (chapter 5, page 154).

Rational-legal authority refers to the kind of power that bureaucracies use to maintain their legitimacy with a population. Legal institutions get their legitimacy from a system of rules that are obeyed because they are consistent with the values of a society and upheld by institutional actors (chapter 4, page 110).

Religion is a unified system of beliefs in which some things are identified as sacred and set apart from everyday items (chapter 3, page 79).

Religious community refers to a group of people who are united by their shared beliefs and practices (chapter 3, page 79).

Religious dysfunction refers to the harmful effects of religion. Social scientists discuss two harmful effects of religious dysfunction: (1) persecution and (2) war and terrorism (chapter 3, page 79).

Religious practices are the rituals around the things that are considered sacred. For example, Muslims pray facing Mecca as a sign of unity and respect, and Jews recognize the transition to adulthood with a bar mitzvah or bat mitzvah (chapter 3, page 79).

Self refers to the relatively stable set of perceptions we have about who we are relative to others. The self is shaped through interaction with others in a variety of settings (chapter 1, page 21).

Self-fulfilling prophesy describes the phenomena where a false assumption occurs because someone else predicted it. In the classroom, this happens when a student performs well (or poorly) because the student meets the expectations of a teacher. If a teacher believes that a student can improve his performance or grade, the student picks up on this positive expectation and improves his performance or grade (chapter 2, page 50).

Social exchange model highlights the importance of relational dynamics, or how the behavior of one actor is shaped by the behaviors of other actors and by changes in the institutional context (introduction, page 1).

Social inclusion refers to the ability of individuals and groups to fully participate in society and control their life chances. Individuals and groups get politically involved to improve their inclusion in political institutions (chapter 6, page 183).

Social institutions are the systems of established social rules that create stable expectations for behavior. Social institutions include family and religion, which provide support and a sense of purpose, and education, government, and law, which help create social order. Mass media also are a social institution (introduction, page 1).

Social networks refer to our networks of social interactions and personal relationships (chapter 6, page 193).

Socialization refers to teaching children the language, social skills, and values of a society so that they can fit into a larger community (chapter 1, page 21).

Structure refers to the rules and practices provided by society and social institutions (introduction, page 1).

Superpanopticon refers to the hyper surveillance that is possible by institutions, such as legal institutions, in the digital age (chapter 4, page 120).

Symbolic interaction refers to sociological theories that examine how individuals use words, body language, and symbols to create a shared understanding with others. Like conflict theorists, sociologists who study interactions think about how power affects the ways in which people relate to one another. In school, for instance, teachers and professors run the classroom and determine whether and how students will be allowed to participate in class discussions (chapter 2, page 50).

Taylorism describes a theory of management developed by Frederick Winslow Taylor in the 1880s and 1890s. Taylor analyzed how workers did their jobs in order to make them more efficient and productive. Unlike Marx, Taylor was not concerned with workers' experiences (chapter 5, page 149).

INDEX

Page numbers followed by *f* and *t* refer to figures and tables, respectively.

Deana A. Rohlinger is a professor of sociology at Florida State University. She is the author of *Abortion Politics, Mass Media, and Social Movements in America* as well as dozens of research articles. Rohlinger writes commentary for a range of news outlets and maintains the blog, www.doubletakesociology.wordpress.com. Learn more about Deana and this book at www.deanarohlinger.com.

CPSIA information can be obtained
at www.ICGtesting.com
Printed in the USA
JSHW012028020223
37214JS00001B/58